MCAT Psychology and Sociology

CONTENT REVIEW AND PRACTICE PASSAGES

NextStep
TEST PREP nextsteptestprep.com

Printed in the United States of America

Second Printing, 2018

ISBN 978-1-944-935-21-4

Next Step Test Prep, LLC
4256 N Ravenswood Ave
Suite 207
Chicago IL 60613

www.nextsteptestprep.com

MCAT is a registered trademark of the American Association of Medical Colleges (AAMC). The AAMC has neither reviewed nor endorsed this work in any way.

Revision Number: 1.2 (2018-04-01)

FREE ONLINE FULL LENGTH MCAT

Want to see how you would do on the MCAT
and understand where you need to focus your prep?

TAKE OUR FREE MCAT DIAGNOSTIC EXAM
and **FREE FULL LENGTH**
Timed practice that simulates Test Day and provides
comprehensive analysis, reporting, and in-depth explanations.

Included with this free account is the first lesson
in Next Step's online course, a free sample
from our science QBank, and more!

All of these resources are provided free to students who have
purchased a Next Step book. Register for your free account at:

http://nextsteptestprep.com/mcat-diagnostic

This page left intentionally blank.

STOP! READ ME FIRST!

The book you're holding is one of Next Step's six MCAT review books and contains both concise content review and questions to practice applying your content knowledge. In order to get the most out of this book, we strongly recommend that you follow a few simple steps:

1. Register for a free MCAT bundle at http://nextsteptestprep.com/mcat-diagnostic and begin your prep by taking the MCAT Diagnostic and Science Content Diagnostic to assess your strengths and weaknesses.

2. Begin working through the Next Step Review set starting with the Verbal, Quantitative, and Research Methods book. Complete this entire book at the start of your prep.

3. Use the Study Plan generator in your free account at nextstepmcat.com to generate a day-by-day study plan to take you through the rest of the Next Step Books.

4. Begin working through the rest of the Next Step MCAT review books, including this one. To get the most value out of these books, use spaced repetition to ensure complete mastery of the material. A spaced repetition approach would look something like this:

> I. Begin by skimming through the chapter to familiarize yourself with the key terms and content in the book. Then go back and read the chapter carefully.
>
> II. Sleep on it! Solidifying those long term memories requires sleep.
>
> III. Come back to the chapter *the next day*, re-skim it and then *complete the questions at the end of the chapter*. Carefully read all of the explanations, even for the questions you got right.
>
> IV. Take notes in your Lessons Learned Journal from the chapter. For a full explanation on what a Lessons Learned Journal is, watch Lesson 1 included in the free online bundle at nextstepmcat.com.
>
> IV. Sleep on it!
>
> V. Two days later, come back, briefly re-skim the chapter, re-do the questions at the end of the chapter, and review your Lessons Learned Journal.

Mastering the MCAT requires more than just a good set of books. You'll want to continue your prep with the most representative practice tests available. Your free bundle includes Next Step Full Length #1. After you've completed that, you can upgrade your account to include additional practice exams.

Finally, if you would like more extensive help, including daily live office hours with Next Step's senior faculty, contact us for more information about our online course. You can reach us at 888-530-NEXT or mcat@nextsteptestprep.com.

This page left intentionally blank.

TABLE OF CONTENTS

This page left intentionally blank.

Biological Basis of Behavior

CHAPTER 1

0. Introduction

The most important science on the MCAT is, by far, biology. It appears in every single science section, and the psych/soc section is no exception. While the bulk of the questions in this section are drawn from psychology and sociology, these facts are grounded in the physical reality of the brain and nervous system. Thus, we start our review of MCAT psychology by looking back to a bit of biology.

> > **CONNECTIONS** < <

Biology chapter 6

1. Conceptual Approaches to Behavior

Humans have understood the behavior of their fellow humans (and themselves) in a variety of ways throughout history. Theories related to bodily humors (fluids like bile and blood), connections to the soul, or even demon possession were all popular among certain groups at certain times. Beginning primarily in the 19th century, however, thinkers began to examine human behavior through the lens of the sciences.

Biologists began using the tools of anatomy and physiology to examine the brain and nervous system and attempted to correlate these physical structures with behavior. Anatomy and physiology included some mis-steps such as phrenology (a field that asserted you could predict personality by feeling bumps on a person's head), but developed through the 19th century via animal experimentation. It determined which parts of the brain served which purpose, and studied the structures of neurons and measured nerve impulses before even the start of the 20th century.

Functionalism, including the work of psychologists such as William James and John Dewey, studied mental processes on the level of whole organism and examined how mental processes respond to and provide adaptive responses to input from the environment. Functionalists were often dismissive of the reductive and over-simplified approaches of the earlier physiologists studying neurons and the brain.

More recently, advances in brain imaging and study techniques have allowed us to tie particular behaviors or behavior patterns into functions or structures of the brain directly. Longitudinal studies and rigorous statistical analyses have allowed us to see the correlations between certain behaviors and genetics. At the same time that scientists were making advances in a physical approach to behavior, the cognitive revolution of the 1960's directed scientists' attention to a deeper interdisciplinary approach to psychology, all but eliminating behaviorism as the dominant paradigm by the early 1980's.

2. Organization of the Nervous System

(note: much of this information is adapted from the nervous system chapter in the Next Step biology review book)

The nervous system is the body's means of taking in information, integrating that information, and then controlling and coordinating much of the body's activity through other physiological systems.

MCAT STRATEGY > > >

Mastering MCAT content involves spaced repetition. Even if you've already gone through the nervous system chapter in the biology book, take this opportunity to review the information again.

We will start with a brief discussion of some general features of the nervous system before moving on to an in-depth discussion neurons, the functional unit in the nervous system. Neurons transmit information through action potentials and send that information to other neurons or to effector cells across synapses. We'll then move on to reviewing the divisions of the peripheral and central nervous systems and discuss some basics related to brain structures and neurotrasmitters.

General Function of the Nervous System

The core function of the nervous system is simple: communication. In this regard, it functions very similarly to the endocrine system, which will be discussed in more detail in a later chapter. The key contrast between nervous and endocrine coordination comes in the speed with which these systems can react to input. Nerves can fire off action potentials in mere fractions of a second, whereas endocrine responses tend to be slower and more long-lasting. For example, in the case of the development of sex characteristics, the body's response to endocrine communication can be life-long.

This communication sifts through the vast data from the environment, and from internal senses (e.g. stretch receptors in the bladder to let you know you need to pee), which lets the body react, both with conscious behaviors and unconscious reflexes to help maintain homeostasis. Neurons and sense receptors in the peripheral nervous system (PNS) take in information and bring it to the brain or spinal cord, which comprise the central nervous system (CNS).

That information is then integrated and the body can respond. Some responses can be so simple they don't even involve the brain. The knee jerk response (patellar tendon reflex) is an example of such a response. In other cases, the information undergoes highly complex processing which may involve conscious reflection and higher judgment or decision-making processes.

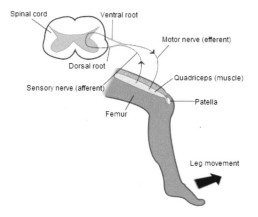

Figure 1. Patellar Tendon Reflex.

Neurons and Glia

The basic functional unit of the nervous system is the neuron. A neuron is a very highly specialized cell designed to integrate inputs and output a signal in the form of an action potential. This level of specialization means that neurons no longer undergo the normal cell cycle and are, like skeletal muscle cells, in the G_0 resting phase and no longer dividing.

The neuron is built out of several components which you should know for the test. The main body of the cell, the soma, houses the cell's nucleus and other large organelles. The cell takes input through dendrites, projections off the cell body which can connect to input from other nerves or other specialized sense organs. A single neuron may have a handful of dendrites or even hundreds or thousands. By contrast, each neuron only has a single axon. The axon is a single, long projection from the soma and is the structure through which a neuron outputs its action potentials. Just before the axon, the cell body tapers into a region called the axon hillock, where a neuron integrates the various input signals it receives and decides whether to send a signal down the axon.

The axon itself can be coated with an insulating sheath of material called myelin. Not all cells are myelinated. Myelin acts as an insulator that allows for much more rapid conduction of action potentials. Breaks in the myelin sheath, called nodes of Ranvier are dotted along the myelinated axon. The axon ends in the nerve terminal where the cell can synapse with (communicate with) either another nerve cell, a muscle, or a gland.

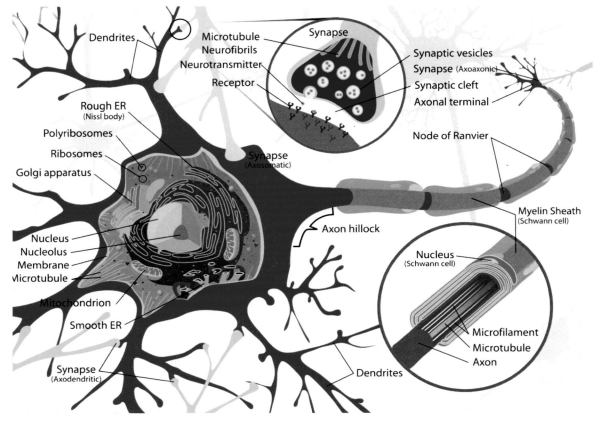

Figure 2. Neuron.

There are six different types of glial cells that provide support to neurons in both the CNS and PNS. While the function of the nervous system was first thought to depend almost entirely on neurons, with glial cells seen as being of secondary importance, more recent research has shown that by managing the microenvironments around neurons and performing other support functions, glial cells are of critical importance in the smooth functioning of the nervous system. The table below provides a brief description of the functions of the glial cells you will be expected to recognize on the exam.

TABLE 1 GLIAL CELLS	
Oligodendrocytes	Provide myelination in the CNS
Schwann Cells	Provide myelination in the PNS
Astrocytes	Provide various support functions to neurons in the CNS
Ependymal Cells	Produce and circulate cerebrospinal fluid in the CNS
Satellite Cells	Control the microenvironment around cell bodies in ganglia in the PNS
Microglia	Macrophages that clean out microbes and debris in the CNS

TABLE 2 NEURON TYPES	
Unipolar	A single dendrite that splits into dendrioles but no axon. Found in cerebellum and associated with balance. More commonly found in insects than humans.
Bipolar	Sensory neuron for smell, sight, taste, hearing, and balance.
Pseudounipolar	Sensory neuron in PNS. One axon splits with one part running to the spinal cord and one running to the periphery. Found in the dorsal root ganglia.
Multipolar	Has a single axon and multiple dendrites. The classic image of a neuron. Includes motor neurons and interneurons.

Membrane Potentials, Action Potentials and Synapses

All of the body's cells maintain a potential difference across their membranes. That is, the area on the inside of the cell membrane maintains a negative voltage potential relative to the area on the outside of the plasma membrane. This potential allows the cell to carry out a number of different functions, and in some cells—neurons and muscle cells—this potential can be manipulated quickly across large portions of the cell to achieve a particular effect (sending an action potential or twitching a muscle fiber).

Neural Membrane and Resting Potential

The nerve cell maintains a resting potential of -70 mV. When the inside of the cell loses this negative potential, the cell is said to be depolarized, and when it drops to a more negative potential (after peaking at +40 mV in an action potential) it is said to be hyperpolarized. This resting potential is maintained by the constant action of the sodium-potassium ATPase (the Na^+/K^+ pump) which pushes three sodium ions out of the cell for every two potassium ions it brings in. This electrochemical gradient is also maintained by the fact that the hydrophobic core of the plasma membrane doesn't allow ions to easily diffuse back across.

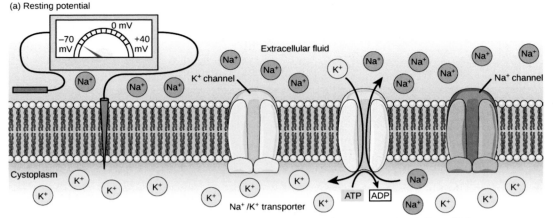

(a) Resting potential

At the resting potential, all voltage-gated Na+ channels and most voltage-gated K+ channels are closed. The Na+/K+ transporter pumps K+ ions into the cell and Na+ ions out.

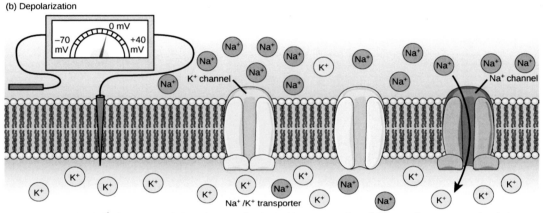

(b) Depolarization

In response to a depolarization, some Na+ channels open, allowing Na+ ions to enter the cell. The membrane starts to depolarize (the charge across the membrane lessens). If the threshold of excitation is reached, all the Na+ channels open.

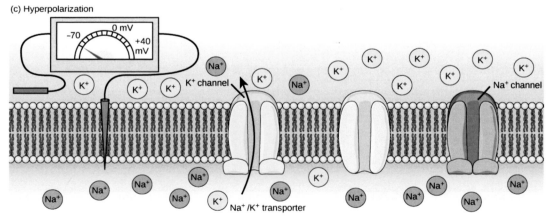

(c) Hyperpolarization

At the peak action potential, Na+ channels close while K+ channels open. K+ leaves the cell, and the membrane eventually becomes hyperpolarized.

Figure 3. Membrane Potential.

During this resting state, the channels which can permit sodium or potassium ions to rush through are held closed. When an excitatory stimulus hits the neuron (typically inputs from dendrites), the cell's potential can be brought up from -70 mV to a more positive state. It is possible for such signals to fail to bring the neuron up to the threshold potential of -55 mV, however. These are shown in the figure below as "failed initiations."

If the excitatory stimulus is strong enough, and the cell's resting potential is brought up to -55 mV, the cell will undergo an action potential (shown below). In the first phase of the action potential, depolarization, the sodium voltage-gated channels open and Na⁺ ions rush into the cell. The sudden influx of positive charges continues until the cell membrane reaches full depolarization at +40 mV, at which point the sodium channels close and potassium voltage-gated channels open.

Now that the interior of the cell is positive, the potassium is pushed by both electrical potential and by its own concentration gradient to rush out, causing repolarization. Repolarization continues until the cell overshoots the -70 mV level, making the cell temporarily hyperpolarized, during what is called the refractory period. Then, the sodium potassium pumps get back to work to re-establish the resting state of the cell.

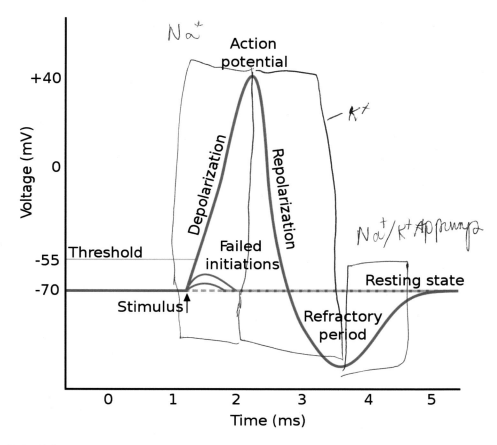

Figure 4. Action Potential

Action potentials begin at the axon hillock and move down the axon towards the synapse. This action potential can either move slowly and smoothly long the cell membrane if the cell is unmyelinated, or can jump very rapidly down the axon from one node of Ranvier to the next if the cell is myelinated.

Remember that for a section of nerve membrane to undergo an action potential, it must have its membrane brought from -70 mV up to -55 mV. The action potential is transmitted from one node of Ranvier to the next because the +40 mV potential of a depolarized section of nerve membrane can transmit some of that positive potential (in the form of sodium ions) towards the next node. This positive potential need only contribute to a 15 mV increase (remember, from -70 to -55 mV) in the next node to get it to experience an action potential and send the signal further down the axon.

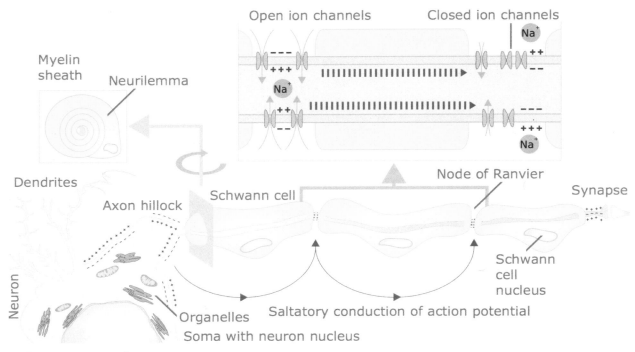

Figure 5. Action Potential Propagation.

When the action potential reaches the end of the axon, it transmits a signal via the nerve's synapse with one of three things—another nerve, a muscle cell, or a gland. Neurotransmitters are stored in vesicles in the axon terminal. When the action potential arrives, calcium voltage-gated channels are triggered, allowing Ca^{2+} to rush into the axon terminal. These calcium ions serve as the signal for the cell to use exocytosis to push the neurotransmitters into the synaptic cleft—the space that exists between the axon and the post-synaptic membrane. The space of the cleft is exceptionally small, such that simple diffusion is enough to very quickly carry the neurotransmitters across the cleft to the post-synaptic membrane. There, the neurotransmitters can act as ligands binding to their receptors.

Neurotransmitters must be cleared out of the synaptic cleft quickly. This allows the body to tightly regulate the strength and timing of the signals sent by nerves. Neurotransmitters can either be broken down by enzymes in the cleft (the classic example being acetylcholinesterase which breaks down acetylcholine) or taken back up by the axon for re-use later. A clinical example of the importance of this re-uptake is seen in the class of antidepressants called selective serotonin reuptake inhibitors (SSRIs), which can selectively block reuptake and enhance the activity of serotonin in certain synapses in the brain.

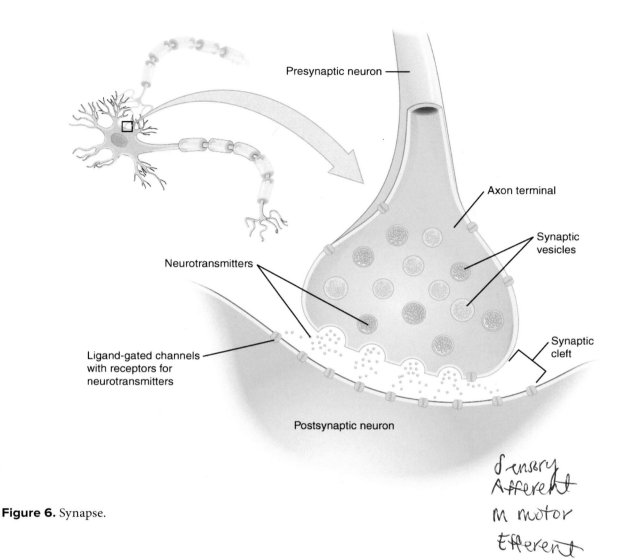

Figure 6. Synapse.

sensory
Afferent
M motor
Efferent

Peripheral and Central Nervous Systems

The nervous system can be understood by looking at its different functional components. First, the system is divided into the central (CNS) and peripheral nervous systems (PNS). The central nervous system includes both the brain and the spinal cord. Everything else is the peripheral nervous system—all of the nerves that carry information into the CNS (afferent fibers) or bring signals out of the CNS to the PNS (efferent fibers). While most cell bodies (somas) are found in the central nervous system, there are clusters of cell bodies outside the CNS. These are called ganglia and are found along the sides of the spinal cord, in the digestive system, and elsewhere in the body.

Nerves, or clusters of axons held together by connective tissue, can be defined as afferent or efferent and also as motor or sensory. Sensory nerves are afferent and bring sensory data into the CNS, carrying information about the environment or about the body's own internal state. Motor neurons are effectors and signal muscle cells to contract.

These sensory and motor nerves either connect to the spinal cord, in which case they are called spinal nerves, or directly enter the skull, in which case they are cranial

MCAT STRATEGY > > >

Remember the word SAME: sensory afferent, motor efferent.

nerves. Nerves can be further classified functionally as either autonomic, somatic, or visceral. Visceral nerves connect to the digestive system to modulate its functioning. Somatic nerves connect to skeletal muscle to allow for voluntary movement. The autonomic nervous system connects to various involuntary responses in the body, including things like sweating, blushing, pupil dilation and so on.

Finally, the autonomic nervous system can be further divided. It is crucial to recognize the difference between the sympathetic and parasympathetic systems. The sympathetic nervous system stimulates the body in the classic "fight or flight" response. If the body needs to get ready for action, it will do things like dilate the pupils, raise the heart rate, and increase blood flow to skeletal muscles to prepare for sudden action. By contrast, the parasympathetic nervous system is the "rest and digest" system that increases blood flow to the digestive system, slows the heart rate, and so on.

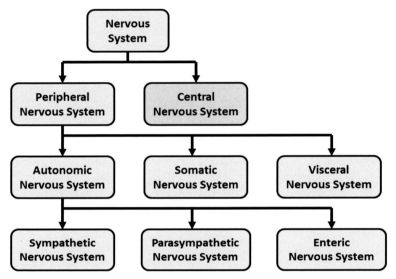

Figure 7. Components of the Nervous System.

The central nervous system—brain and spinal cord—are protected by bones (skull and vertebral column, respectively), tough membranes called meninges, and cushioned by cerebrospinal fluid (CSF). CSF is secreted by specialized glial cells called ependymal cells and circulates across the brain and down the spinal cord.

The Central Nervous System

The brainstem (consisting of the midbrain, pons, and medulla oblongata), provides the connection from the brain to the spinal cord. It serves to regulate crucial functions basic to the survival of the organism—things like heart rate, respiration, sleep, and overall activation of the rest of the CNS. The cerebellum, found just underneath the occipital lobe, serves to direct complex coordinated movement, such as walking or playing the piano. The basal ganglia are located just under the cortex and connect to both the brainstem and the cortical lobes. The basal ganglia are involved in a number of different functions, including voluntary movement, habitual behaviors, learning, and emotion.

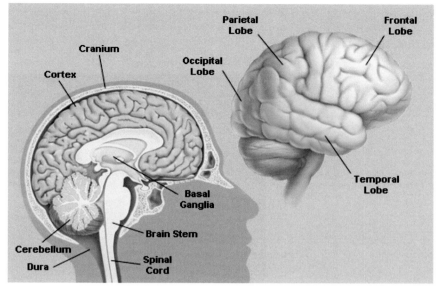

Figure 8. The Brain.

The cerebral cortices overlay the rest of the brain's structures and are responsible for much of the higher functions seen in humans. The cortices can be divided into four lobes: frontal, parietal, occipital, and temporal. Each lobe is associated with a wide variety of functions related to sensation, motor activity, and cognition. In particular, the frontal lobe is associated with making judgments and regulating behavior as a part of executive functioning. The occipital lobe is most closely related to visual processing, as data from the optic nerves are sent directly there. The parietal lobe is associated with integrating various sensory input, and both the parietal and temporal lobes are important for language.

TABLE 3 PARTS OF THE BRAIN		
Hindbrain	Cerebellum	Coordinated movement
	Medulla Oblongata	Autonomic functions such as breathing, heart rate, blood pressure.
	Pons	Relays signals between the cerebellum, medulla and the rest of the brain. Involved in sleep, respiration, swallowing, taste, bladder control, and balance.
Midbrain	Inferior Colliculus	Processes auditory signals and sends them to the medial geniculate nucleus in the thalamus.
	Superior Colliculus	Process visual signals and participate in control of eye movements.

Forebrain	Amygdala	Process memory, emotions, and decision-making.
	Basal Ganglia	Participate in motivation, in controlling eye movements, and modulate decision-making
	Frontal Lobe	Involved in voluntary movement, memory processing, planning, motivation, and attention.
	Hippocampus	Consolidation of short-term memory into long-term memory
	Hypothalamus	Links the nervous system to the endocrine system via the pituitary gland.
	Occipital Lobe	Visual processing.
	Parietal Lobe	Sensory processing.
	Pineal Gland	Modulates sleep through melatonin production.
	Posterior Pituitary	Projection through which the hypothalamus secretes oxytocin and vasopressin.
	Septal Nuclei	Part of the reward pathway.
	Temporal Lobe	Involved in processing sense information to help form memory and attach meaning to information. Includes Wernicke's area.
	Thalamus	Relays sense and motor signals and regulates sleep and alertness

Neurons in both the central and peripheral nervous systems must communicate with each other via neurotransmitters. Make sure you're familiar with the following neurotransmitters for Test Day.

TABLE 4 NEUROTRANSMITTERS	
Acetylcholine	Activates muscle contraction at the neuromuscular junction. Used in all autonomic outputs from the brain to autonomic ganglia. Used in the parasympathetic nervous system for post-ganglionic connections.
Dopamine	Used in reward pathways and motor pathways. Particularly associated with Parkinson's disease and the loss of dopaminergic neurons in the substantia nigra.
Endorphin	Pain suppression and can produce euphoria
Epinephrine	Stimulates fight-or-flight response
GABA	Main inhibitory neurotransmitter of the CNS that hyperpolarizes cells to reduce action potential firing. Associated with many of the physiological effects of alcohol intoxication.
Glutamate	Excitatory neurotransmitter and most common neurotransmitter (90% of brain cells are glutaminergic).
Glycine	Inhibitory neurotransmitter of the spinal cord and brainstem. Can work in conjunction with GABA.

Norepinephrine	Used in post-ganglionic connections in the sympathetic division of the autonomic nervous system. Increases arousal, alertness, and focuses attention.
Serotonin	Regulates intestinal movement in the GI tract and regulates mood, appetite, and sleep in the brain. Low levels particularly associated with depressive mood disorders.

Studying the Brain

Scientists have been examining the brain for well over a century, using a variety of techniques. At first, such explorations were limited to crude anatomical manipulations—destroying chunks of the brain in animals and studying the effects.

Throughout the early 20th century, doctors began carefully studying human patients who had suffered brain trauma. By meticulously cataloguing the patient's various abilities and deficiencies, doctors could then associate such deficiencies with areas of the brain that showed trauma by performing an extensive autopsy of the brain.

This process provided a wealth of information about which areas of the brain were associated with certain functions, and allowed scientists to take the next step—surgically opening the skull and stimulating regions of the brain with small electrodes. By keeping the patient awake and lucid throughout the process, doctors could have the patient report what subjective experience was associated with such stimulation.

In the latter part of the 20th century and moving into the 21st century, scientists have been able to study the brain in even more detail through imaging techniques that don't require any surgical intervention.

An EEG measures electrical impulses in the brain by covering the scalp with small sensors. Researchers can then present the subject with various stimuli and record which areas of the brain demonstrate increased electrical activity. Instead of measuring electrical activity, scientists can watch the level of blood flow in parts of the brain. By injecting a tracer molecule, scientists are able to image which parts of the brain are more active in response to certain stimuli. More active brain areas will see an increase in blood flow, and thus an increase in the tracer molecule.

13

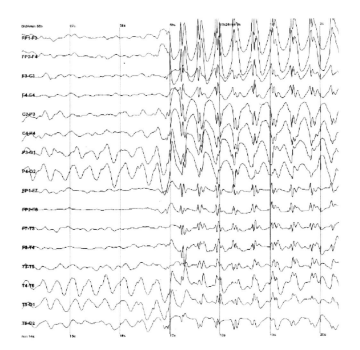

Figure 9. EEG.

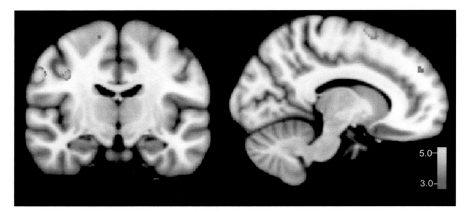

Figure 10. Regional cerebral blood flow.

MCAT STRATEGY > > >

Focus on exactly what's measured in various techniques. EEG: electrical activity; PET: metabolic activity through glucose uptake; fMRI: metabolic activity through oxygen utilization (hemoglobin in the blood)

Brains can also be imaged using MRI, PET, and CT scans. MRI scans use magnetic fields and radio waves to image parts of the brain while avoiding the dangers of bombarding the body with ionizing radiation such as X-rays. Functional MRI, or fMRI trades spatial resolution for temporal resolution and allows scientists to map active parts of the brain. It does so by analyzing the differences in oxyhemoglobin and deoxyhemoglobin concentration in parts of the brain. PET scans work by injecting the patient with a radioactive analogue of glucose, and then measuring the radioactive emissions from the body. Much like MRI and fMRI, PET scans work on the principle that more active areas of the brain will show increased metabolism, and thus increase uptake of glucose. Such uptake can then be converted into a false-color "heat map" of the brain to show areas of increased or decreased activity. Finally, CT scans use X-rays, but unlike a typical single two-dimensional X-ray film, CT machines use computer processing to take many X-ray measurements from multiple different angles, generating images that can be used for diagnosis.

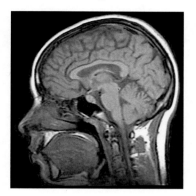

Figure 11. Brain MRI.

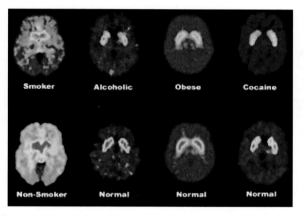

Figure 12. PET scans comparing brains of smokers, alcoholics, obese individuals, and cocaine addicts to corresponding controls.

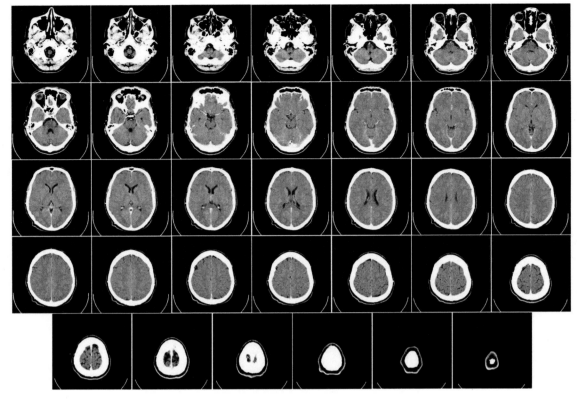

Figure 12. CT scan of the head.

4. Hormones

The final topic to consider when discussing the biological determinants of behavior is hormones. An in-depth discussion of hormones is available in the Next Step biology review book in the endocrine system chapter. For your convenience, we've reproduced the hormone chart here that you can use to memorize this crucial MCAT information.

TABLE 5 HORMONES				
Hormone	**Secreted by**	**In response to**	**Effect**	**Type**
Oxytocin	Posterior Pituitary	Childbirth	Uterine contraction, Emotional Bonding	Peptide
Vasopressin (ADH)	Posterior Pituitary	High plasma osmolality	Retain water, ↑ aquaporin channels in collecting duct, DCT	Peptide
FSH	Anterior Pituitary	GnRH	♀: initiate follicle growth ♂: ↑ spermatocyte development ♀, ♂: maturation of germ cells	Glycoprotein
LH	Anterior Pituitary	GnRH ♀: estrogen spike from follicle just before ovulation	♀: ovulation, follicle becomes corpus luteum ♂: Leydig cells ➡ ↑testosterone	Glycoprotein
ACTH	Anterior Pituitary	CRH, Stress	↑ adrenal release of corticosteroids	Peptide
TSH	Anterior Pituitary	TRH, low plasma levels of T4 and T3	↑ thyroid release of T4 and T3	Glycoprotein
Prolactin	Anterior Pituitary	Falling progesterone at end of pregnancy	Mammary gland enlargement, milk production	Peptide
Endorphin	Anterior Pituitary	Pain	Pain relief	Peptide
Growth Hormone	Anterior Pituitary	GHRH	Growth of long bones, general anabolism	Peptide
Calcitonin	Thyroid	High plasma [Ca2+]	Reduce plasma [Ca2+]	Peptide
T_4 & T_3	Thyroid	TSH	↑ metabolic rate	Amino Acid Tyr, but act like steroid
Parathyroid Horm.	Parathyroid	Low plasma [Ca2+]	↑ plasma [Ca2+]	Peptide
Glucagon	Pancreas α cells	Low blood [Glucose]	↑ blood [Glucose]	Peptide
Insulin	Pancreas β cells	High blood [Glucose]	↓ blood [Glucose]	Peptide
Somatostatin	Pancreas δ cells	Various, usually high hormone levels	Suppress: GH, TSH, CCK, insulin, glucagon	Peptide

Hormone	Secreted by	In response to	Effect	Type
Cortisol	Adrenal Cortex	Stress	↑ [Glucose], Immune suppression	Steroid
Aldosterone	Adrenal Cortex	ACTH, ATII, low bp	Collecting Duct, DCT: reabsorb Na^+, Secrete K^+, water retention, ↑ bp	Steroid
Epinephrine	Adrenal Medulla	Sudden stress	Sympathetic response: ↑ heart rate, breathing, etc.	Peptide / Tyr derivative
Estrogen	♀: Ovaries, ♂: Adrenal	FSH	♀: secondary sex characteristics, endometrial development during menstrual cycle, surge leads to LH surge	Steroid
Progesterone	♀: Ovary: Corpus Luteum, ♂: Adrenal	Ovulation	Thicken, maintain endometrium in preparation for implantation	Steroid
Testosterone	♂: Leydig cells of testes, ♀: Ovaries	GnRH→LH→Testos.	Development, maintenance of secondary sex characteristics	Steroid
Norepinephrine	Adrenal Medulla	Sudden stress	Sympathic responses of fight or flight	Peptide / Tyr derivative
hCG	Placenta	Implantation	Maintains corpus luteum at start of pregnancy	Glycoprotein
GnRH	Hypothalamus	Puberty, Menses	↑ LH, FSH release	Peptide

This page left intentionally blank.

Practice Passage

There are three types of aggression: premeditated aggression, in which the aggression is consciously planned and executed for some expected gain, such as a planned robbery; medically related aggression, where aggression is symptomatic of some medical condition; and third is impulsive aggression, which results from children having difficulty controlling their actions and reacting impulsively. Studies were conducted to assess the connection between specific brain region dysfunction and aggressive behavior.

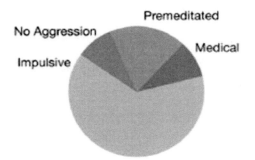

Figure 1. Aggression type in patients with prefrontal cortical dysfunction

The prefrontal cortex (PFC) helps control affect. The left PFC primarily connects words to emotional experiences and encodes memories. The right PFC cortex controls the retrieval of memory and visuospatial information, important in nonverbal problem solving. Around age 4, the left PFC comes to dominate, resulting in good interpretation of events and decision making. Decreased PFC function is tied to inattention, impulsivity, and disorganization, which can lead to aggression for two reasons. First, by making it difficult for the individual to choose non-aggressive responses and second, having deficits in executive decision making can lead a child to have a number of social problems. The resulting isolation from peers can prevent social skill building, and predispose the child to aggression due to a lack of alternative methods to deal with challenges.

The anterior cingulate gyrus (aCG) is involved with processing emotional experience, and connects the limbic system with the PFC. The aCG helps the brain to shift attention to relevant stimuli, and serves to modulate attention between affect and cognition. When an individual encounters provocative situations that may cause frustration, the aCG allows them to reflect on internal controls and modulate this arousal. If one is unable to focus on the social expectations of a peer group, for example, an individual uninhibited by social constraints is more likely to react with aggression.

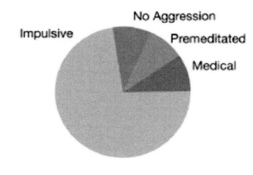
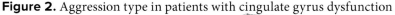

Figure 2. Aggression type in patients with cingulate gyrus dysfunction

The amygdala region of the temporal lobe that is especially involved in aggression. Low amygdala activity has been found in people with antisocial personality disorder. It is hypothesized that deficits in the amygdala lead to a lack of feeling aversive behaviors, such as fear. Without experiencing these aversive emotions an individual may be inclined to behave in self-serving ways without fear of outcomes.

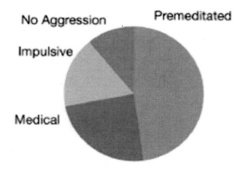

Figure 3. Aggression type in patients with amygdala dysfunction

1. Why might those with amygdala deficits predominantly show the kind of aggression they do?
   A. Lack of social skills
   B. Lack of executive functioning skills
   C. Lack of fear-based learning
   D. Lack of memory

2. What would likely be an area in which an individual with impulsive aggression might have deficits?
   A. Immune functions
   B. Physical development
   C. Vestibular sense
   D. Language

   check both PFC and ACG

3. Which of the following disorders could lead to problems with aggression via the temporal lobe?
   A. Schizoid disorder
   B. Schizophrenia
   C. Epilepsy
   D. Anxiety

   epilepsy can affect temporal lobe
   ↳ cause aggression via temporal lobe

4. What type of intervention would NOT be helpful for an individual demonstrating aggression as a result of aCG dysfunction?
   A. Affect arousal modulation skill instruction
   B. Social skills training
   C. Weighing the pros and cons of engaging in deviant behavior ← *better for premeditated aggression*
   D. Connecting thoughts, feelings, and behaviors

5. Why might an individual with impulsive aggression also have low scores on visuospatial tasks on an IQ test?
   A. There is damage to the right PFC.
   B. There is damage to the left PFC.
   C. There is right temporal lobe damage.
   D. There is left temporal lobe damage.

6. Which of the following correlational findings would most strongly support the passage regarding the relationship between the PFC and aggression?
   A. PFC activity vs. yelling during arguments; R = +0.56; p = 0.06
   B. PFC activity vs. yelling during arguments; R = -0.80; p = 0.06
   C. PFC activity vs. physical assault incidents; R = +0.73; p = 0.03
   D. PFC activity vs. bullying behavior; R = -0.80; p = 0.03 ← *want less than .05*
   ↳neg R ↑PFC ↓bullying

7. In order to reduce aggression in children and replace it with more socially acceptable behavior, many studies will observe child behavior and take away scheduled playtime from a child when aggressive behavior is displayed.
   A. Positive punishment
   B. Negative punishment
   C. Positive reinforcement
   D. Negative reinforcement

Practice Passage Explanations

There are three types of aggression: premeditated aggression, in which the aggression is consciously planned and executed for some expected gain, such as a planned robbery; medically related aggression, where aggression is symptomatic of some medical condition; and third is impulsive aggression, which results from children having difficulty controlling their actions and reacting impulsively. Studies were conducted to assess the connection between specific brain region dysfunction and aggressive behavior.

Key terms: chronic violence, neurobiological issues

Contrast: premeditated vs. medical vs. impulsive aggression

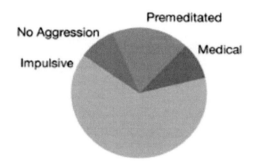

Figure 1. Aggression type in patients with prefrontal cortical dysfunction

Figure 2 shows PFC dysfunction → more impulsive aggression

The prefrontal cortex (PFC) helps control affect. The left PFC primarily connects words to emotional experiences and encodes memories. The right PFC cortex controls the retrieval of memory and visuospatial information, important in nonverbal problem solving. Around age 4, the left PFC comes to dominate, resulting in good interpretation of events and decision making. Decreased PFC function is tied to inattention, impulsivity, and disorganization, which can lead to aggression for two reasons. First, by making it difficult for the individual to choose non-aggressive responses and second, having deficits in executive decision making can lead a child to have a number of social problems. The resulting isolation from peers can prevent social skill building, and predispose the child to aggression due to a lack of alternative methods to deal with challenges.

Key terms: executive function, PFC

Cause and effect: PFC deficiencies → aggression/inappropriate behavior → socially ostracized → further problems

The anterior cingulate gyrus (aCG) is involved with processing emotional experience, and connects the limbic system with the PFC. The aCG helps the brain to shift attention to relevant stimuli, and serves to modulate attention between affect and cognition. When an individual encounters provocative situations that may cause frustration, the aCG allows them to reflect on internal controls and modulate this arousal. If one is unable to focus on the social expectations of a peer group, for example, an individual uninhibited by social constraints is more likely to react with aggression.

Key terms: aCG, limbic system

Cause and effect: when an individual encounters a situation that would provoke anger, the aCG lets them calm down and think about the situation

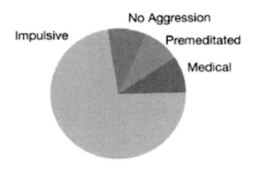

Figure 2. Aggression type in patients with cingulate gyrus dysfunction

Figure 2 shows aCG dysfunction → more impulsive aggression (similar to PFC)

The amygdala region of the temporal lobe that is especially involved in aggression. Low amygdala activity has been found in people with antisocial personality disorder. It is hypothesized that deficits in the amygdala lead to a lack of feeling aversive behaviors, such as fear. Without experiencing these aversive emotions an individual may be inclined to behave in self-serving ways without fear of outcomes.

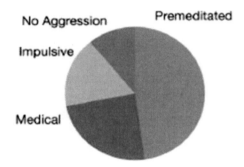

Figure 3. Aggression type in patients with amygdala dysfunction

Figure 3 shows amygdala dysfunction → more premeditated aggression

1. C is correct. The amygdala is responsible for experiencing aversion responses, including fear. Without feeling fear, an individual may commit premeditated aggression without concern.

2. D is correct. According to the data, individuals with impulsive aggression likely have trouble with the PFC or aCG. The PFC also regulates language, therefore there could be a deficit in both language and impulsive aggression.

3. C is correct. Epilepsy can affect the temporal lobe. Aggression can result due to dysfunction in the temporal lobe, as described in the passage.

4. C is correct. According to Figure 2, aCG dysfunction most commonly manifests as impulsive aggression. Using cognition to evaluate the consequences of behavior beforehand is more in line with someone who demonstrates premeditated aggression, not the impulsive aggression associated with aCG dysfunction.

5. A is correct. According to the passage, the right PFC damage is associated with both impulsive behavior and visuospatial tasks.

6. D is correct. According to the paragraph 2 and Figure 1, PFC dysfunction (decreased PFC activity) is associated with greater aggression. Thus, we would expect to see a negative correlation ($R < 0$) between PFC activity and aggressive behavior. In addition, for the results to have meaning, we want them to be statistically significant ($p < 0.05$). Only choice D fits these criteria.

7. B is correct. In the example given, we have the researchers taking away something positive (playtime) when an undesired behavior (aggression) is displayed. Negative punishment happens when a certain desired stimulus is removed after a particular undesired behavior is exhibited, resulting in the behavior happening less often in the future.

Independent Questions

1. Sensory neurons in the periphery have their cell bodies aggregated in a structure known as the dorsal root ganglion. These neurons have projections into the periphery (for sensation) and also projections into the CNS for processing. What type of neuron is the typical sensory neuron?
   A. Unipolar
   B. Bipolar
   C. Interneuron
   D. Pseudounipolar
   ↳ sensory neurons

2. The botulinum toxin is a potent neurotoxic protein that prevents acetylcholine release at the neuromuscular junction. What condition would this result in?
   A. Flaccid paralysis
   B. Spastic paralysis
   C. Lower limb numbness
   D. Muscular dystrophy

3. Irreparable damage to the midbrain would most likely disrupt which functions?
   A. Balance and coordination
   B. Movement of the lower limb
   C. Visual and auditory processing
   D. Body temperature and reproductive functions

4. Charlie has been feeling increasingly depressed over the past few months. Which one of the following medications may be the most effective in treating his depression?
   A. L-Dopa
   B. A benzodiazepine
   C. A selective serotonin reuptake inhibitor
   D. A GABA analog

5. A resting tremor is a classic sign of Parkinson's disease. This is due to a specific degeneration of the basal ganglia, which leads to reduced transient inhibition of the tonically active globus pallidus. Which part of the basal ganglia degenerates, promoting lower levels of dopamine and an increasingly pronounced resting tremor?
   A. The internal capsule
   B. The caudate nucleus
   C. The amygdala
   D. The substantia nigra *← dopamine produced here*

6. Mr. Lin slips in the bathroom and hits his head on the edge of the sink. He blacks out briefly and subsequently develops intense headaches. Upon arriving at the hospital, which of the following imaging techniques would be most appropriate to examine the integrity of Mr. Lin's arteries in his head?
   A. fMRI *— blood flow → visually for research*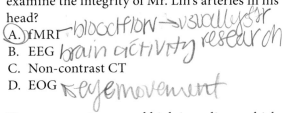
   B. EEG *brain activity research*
   C. Non-contrast CT
   D. EOG *eye movement*

7. Upon consuming a meal high in sodium, which one of the following physiological responses is most appropriate?
   A. ADH is released by the posterior pituitary gland.
   B. Atrial natriuretic peptide is released by cardiac muscle.
   C. Renin is released by the juxtaglomerular cells of the kidney.
   D. Histamine is released by mast cells.

8. A patellar reflex is a monosynaptic reflex that first enters the spinal cord. Within the spinal cord, there is excitation of the motor neuron controlling the quadriceps muscle and inhibition of the motor neuron controlling the antagonist (hamstring) muscle. Which neurotransmitter(s) are responsible for excitation and inhibition?
   A. Dopamine / GABA
   B. Glutamate / GABA
   C. Glutamate / glycine
   D. Dopamine / glycine

Independent Question Explanations

1. D is correct. Sensory neurons are pseudounipolar, which means they have an axon that splits both into the periphery and the spinal cord.

2. A is correct. Preventing acetylcholine release at the neuromuscular junction would prevent the ability to control the muscle and would result in a reduction of muscle tone. Choice B is seen with the tetanus toxin. Choice C does not work because although this process would paralyze movement, it would not necessarily limit sensation. Additionally, since this toxin acts at neuromuscular junctions (NMJ) in general, it would not specifically target the lower limbs. Choice D refers to a disorder that does affect muscle, but has a variety of different causes not limited to acetylcholine release at the NMJ.

3. C is correct. The midbrain contains the superior and inferior colliculi. The superior colliculus is involved in visual processing, while the inferior colliculus is involved in the auditory relay. Balance and coordination are controlled by the cerebellum, which is located in the hindbrain (eliminate choice A). Choice B would be correct if the pyramids of the medulla (which is a part of the hindbrain) were damaged, as they form the descending motor tracts. Choice D is controlled by the hypothalamus, which is a part of the forebrain.

4. C is correct. SSRIs are considered front-line antidepressants that function by presumably increasing extracellular levels of serotonin by limiting its reuptake by the presynaptic cell. L-Dopa is used in the treatment of Parkinson's disease (eliminate choice A), while benzodiazapenes are sedative medications used in the treatment of anxiety (eliminate choice B). GABA analogs are used as anxiety medication, not antidepressant medication (eliminate choice D).

5. D is correct. Dopamine is produced by the substantia nigra, and so it is the degeneration of the substantia nigra that leads to reduced dopamine levels. This ultimately results in the resting tremor. Note that you do not need to know the functions of choices A and B, and the amygdala is not part of the basal ganglia.

6. C is correct. A CT scan is the best choice to visualize blood vessels or hemorrhage. The other options can be eliminated. A functional MRI scan (fMRI) is used to compare blood flow to different regions of the brain. This is generally used to assess brain activity (often for research purposes), not to diagnose injuries. An electroencephalogram (EEG) is also used to monitor brain activity, although it does so using the electrical activity of brain waves. Finally, an electrooculogram (EOG) records eye movements. If you are interested, note that it is highly probable that Mr. Lin suffered an epidural hematoma, a condition that you are almost certain to see in medical school.

7. A is correct. ADH (antidiuretic hormone, also called vasopressin) is a hormone that causes the body to retain water, and is released in response to an increase in plasma osmolality, which will likely happen after consuming a high-sodium meal. Atrial natriuretic peptide's main function is to reduce high blood pressure, which is not necessarily true in this case (eliminate choice B). Renin also has water-conservation effects, but it responds principally to a decrease in arterial blood pressure, reduction in sodium load to the distal tubule, and sympathetic nervous system activity (eliminate choice C). Finally, histamine is a cellular signal that is released in response to an allergic reaction, not sodium levels (eliminate choice D).

8. C is correct. While dopamine is an excitatory neurotransmitter in the brain, glutamate is excitatory in the brain and the spinal cord. Similarly, GABA is inhibitory in the brain, while glycine is the inhibitory neurotransmitter in the spinal cord.

This page left intentionally blank.

Sensation and Perception

0. Introduction

Though they may seem interchangeable in every day usage, in psychology, the words "sensation" and "perception" have specific meanings and are sometimes even contrasted with one another.

Sensation is an effect of **transduction,** the process by which auditory, electromagnetic, physical, and other kinds of information from the environment are converted into electrical signals within the human nervous system. Sensation provides the raw signal, communicating information, entering the nervous system through receptors in the peripheral nervous systems. This raw information is sent to the central nervous system by action potentials and neurotransmitters.

Perception is the processing of this raw information. Therefore, it is sensation that gives us information from the world around us and perception that allows us to make sense of it.

> **MCAT STRATEGY > > >**
>
> Remember that *p*erception involves *p*rocessing sense information.

1. Sensory Processing and Perception

I. Sensory Receptors

Sensory receptors are the neurons that trigger electrical signals in response to stimuli from the environment. These receptors can encode multiple aspects of a stimulus. For example, a single hair call responsible for sound perception can transmit information about volume, frequency, and pitch. Sensory receptors receive stimuli and transmit information about them through ganglia, which are groups of nerve cells found outside of the central nervous system. Once received by the central nervous system, the information is sent via neural pathways to projection areas in the brain where the sensation is further analyzed.

There are four properties that sensory receptors communicate to the central nervous system: **modality**, which is the type of stimulus, **location**, which is where the stimulus is coming from, **intensity**, which is the frequency of action potentials produced by the stimulus, and **duration**, which is how long the stimulus lasts.

Broadly, sensory receptors are divided into **exteroceptors**, which respond to stimuli from the outside world, and **interoceptors**, which respond to internal stimuli. Here are the sensory receptors that most commonly appear on the MCAT:

> Hair cells (hearing; linear and rotational acceleration): respond to movement of fluid in the inner ear
> Olfactory receptors (smell): respond to volatile compounds in the air
> Osmoreceptors (water homeostasis): respond to the osmolarity of blood
> Nociceptors (somatosensation, a.k.a. touch): respond to painful stimuli
> Photoreceptors (sight): respond to the visible spectrum of the electromagnetic waves
> Taste receptors (taste): respond to dissolved compounds in substances

II. Thresholds

Threshold is the minimum amount of stimulus required to deliver a difference in perception. Because the same sensation can be perceived in very different ways in different people, and because these variations between people must be explained by central system activity, thresholds represent an example of why perception is considered to be an element of psychology.

There are three types of thresholds:

Absolute threshold is the minimum amount of stimulus energy that is needed to activate a sensory system. The absolute threshold is one of sensation, not perception. For example, very low frequency sounds may cause slight vibrations in the hair cells of the inner ear but they may not be significant enough for transduction of the stimulus to occur.

Threshold of conscious perception is the minimum amount of stimulus energy that is needed for a signal to be sent to the central nervous system and perceived. If a stimulus is above the absolute threshold but below the threshold of conscious perception, sometimes called subliminal perception, it will activate a sensory system that will send a signal to the central nervous system, but it will not reach the regions of the brain responsible for attention and consciousness. Therefore, stimulus energy under the threshold of conscious perception is sensed, but not perceived

Difference threshold is the minimum difference in magnitude between two different stimuli before the difference can be perceived. This is also referred to as **just-noticeable difference** (jnd). An important element to this type of threshold is **Weber's law**, which states that the change in magnitude of a stimulus that will make it noticeable is a constant ratio of the magnitude of the original stimulus. It is important to note that Weber's law does not work for sensations of an extremely high or low magnitude, i.e. extremely high or low frequency sounds.

III. Signal Detection Theory

According to **signal detection theory**, perception of stimuli can be affected not only by the stimuli themselves, but also nonsensory considerations like expectations, experiences, and motives. In this way, psychological and environmental context can alter our perception of stimuli. Signal detection theory accounts for response bias, which is the tendency of people to habitually respond to a certain stimulus in a certain way because of nonsensory factors.

IV. Adaptation

Adaptation refers simply to how the detection of stimuli can change over time, either through physiological or psychological means, which affect, respectively, sensation and perception. For example, pupils dilate in the dark to take in more sensory information. For another example, when you walk into a kitchen and pizza is baking in the oven, odor molecules stimulate your olfactory receptors and you smell the pizza. However, as time goes by, you notice the smell less, though those odor molecules are still in the air. Adaptation allows the brain to focus attention on relevant stimuli, which are typically changes in the environment.

> **MCAT STRATEGY > > >**
>
> Under signal detection theory, we can have false alarms (got a "hit" even though there was no signal) and misses (didn't get a "hit" even though the signal was sent).

2. Vision

Vision is one of most highly adapted senses in humans, so much so that it is the only sense which has an entire lobe of the brain, the occipital lobe, dedicated to it.

I. The Structure and Function of the Eye

The eye is the organ that detects visual stimuli, converts the stimuli into action potentials, and sends them to the brain via visual pathways. Below is a diagram of the eye:

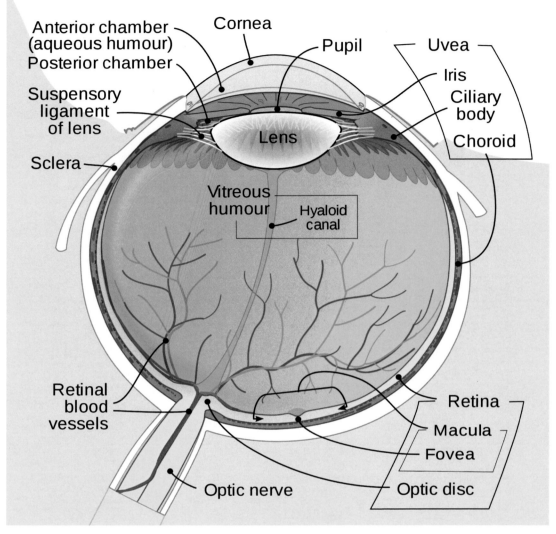

Figure 1. The Anatomy of the Eye.

Light enters the eye through the clear portion at the front of it, the **cornea**. Because the cornea is highly curved, light is refracted as it passes through it. The cornea is directly continuous with the **sclera**, the white part of the eye. There is a layer underneath the sclera called the **choroid**, responsible for absorbing excess light with darkly-pigmented cells. One layer deeper is the surface upon which the light entering the eye is focused, the **retina**. It is the retina, part of the central nervous system, that contains the photoreceptors that convert light into electrical impulses to be sent to the brain.

When it enters through the cornea, light passes through the **anterior chamber**, the space in front of the iris, the **iris**, the colored part of the eye which has an opening called the **pupil**, the **posterior chamber**, which is between the iris and the lens, the **lens**, which helps control the further refraction of the incoming light, and the **vitreous chamber** which contains **vitreous humor**, a transparent gel that supports the retina, on its way to the retina.

Several parts of the eye help to optimize this process. The **dilator pupillae** opens the pupil when stimulated sympathetically. Inversely, the **constrictor pupillae** constricts the pupil when stimulated parasympathetically. The

ciliary body is the tissue that produces the **aqueous humor**, the liquid that bathes the front part of the eye before it drains into the **canal of Schlemm**. The **ciliary muscle**, part of the ciliary body, is responsible for changing the shape of the lens via parasympathetic movements of the **suspensory ligaments**. **Accommodation** is the name of the process by which the shape of the lens is changed.

Once light reaches the retina, it is received by the **cones** and **rods**, the photoreceptors of the eye. The retina typically contains 6 million cones and 120 million rods.

Cones perceive color and fine detail. There are three types of cones, named for the wavelengths of light that they primarily absorb, those being short (absorbing blue), medium (absorbing green), and long (absorbing red).

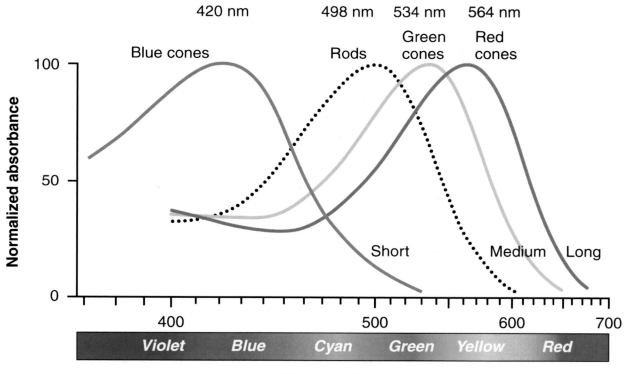

Figure 2. Absorption of the Three Types of Cones from Wavelengths of 400 to 700.

Rods, containing the pigment rhodospin, allow for the perception of light and dark. They are not sensitive to details, have no involvement in color vision, but do permit humans to see in reduced illumination.

The central section of the retina, the **macula,** contains a high concentration of cones, and at its central point, the **fovea**, no rods are present. Moving outward from the fovea, the concentration of cones decreases as the concentration of rods increases. For this reason, vision is most clear and acute at the fovea. And, as there are no cones or rods in the **optic disc**, the area where the optic nerve leaves the eye, this region is a blind spot.

Between the cones and rods and the optic nerve are several layers of neurons through which information must be sent. Rods and cones synapse with **bipolar cells**, nerve cells that have only one axon and one dendrite. The bipolar cells then synapse with **ganglion cells,** the axons of which form together to make up the **optic nerve**, which takes information from the eye to the occipital lobe to be processed. There are far more rods and cones than there are ganglion cells, and therefore, the ganglion cells must receive information from many photoreceptors. As more and more photoreceptors converge on one ganglion, the resolution decreases.

Amacrine and **horizontal cells** help to optimize this process: they receive input from retinal cells before any information is passed onto to ganglion cells. This allows them to accentuate subtle differences between the information being transferred to each bipolar cell. In this way, amacrine and horizontal cells can increase our perception of visual contrasts, making them important for edge detection.

II. Visual Pathways

The term visual pathways refers both to the physical connections between the eyes and the occipital lobe and the movement of information through them.

Each eye is divided down the middle, vertically, into two visual fields, left and right. Each eye's right visual field is projected onto the left half of the eye's retina. As the electrical signals carrying visual information travel on their way to the occipital lobe, the first major event happens at the **optic chiasm**. It is here that optical fibers from the nasal half (the visual field closer to the nose) of each retina cross paths. Because of the aforementioned crossing of visual fields, these optical fibers from the nasal half of each eye carry the temporal vision (the visual field closer to the temple) from each eye. On the other hand the temporal fibers (which carry the nasal visual field) do not cross paths, meaning that once optic fibers get through the optic chiasm, the fibers corresponding to the left visual field from both eyes are projected onto the right side of the brain, and vice versa. Once they have passed through the optic chiasm, the reorganized optic pathways are referred to as **optic tracts**.

At this point, visual information passes to the brain. First, it meets the **lateral geniculate nucleus (LGN)**, which is in the thalamus and is the primary relay center for information received from the retinae. The LGN then radiates the information through the temporal and parietal lobes to the **occipital lobe**, where it finally reaches the **visual cortex**.

The chart below can help to visualize this process:

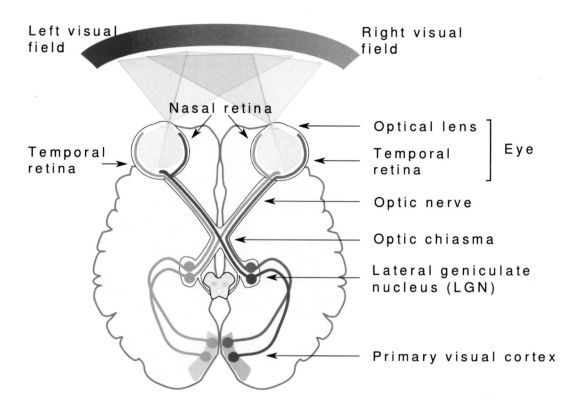

Figure 3. Visual Pathways.

III. Information Processing

The brain is able to create a cohesive image of the world through **parallel processing**, the ability to analyze and combine several pieces of information regarding color, motion, and shape at once. Through this process, the new information that is received through the visual pathways can be compared with memories. In this way, the brain can rapidly come to the conclusion that, for example, not only are you looking at a dog, but it is your dog that you've had for years.

The psychological model of parallel processing comes hand in hand with the neuroscientific **feature detection theory,** which explains why different areas of the brain are activated when a person is looking at different things. Different parts of the visual pathway contain different kinds of cells that are specialized to detect either color, shape or motion.

As we've said before, color is detected by cones.

Shape is detected by **parvocellular cells**. As these cells have high **spatial resolution**, they allow us to see very fine detail when looking at a stationary object (they cannot work with fast moving object because they have low **temporal resolution**). This allows us not only to see the full three-dimensional shape of an object, but it also allows us to differentiate the object from the background, letting us clearly see its boundaries.

Motion is detected by **magnocellular cells** because, as opposed to parvocellular cells, they have high temporal resolution. Furthermore, mangocellular cells have low spatial resolution, meaning the detail of an image is lessened when it is in motion.

The human brain commits a great deal of resources to vision, so much so that 30% of the cortex is committed to processing visual information, whereas 8% is committed to touch information, and 3% to auditory information.

3. Hearing and Vestibular Sense

I. The Structure and Function of the Ear

The ear is the organ responsible not only for hearing, but also for sensing linear and rotational acceleration (also known as kinesthetic sense). It is divided into three major parts, the outer, middle, and inner ear.

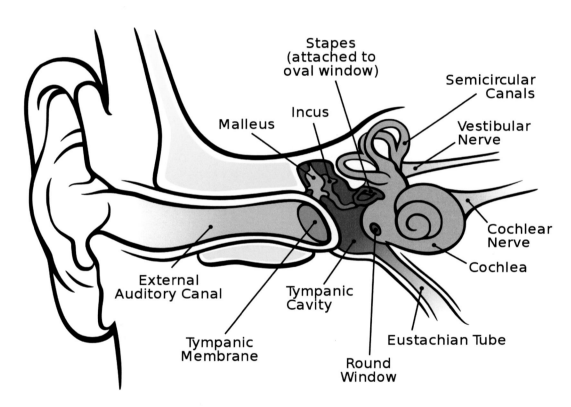

Figure 4. The Anatomy of the Ear.

The outer ear begins with **the pinna** (also known as the **auricle**), which is the outwardly visible part of the ear. It functions as a kind of funnel for sound, channeling sound waves through the **external auditory canal** and to the **tympanic membrane** (colloquially known as the **eardrum**). Once sound waves reach the membrane, they cause it to vibrate; the frequency of those sound waves determines the rate of vibration of the tympanic membrane, with high-frequency sounds causing high-speed vibration and low-frequency sounds causing low-speed vibrations. And the louder a sound is, the higher the amplitude of the vibration on the eardrum.

Once past the tympanic membrane, sound waves enter the middle ear and are met by the three smallest bones in the body, the **ossicles**. First is the **malleus** (or **hammer**), which is connected to the tympanic membrane. It sends vibrations on to the **incus** (or the **anvil**), which in turn sends them on to the **stapes** (or the **stirrup**). The stapes is the connection between the middle and the inner ear, with its baseplate connected to the **cochlea** on the **oval window**. Additionally, the **Eustachian tube** connects the middle ear to the nasal cavity and helps to equalize pressure between the ear and the environment.

The inner ear contains the cochlea, which is crucial for hearing, and the **vestibule** and the **semicircular canals**, which account for linear and rotational acceleration, respectively. The inner ear is protected by a thick layer of bone called the **bony labyrinth.** Together, the structures of the inner ear form a mass called the **membranous labyrinth**, which is filled with **endolymph**, a potassium rich fluid. Outside of the membranous labyrinth, between it and the bony labyrinth, is a thin layer of another fluid called **perilymph**. Perilymph transmits vibrations from the stapes, but also protects the membranous labyrinth.

The spiral-shaped cochlea is divided into three **scalae**, or sections. Inside of the central scala, and protected by the flexible **basilar membrane**, is the **organ of Corti**, the actual hearing apparatus of the ear. The organ of Corti is made up of hair cells that are bathed in the potassium-rich fluid mentioned before, endolymph. The two other scalae are filled with perilymph, surround the organ of Corti, and are continuous with the oval and round windows of the cochlea, which connect to the middle ear.

When sound waves are moved from the stapes through the oval window of the cochlea, the perilymph vibrates. Then, the hair cells of the organ of Corti, just as the rods and cones do in the eye, convert physical stimulus into electrical information, which is transferred to the central nervous system by the **auditory nerve** (also called the **vestibulocochlear nerve**).

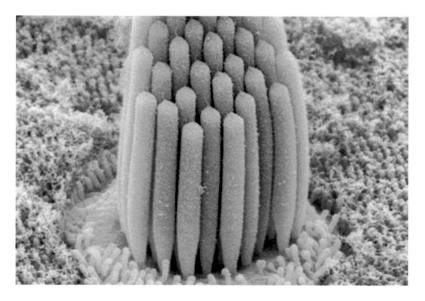

Figure 5. A Hair Cell.

Now, for hair cells: they take their name from the long **stereocilia** that cover their surface (pictured above). Vibrations in the endoylpmh cause the stereocilia of the hair cells to sway from side to side, causing ion channels to open, which in turn creates a receptor potential.

The cochlea is arranged tonotopically, meaning that different hair cells in different parts of the cochlea pick up different kinds of sounds. Therefore, the brain can assess the quality of a sound based upon which hair cells are vibrating.

Meanwhile, the vestibule, which contains the **utricle** and **saccule**, is responsible for sensing linear acceleration, which helps us balance and determine our orientation in space. The utricle and saccule contain specialized hair cells, otoliths, that resist motion as the body accelerates, and send information to the brain.

The semicircular canals sense rotational acceleration. Each canal ends in an **ampulla**, which houses hair cells. Endolymph in the ampullas resist motion when the head rotates, stimulating hair cells to send information to the brain.

II. Auditory Pathways

Once the hair cells of the organ of Corti have converted physical vibrations into electrical information, it is sent via the auditory nerve, along the brainstem, to the **medial geniculate nucleus** (MGN) of the thalamus. At this point, the information is primarily sent to the temporal lobe of the brain, where it is processed in the **auditory cortex**, but some is also sent to the **superior olive** and the **inferior colliculus** as well. The former serves to localize sound information, and the latter is responsible for the startle reflex. Moreover, the inferior colliculus works with both the eyes and ears for what is called the **vestibulo-ocular reflex**, helping to keep the eyes fixed on a single point in space while the head rotates.

MCAT STRATEGY > > >

Mental illness is much more commonly associated with auditory hallucinations rather than visual ones in part because the auditory pathway has to pass through several more steps—so there's more places where things can go wrong.

4. Other Senses

The other senses include smell and taste, somatosensation (touch), and the kinesthetic sense.

I. Smell

The sense of smell is the result of aerosolized (volatile) compounds, which are dissolved in the air, binding to **olfactory chemoreceptors**, which are located in the olfactory epithelium in the upper part of the nasal cavity. Just like seeing and hearing, the sense of smell relies upon an **olfactory pathway**. Once the chemoreceptors convert physical stimuli into electrical information, it is sent to the **olfactory bulb**, which is located in the front of the brain, and is then passed along the **olfactory tract** to be processed by higher parts of the brain, including the **limbic system**, a complex structure located on both sides of the thalamus.

II. Taste

Taste is the result of groups of cells on the tongue, called taste buds, that bind with dissolved chemicals. The taste buds occur in small groups called papillae. Once the chemoreceptors of the taste buds have transduced stimuli into information, it is sent to the **taste center** of the thalamus. From there, it is processed and sent to other high-order brain regions.

Taste and flavor are not synonymous: flavor represents a confluence of both smell and taste.

III. Somatosensation

Somatosensation is more complex than simply being the sense of touch, as it includes four modalities: pain, pressure, temperature, and vibration. There are several different types of receptors that receive tactile stimulus and convert it to electrical information, including **free nerve endings** (pain and temperature), **Miessner's corpuscles** (light touch),

Merkle discs (deep pressure and texture), **Pacinian corpuscles** (deep pressure and vibration), and **Ruffini endings** (stretch).

Due to its complexity, there are a few additional concepts that scientists use to explain and study somatosensation.

Two-point threshold is the minimum distance between two points being stimulated concurrently on the skin where those two points will be felt distinctly from one another. This distance varies with the density of nerves in the skin.

Physiological zero is the normal temperature of the skin, ranging between 86° and 97° Fahrenheit.

The gate theory of pain holds that our bodies have the ability to "gate" pain signals, turning them on or off with a special mechanism in the spinal cord, which can be preferential of which signals from which modalities of somatosensation it sends to the brain. This can explain how pain thresholds vary from person to person.

Once stimuli are transduced, electrical information from somatosensation is sent to the **somatosensory cortex** in the parietal lobe of the brain.

IV. Kinesthetic Sense

Also known as **proprioception**, this sense, with its receptors found mostly in the muscles and joints, allows us to perceive our bodies are in space. For example, even with your eyes and ears covered, you can know where your foot is in space.

Practice Passage

Gate Control theory posits that pain is both psychogenic and somatic, originating both in perception and the body. Prior theories considered psychological factors were only reactions to pain. In Gate Control theory, these factors are understood to influence the perception of pain.

Depression is a prominent disorder involved with chronic pain, impacting as many as 40-50% of individuals experiencing pain. There is a cyclic relationship between experiencing pain and depression, where chronic pain can cause depression, but depression also impacts the perception of pain. For individuals experiencing depression and chronic pain, it can be hard to generate strategies for addressing the pain, leading to a sense of helplessness. As a result, many individuals may utilize passive coping strategies for managing pain, such as abusing medication, illicit drugs, alcohol, or being inactive.

Pain is typically assessed by a "pain thermometer" on which patients are asked to rate the severity of their pain from 1 to 10. In a study which examined patients with chronic pain, researchers emphasized using coping strategies, developing a sense of self-efficacy, and being active. Patients were asked to rate their level of pain before and after the program. Table 1 shows results of the experiment, with results from group pain thermometers compared (Note: t-test comparison of pre- vs. post-treatment, $p = 0.009$).

Table 1. Effect of Treatment on Pain Perception

Group	Before Treatment	After Treatment
Treatment	1=Less Severe — More Severe=10 : 7.9	1=Less Severe — More Severe=10 : 5.3
Control	1=Less Severe — More Severe=10 : 6.1	1=Less Severe — More Severe=10 : 5.1

Cognitive factors are also associated with pain. Patients who realize their pain signifies a progressive disease experience more severe pain compared to those who see their condition as stable or improving. In addition, patients who experience pain when involved in physical activity have a learned expectation that future activity will result in pain, resulting in decreased voluntary physical activity.

There are two types of coping strategies that patients can employ, overt and covert coping strategies. Overt coping strategies are active strategies to manage pain, such as engaging in healthy behavior. Covert strategies involve distracting oneself from the pain, such as through meditation or obtaining information about the chronic condition.

1. A patient assumes his pain will not get better. In his treatment he is asked to find research about his condition each day for a week to help develop personal coping strategies to change this belief. This is an example of what type of strategy?
   A. Humanistic
   B. Psychodynamic
   C. Cognitive behavioral
   D. Neurobiological

2. Which of the following best summarizes the reported results of the study?
   A. The treatment group had a greater decrease in pain than the control group
   B. The control group had a greater decrease in pain than the treatment group
   C. The treatment group had a greater increase in pain than the control group
   D. The control group had a greater increase in pain than the treatment group

3. What best accounts for the results seen in the control group, who were told they were receiving treatment but actually were not?
   A. Avoidance learning
   B. Expectancy theory
   C. Placebo effect
   D. Conditioned learning

4. This passage suggests that what else should be assessed in addition to assessing a patient's level of pain?
   A. Somatic issues
   B. Psychogenic issues
   C. The area of the body in which the pain is occurring
   D. The neurobiological factors involved with pain

5. The example of understanding the severity and progress of disease and its effect on pain perception is most accurately an example of:
   A. top-down processing. — *perception driven by cognition*
   B. bottom-up processing. — *processing info as its coming in*
   C. perceptual organization.
   D. somatosensation.

6. If neurologists were looking to quantify the levels of pain receptor activation that correlates to a specific level on the pain thermometer would be best served by targeting and measuring which receptor type?
   A. Chemoreceptors
   B. Mechanoreceptors
   C. Gustatory receptors
   D. Nociceptors

7. The figure below, which displays the level of electric shock sensation reported by subjects holding on to a current-carrying wire, exemplifies which sensory processing phenomena?

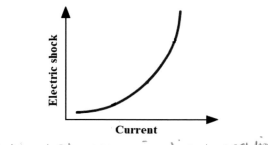

   A. Psychophysics — *relationship between stimuli & sensations/perceptions*
   B. Feature detection
   C. Parallel processing
   D. Pheromones

Practice Passage Explanations

Gate Control theory posits that pain is both psychogenic and somatic, originating both in perception and the body. Prior theories considered psychological factors were only reactions to pain. In Gate Control theory, these factors are understood to influence the perception of pain.

Key terms: Gate control theory, psychogenic, somatic

Contrast: psychological factors used to be considered only reactions to pain, now we know they contribute to pain perception

Depression is a prominent disorder involved with chronic pain, impacting as many as 40-50% of individuals experiencing pain. There is a cyclic relationship between experiencing pain and depression, where chronic pain can cause depression, but depression also impacts the perception of pain. For individuals experiencing depression and chronic pain, it can be hard to generate strategies for addressing the pain, leading to a sense of helplessness. As a result, many individuals may utilize passive coping strategies for managing pain, such as abusing medication, illicit drugs, alcohol, or being inactive.

Key terms: depression, passive coping, cyclic relationship

Cause and effect: depression leads to helplessness and passive approaches to pain management

Pain is typically assessed by a "pain thermometer" on which patients are asked to rate the severity of their pain from 1 to 10. In a study which examined patients with chronic pain, researchers emphasized using coping strategies, developing a sense of self-efficacy, and being active. Patients were asked to rate their level of pain before and after the program. Table 1 shows results of the experiment, with results from group pain thermometers compared (Note: t-test comparison of pre- vs. post-treatment, $p = 0.009$).

Key terms: pain thermometer, treatment program, coping strategies

Table 1. Effect of Treatment on Pain Perception

Group	Before Treatment	After Treatment
Treatment	1=Less Severe More Severe=10 7.9	1=Less Severe More Severe=10 5.3
Control	1=Less Severe More Severe=10 6.1	1=Less Severe More Severe=10 5.1

Table 1 shows us that both groups saw a decrease in pain, but the treatment group had a larger decrease

Cognitive factors are also associated with pain. Patients who realize their pain signifies a progressive disease experience more severe pain compared to those who see their condition as stable or improving. In addition, patients who experience pain when involved in physical activity have a learned expectation that future activity will result in pain, resulting in decreased voluntary physical activity.

Key terms: cognitive factors

Cause and effect: people who view their disease as progressive and getting worse will experience greater pain; those who associate pain with physical activity will engage in less activity

There are two types of coping strategies that patients can employ, overt and covert coping strategies. Overt coping strategies are active strategies to manage pain, such as engaging in healthy behavior. Covert strategies involve distracting oneself from the pain, such as through meditation or obtaining information about the chronic condition.

Key terms: coping strategies, overt, covert

Cause and effect: coping strategies can actually help reduce pain perception; overt ~ active, covert ~ passive

1. C is correct. In this strategy the patient is asked to address his catastrophic thoughts by engaging in a behavior that is designed to change his thinking, which is a cognitive behavioral strategy.

2. A is correct. According to Figure 1, both groups decreased in their pain level, but the treatment group decreased in pain more than the control group.

3. C is correct. The placebo effect occurs when participants in an experiment demonstrate a certain benefit after expecting to benefit, even though they are not receiving the treatment.

4. B is correct. The passage illustrated that pain involves psychological factors as well as physical ones. In addition, psychological factors can have a causative influence on pain, not just be reactions to pain.

5. A is correct. In the 4th paragraph, we are told that cognition can affect the perception of pain. There are two general processes involved in sensation and perception. Bottom-up processing refers to processing sensory information as it is coming in. Top-down processing, on the other hand, refers to perception that is driven by cognition. Your brain applies what it knows and what it expects to perceive and fills in the blanks, so to speak.

6. D is correct. A nociceptor is a receptor found at the end of a sensory neuron's axon that responds to damaging or potentially damaging (i.e. painful) stimuli by sending danger signals to the central nervous system.

7. A is correct. Psychophysics is the scientific study of the relationship between stimuli (quantified in physical terms) and the sensations and perceptions evoked by these stimuli. Here we have the quantified stimuli (current) and the corresponding perception/sensation of "electricity" reported by the patient.

Independent Questions

1. Pouring cold water into one ear and then attempting to sit up and turn one's head is reported to elicit symptoms consistent with motion sickness, vertigo, and dizziness. Why does this phenomenon occur?
   A. Hair cells of the ossicles are stimulated at different rates, leading to an inaccurate sense of position.
   B. Temperature differences in the ear disrupt the balance of the proprioceptive system.
   C. Cold water disrupts the function of the cochlea, which detects rotational motion.
   D. Endolymph flow in the semicircular canals is disturbed, reducing their ability to accurately detect angular acceleration.

   8×3   .5×3

2. A woman carrying an 8-kg gym bag just barely notices when a 0.5-kg weight is added to it. When holding a 24-kg suitcase in a similar way, which of the following is true of this woman?
   A. She would begin to notice a difference if a 0.5-kg weight were added, because it would surpass her absolute threshold.
   B. She would begin to notice a difference if a 1.5-kg weight were added, because it would surpass her absolute threshold.
   C. She would begin to notice a difference if a 0.5-kg weight were added, because it would surpass her difference threshold.
   D. She would begin to notice a difference if a 1.5-kg weight were added, because it would surpass her difference threshold.

   processed by relevance

3. When scanning a busy street, the feature detection ability of the human visual system would most likely pick up on which of the following stimuli?
   A. A person waving
   B. A police car with its lights flashing
   C. Fast-moving clouds signifying rain
   D. This question cannot be answered without more information. *need context*

4. What is the benefit of the crossing over of optic nerve fibers at the optic chiasm?
   A. It provides for ocular sparing, which allows one optic nerve to accommodate the other if it is damaged
   B. The eyes can share the same blood supply in case of a tumor or aneurysm.
   C. It generates binocular and stereoscopic vision.
   D. It allows vision to take place in a monocular fashion.

5. In the visual system, motion is detected in part by:
   A. parvocellular cells.
   B. magnocellular cells.
   C. bipolar cells.
   D. cones.

6. Afferent nerve fibers are responsible for transmitting somatosensory information to the brain for processing. While taking a hot shower, warm water can be interpreted as pleasant; however, water too hot can cause pain. Which receptors in the skin, which are characterized by free nerve endings, are responsible for transmitting this sudden pain?
   A. Pacinian corpuscles
   B. Thermoreceptors
   C. Nociceptors — *pain!*
   D. Meissner's corpuscles *mechano - light*

7. Proprioception would most likely be used to:
   A. know that one's foot was elevated even without looking at it.
   B. notice that deep pressure was being applied to one's arm.
   C. sense that a plane was entering a downward spin.
   D. balance on a tightrope.

8. Which of the following situations best exemplifies top-down processing?
   A. Walking into a bookstore and browsing the bookshelf
   B. A child stepping into an airplane for the first time
   C. Seeing "ton" on a partially obscured road sign and knowing that it says "Dayton" because you are familiar with the area
   D. A blindfolded person petting an animal and determining from its size, shape, and the "meow" noise that it makes that the animal is a cat. *BOTTOM UP*

Independent Question Explanations

1. D is correct. The semicircular canals are components of the inner ear. They are filled with endolymph, and the movement of this fluid against hair cells is responsible for the detection of angular acceleration. Pouring cold water into one ear will generate opposite convective currents, leading to reduced ability to interpret angular acceleration, which is initiated when turning the head. Alternatively, you can answer this question using process of elimination. The ossicles are bones and thus do not contain hair cells (eliminate choice A); proprioception is not related to balance or the ear, and the cochlea does not primarily detect rotational motion (eliminate choice B and C).

2. D is correct. Noticing a difference in the amount of weight one is carrying relates to the difference threshold, not the absolute threshold; thus, choices A and B can be immediately eliminated. Weber's law states that the percent change in intensity of a stimulus required to reach the just-noticeable difference is constant along a range of intensities. In other words, the *percent* of 8 kg that 0.5 kg represents should be the same as the percent change required to notice an addition to a 24-kg suitcase. Since 24 kg is three times 8 kg, a 1.5-kg addition is required to represent the same percent change.

3. D is correct. Feature detection is a phenomenon in which external visual stimuli are filtered and processed by relevance. This can be used to detect stimuli of certain colors, of certain shapes, or with certain motion patterns. Which stimulus is detected first depends largely on the context of the situation. An individual waiting for a friend may be more likely to quickly identify someone waving, while someone who has been in a car accident may see the police car first.

4. C is correct. Crossing over at the optic chiasm allows for the visual cortex to receive visual information from the same hemispheres of both eyes. This allows for vision from one eye to be processed by both hemispheres of the brain, ultimately generating binocular and stereoscopic vision. Keep in mind that not all optic nerve fibers cross at the optic chiasm. The other options can also be eliminated; one optic nerve cannot take over the functions of the other if it has been damaged (eliminate choice A), and nerve fibers do not carry blood (eliminate choice B). Additionally, monocular vision refers to vision that utilizes each eye separately, which is not an advantage of the crossing over of nerve fibers (eliminate choice D).

5. B is correct. Magnocellular cells have low spatial resolution but high temporal resolution, allowing them to form a basis for our detection of objects in motion. In contrast, parvocellular cells have high spatial resolution but low temporal resolution; these are used to detect details and the boundaries of objects. Bipolar cells transmit information obtained by rods and cones, but they do not sense motion. Cones detect color.

6. C is correct. Nociceptors are responsible for transmitting painful stimuli to the brain. While thermoreceptors, or receptors that detect changes in temperature, is a tempting answer, remember that the question is asking about the pain associated with hot water, not its temperature (eliminate choice B). Pacinian corpuscles refer to receptors that detect pressure and vibration (eliminate choice A). Meissner's corpuscles are mechanoreceptors that react to light touch (eliminate choice D).

7. A is correct. Proprioception is our sense of where our own body parts are in space. Choice A is a direct use of proprioception. Option D is close, but balance is more closely related to the vestibular sense. Similarly, the vestibular sense (specifically the semicircular canals in the ear) would be used to sense that a plane one was traveling in was spinning downwards. Finally, deep pressure is sensed by Merkel disks as part of somatosensation.

8. C is correct. Top-down processing is driven by previous experience and expectations. It is often used to recognize something familiar without needing to look at all of its individual parts. Here, if you are able to recognize the city name "Dayton" due to its familiarity, that exemplifies top-down processing. In contrast, bottom-up processing involves piecing together larger concepts from their component parts. Choice D is a good example of bottom-up processing; additionally, infants and children, like that in choice B, often use bottom-up processing if they are seeing a new object for the first time. Choice A is not an example of top-down processing because there is no evidence that we are using prior knowledge or experiences to make decisions about the books on the bookshelf.

Consciousness

0. Introduction

Consciousness is the awareness that we have of our surroundings, our internal states, and our selves. There are commonly accepted to be four general states of consciousness: alertness, sleep, dreaming, and altered states of consciousness.

1. Consciousness and Alertness

Alertness is the state of being awake, being attentive to what is going on within us and around us, and being able to think. Alertness is the function of an interplay between the **reticular formation**, which is located in the brainstem, and the prefrontal cortex of the brain.

When alert, the body experiences physiological stimulation, with cortisol levels higher than in other states of consciousness. Moreover, scientists can measure the electrical activity of the brain through **electroencephalography**, which shows that the brain is more active when we are alert.

2. Sleep

Sleep is a state of consciousness in which the nervous system is relatively inactive and the normal brain activity that is typical during consciousness is, for the most part, suspended.

I. Stages of Sleep

In order to study the nature of sleep, scientists employ **polysomnography** (PSG), a multi-faceted method for examining and measuring physiological processes that occur during sleep. Using PSG, scientists can measure electrical impulses in the brain with **electroencephalogram** (EEG), skeletal and muscular movements with **electromyogram** (EMG), and eyes movement with **electrooculogram** (EOG).

When a person is fully awake, and EEG will pick up **beta waves** (high frequency, low amplitude). These waves, which have the highest frequency of all brain waves, are not very consistent in their pattern, and are therefore considered desynchronous.

When a person is awake but tired and less alert, an EEG will pick up **alpha wave** (low amplitude, high frequency) readings, showing that the person's brain is behaving differently from when the person is fully alert. Alpha waves are more consistent than beta waves (synchronous).

When this person actually falls asleep, they enter **Stage 1 sleep**, and their EEG readings primarily show **theta waves** (low amplitude and irregular frequency). In this stage, EOG readings show slow, rolling movement of the eyes while EMG readings show moderate activity.

MCAT STRATEGY > > >

Remember K-complexes and sleep spindles for Stage 2 non-REM sleep. The MCAT loves asking about them!

In **Stage 2 sleep,** theta waves continue to show up on the EEG, but are now interspersed with **K-complexes**, single high amplitude, low frequency waves, and **sleep spindles**, bursts of multiple high-frequency, moderate amplitude waves. A typical K-complex lasts for half a second while a typical sleep spindle lasts for half to one and a half seconds. During this stage, the EOG picks up no eye movement and the EMG continues to show moderate activity. It is during this stage that heart rate, temperature, and respiration decrease.

Stage 3 sleep marks the transition into **slow wave sleep** (SWS), containing both Stage 3 and Stage 4. In this stage, EEG readings primarily detect **delta waves** (high amplitude, low frequency). At the beginning of Stage 3 sleep, delta waves are mixed with higher frequency waves, but as it progresses, these higher frequency waves phase out and **Stage 4 sleep** begins. During this stage, EOG readings continue to show no eye movement while EMG continues to show moderate muscular and skeletal activity. Meanwhile, digestion and heart rate slow and growth hormones are released.

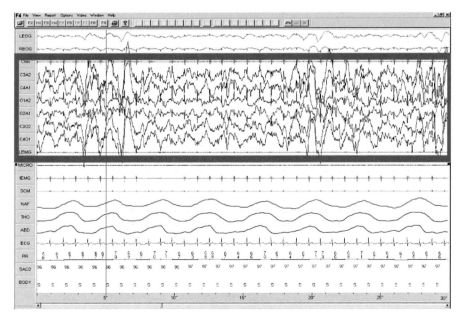

Figure 1. Screenshot of a PSG Reading From Stage 3, Slow Wave Sleep, (EEG Readings are in the Red Rectangle, Showing High Amplitude Delta Waves).

In the next stage, **REM sleep**, EEG readings show waves that are similar to the beta waves present when a person is awake, but have a more variable frequency. EOG readings show bursts of rapid eye movements (which is where REM sleep gets its name), and EMG readings show very low skeletal movement. Given this combination of brainwaves, heart rate, and respiration that are similar to that of being awake, and of muscular skeletal readings that are very low, a person in REM sleep appears to be physiologically awake, but also paralyzed. This is the stage when a person typically dreams.

Missing REM sleep in a night will cause **REM rebound**, meaning that the next night a person will spend more time in REM sleep than they typically do.

II. Sleep Cycles

A **sleep cycle** is a complete progression through all of the stages of sleep, from Stage 1 to REM and over again. At the beginning of the night, a person spends most time in deep sleep, Stage 4, but as the night progresses, REM predominates, and a person may even have very brief moments of being awake. The length of the sleep cycle increases from childhood to adulthood, from about 50 minutes to 90 minutes, respectively.

The following chart, a hypnogram, illustrates the progression of sleep cycles throughout the night.

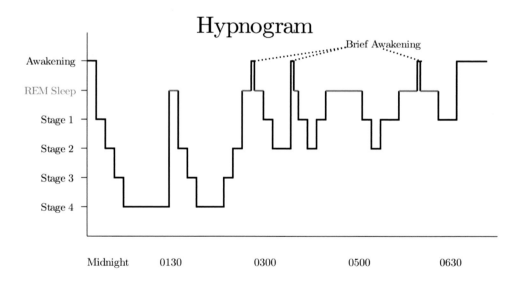

Figure 2. Hypnogram Depicting Sleep Cycles.

III. Circadian Rhythms

Circadian rhythm is the 24-hour cycle that, influenced by biochemical signals, regulates the daily progression from sleep to being awake and back to sleep. External stimuli, like light, also play a part in regulating this daily cycle.

Melatonin, a hormone derived from serotonin and produced in the **pineal gland** of the brain, plays a role in causing sleepiness. When external light decreases, the pineal gland releases melatonin (it can do this because the pineal gland is controlled by the hypothalamus, which has direct neural connections to the eyes).

On the other hand, the **adrenal cortex**, found in the adrenal glands, which rests atop the kidneys, produces the steroid hormone **cortisol**. As the retinas of the eyes take in more light, the hypothalamus releases **corticotropin releasing factor** (CRF), which causes the anterior pituitary gland of the brain to release **adrenocorticotropic** hormone (ACTH), which finally causes the release of cortisol from the adrenal cortex.

IV. Dreaming

Dreaming initially begins after a person enter Stage 2 sleep, but a full 75% of dreaming doesn't take place until REM sleep. There are several theories that scientists use to help them understand dreams.

Activation-synthesis theory holds that random activation of neurons throughout the brain, which can emulate sensory information being sent from receptors to the brain, causes dreams. Additionally, experiences, memories, and preoccupations are also included and mixed in with the false sensations, creating the odd details we encounter in dreams.

Problem-solving dream theory holds that dreams are a way for the brain to find solutions to problems without the constraints of reality.

Cognitive dream theory holds that dreams are simply stream-of-consciousness events that happen while we sleep.

Freud believed that dreams were divided into **manifest content**, which were the plotlines and details of dreams, and **latent content**, the hidden drives and desires that informed the manifest content. Therefore, he believed that analyzing manifest content might help elucidate underlying problems, passions, and desire.

How do scientists put it all together? They use **neurocognitive models of dreaming** to combine anatomical and psychological perspectives by relating the actual experience of dreaming with physiological changes that can be measured with PSG.

V. Sleep Disorders

There are two kinds of sleep disorders: **Dyssomnias** include insomnia, narcolepsy, and sleep apnea. They make it more difficult to fall asleep, stay asleep, or in the case of narcolepsy, avoid sleep. **Parasomnias** include sleeping walking and night terrors. They cause abnormal behaviors and movement during sleep.

Related to anxiety, depression, and certain medications, **insomnia** makes it difficult to fall asleep and is the most common sleep disorder.

Conversely, a person with **narcolepsy** has no control over when they fall asleep. There are several symptoms, which include **cataplexy**, when the body reacts to an emotional trigger and goes suddenly from being awake into REM sleep, causing total loss of muscle control, **sleep paralysis**, which is causes an inability to move while a person is awake but entering or leaving sleep, **hypnagogic hallucinations**, which occur when going to sleep, and **hypnopompic hallucinations**, which occur when waking up.

Sleep apnea causes a person to be unable to breath during sleep, making them wake up throughout the night to catch their breath. Sleep apnea is either obstructive, meaning it is caused by a physical blockage in the pharynx or trachea, or central, meaning the brain does not actually send the proper signals to make the body breathe.

MCAT STRATEGY > > >

Hypnagogic hallucinations occur when *going* to sleep.

Sleep walking (or **somnambulism**), occurs during Stages 3 and 4, or slow wave sleep (SWS). It causes the sleeper to walk, talk, and engage in other daily activities while being soundly asleep. This activity is typically not remembered in the morning.

Night terrors also occur during SWS and are brief bouts of intense anxiety that cause a person's heart rate and respiration to increase to high levels. It is difficult to wake up someone having a night terror as they are in SWS. During normal dreams, the **pons**, a part of the brainstem, keeps the body from acting out dreams. The pons does not do this during night terrors. Night terror sufferers typically do not remember them the next morning.

3. Attention

Attention is the ability to focus on a single aspect of the **sensorium**, or the sensory environment around us.

I. Selective Attention

Because we cannot possibly pay attention to all of the stimuli in our environment, **selective attention** is necessary, allowing us to sense and perceive one input at a time.

The **Broadbent Model of Selective Attention**, an early model for selective attention developed by the British experimental psychologist Donald Broadbent, considered the brain a low capacity processing system and sought to trace the process by which the brain makes sensory data into memories. Multiple sensory inputs entered what Broadbent called a sensory buffer, where one of them was selected, while the others that were not selected decayed. The chosen information then entered into short-term memory storage, from where it was processed semantically (for meaning).

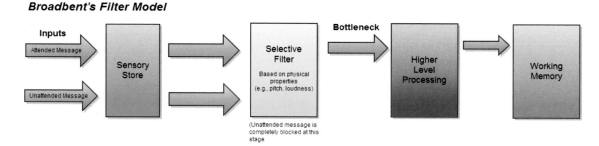

Figure 3. Broadbent's Filter Model.

Where Broadbent's model worked in an all-or-nothing way, modern psychologists have found that selective attention allows us to focus on one single thing while physical stimuli are processed to a lesser degree in the background.

The **cocktail party phenomenon** provides evidence for this: say you are talking with a group of friends at a cocktail party, focused on your conversation, when all the way across the room, you hear someone say your name. Though your focus was dedicated to the conversation at hand, you were able to hear your name. So, selective attention lets us focus on a single thing while other stimuli are still processed, though to a lesser degree, and if one of those other stimuli happens to be significant to us, we can attune to it.

Anne Treisman's Attenuation Model essentially updated Broadbent's, attempting to account for the cocktail party effect, claiming the brain had an attenuator which can turn down the intensity of an unattended to stimulus.

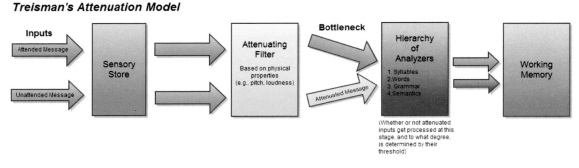

Figure 4. Treisman's Attenuation Model.

II. Divided Attention

Divided attention is the ability to multi-task. According to the **resource model of attention**, the brain has a limited set of resources available for handling tasks: if the resources required to handle two tasks at once are greater than that limited set, the tasks will not be able to be carried out simultaneously. Task similarity, task difficulty, and task practice are the three factors that are typically connected with multi-tasking ability.

Most tasks that are new to us will be difficult and unpracticed, and therefore, it is difficult to undertake another task at the same time. These new tasks utilize **controlled processing**, meaning they take a lot of effort and focus to get right. On the other hand, tasks that are easy, well known, or practiced utilize **automatic processing**, which allows us to divide our attention and focus on other tasks.

4. Consciousness-Altering Drugs

Consciousness-altering drugs work by altering the regular processes that take place at the synapses of neurons.

I. Depressants

Depressants cause relaxation by reducing the activity of the nervous system.

Alcohol is the most commonly used depressant. It works by stimulating the production of gamma-aminobutyric acid (GABA), an inhibitory transmitter associated with reduced anxiety, and dopamine, which leads to a feeling of euphoria. Though people may occasionally seem to become hyperactive while drinking alcohol, this is because the activity of the frontal lobe, which plays a role in judgment and inhibition, is slowed down. While drinking, people can become unable to recognize the consequences of actions, creating **alcohol myopia**, a short-sighted view of the world. With more consumption, the activity of the cerebellum is suppressed, causing slurring of speech, slower reaction times, and diminished skilled motor ability. With even more consumption, alcohol can suppress recent memories that have not yet been transferred to long-term memory, causing a blackout. Additionally, alcohol inhibits REM sleep, which contributes both to loss of short-term memory, which is consolidated during REM sleep, and problems staying asleep. An overdose of alcohol can occur if enough is consumed to depress the respiratory control center of the medulla enough to completely stop sending signals for breathing.

Barbiturates and benzodiazepines also increase the production of GABA, causing a feeling of relaxation, but are more addictive than alcohol. Barbiturates like amobarbital, phenobarbital used to be commonly used for reducing anxiety, but now, they have been mostly replaced by benzodiazepines such as alprazolam, clonazepam, diazepam, and lorazepam as they carry less risk of overdose.

Opiates are derived from poppy and include such drugs as morphine and codeine. **Opioids**, including oxycodone, hydrocodone, and heroin, are semisynthetic versions of opiates. Opiates and opioids cause a sense of euphoria and a decreased reaction to pain by binding to opioid receptors in the nervous system. Like alcohol overdose, opiate overdose can cause death when the brain stops sending signals for respiration. After prolonged use, opiates and opioids can cause the brain to entirely stop producing endorphins, meaning that withdrawal is very painful.

> ## MCAT STRATEGY > > >
>
> We don't have to know every single neurotransmitter found in the brain, but we certainly should recognize GABA as the inhibitory neurotransmitter that mediates alcohol's effect. This is a popular one on the exam.

II. Stimulants

Stimulants increase arousal in the nervous system by either increasing the release of a particular neurotransmitter, reducing the release of a particular neurotransmitter, or both.

Amphetamines release dopamine, norepinephrine, and serotonin while simultaneously inhibiting their reabsorption, effectively increasing arousal, increasing heart rate and blood pressure, and creating effects of anxiety, delusions of grandeur, euphoria, hypervigilance, and paranoia. Meanwhile, appetite and need for sleep are decreased. Brain damage and stroke can result from prolonged, heavy use, as well as withdrawal symptoms after stopping intake.

Cocaine, like amphetamines, releases large quantities of dopamine, norepinephrine, and serotonin, creating intense pleasure for a short duration, which is then followed by a depressive crash. Additionally, cocaine has vasoconstrictive properties (it constricts blood vessels), meaning it can lead to heart attacks and strokes. However, this quality also means it can be used during surgery to constrict vessels in highly vascularized areas like the nose and throat.

MDMA, or **ecstasy**, is both an amphetamine and a mild hallucinogenic, stimulating the release of dopamine and serotonin while blocking the reabsorption of serotonin. Using ecstasy can cause emotional elevation, euphoric feelings, alertness, and a sense of wellbeing. If used long-term, it can damage the neurons that produce serotonin, which reduces its production and can cause depression.

III. Hallucinogens

Hallucinogens like **lysergic acid diethylamide (LSD)**, ketamine, mescaline, peyote, and psilocybin (the chemical that makes certain mushrooms hallucinogenic) distort perception, enhance sensory experiences, and cause introspection, all while increasing heart rate and blood pressure, increased body temperature, and a dilation of the pupils.

IV. Marijuana

Marijuana has qualities of a stimulant, depressant, and hallucinogenic. Marijuana, which is the name used for the leaves and flowers of the plants *Cannabis sativa* and *Cannabis indica*, has an active chemical called tetrahyrdocannabinol (THC) which affects cannabinoid, glycine, and opioid receptors in the brain, though scientists are not exactly sure how. Additionally, THC increases the production of GABA and dopamine. Physiologically, THC can cause an increase in appetite, dry mouth, fatigue, eye redness, lowered blood pressure, and increased heart rate.

V. Drug Addiction

Addiction has a physiological basis: the **mesolimbic pathway** (sometimes referred to as the mesolimbic reward pathway). This pathway, made up by the nucleus accumbens, the ventral tegmental area (VTA), and the area that connects them, the medial forebrain bundle, is one of the four dopaminergic pathways in the brain that is involved in motivation and emotional response. When activated by addictive drugs, it can give chemical, positive reinforcement for their continued usage. All activities that produce psychological independence, including drug use, gambling, and even falling in love, activate the mesolimbic reward pathway.

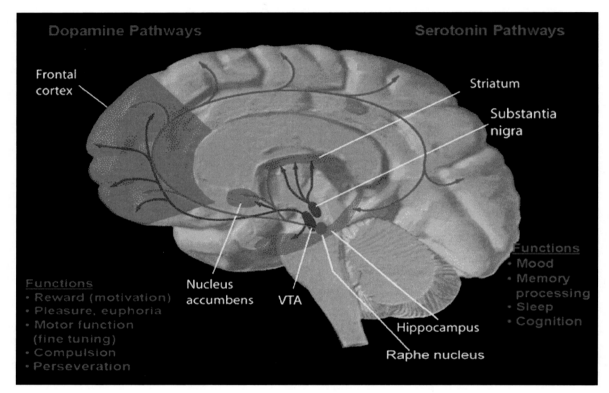

Figure 5. The Dopamine and Serotonin Pathways of the Brain (One Part of the Mesolimbic Pathway, the Medial Forebrain Bundle, is Not Pictured, but Is Between the Nucleus Accumbens and the VTA.

This page left intentionally blank.

Practice Passage

Both Freud and Jung believed in the usefulness of analyzing dreams to understand the unconscious. Both viewed the unconscious as expressing itself in the forms and images of the dream. However, they disagreed about the form and function of dreams and how to interpret them.

Freud viewed dreams as a disguised representation of a person's wishes. He stated that the dream is disguised because if the wish was presented in its natural form, it would be too disturbing for the person. Jung viewed dreams as a direct representation of the dreamer's mental state, represented in symbols. Jung believed that dreams represent the objective and subjective reality, both the events that happen and the person's interpretation of them. This contrasted with Freud, who viewed dreams as only representing individual's wishes.

Jung viewed the dream as having a compensatory function, in which the dream represents an aspect of the person that is perceived as lacking. For example, a person who feels stifled may dream of flying. Freud viewed the dream as presenting both manifest and latent content. The manifest content consists mainly of "day residue," which is experiences that the person had during the day. The latent content is the unconscious wishes that the person has, which is disguised in the manifest content, often through condensation, or several aspects of the unconscious representing itself in similar forms.

In the method of interpreting dreams, Freud advocated for using free association to interpret, in which the patient talks about the dream and in so doing the significance of the dream comes to be realized only with the help of an analyst. Jung posited that one can interpret their own dreams, and encouraged patients to immediately record their dreams in a dream journal upon waking. This is not to say that Jung did not value the associations a person made with the dream, which he termed amplifications. Rather, Jung wanted to focus more on the dream, while free associations could lead thoughts to almost infinite destinations.

1. It can be inferred that both Jung and Freud desired to bring the meaning of dreams into a person's:
   A. consciousness.
   B. free association.
   C. hypnogogic state.
   D. dream journal.

2. According to Freud, which of the following could be the latent meaning of a child's dream of a lake?
   A. A uniting force of mankind
   B. A lake the child saw on a map
   C. Attachment to a childhood vacation place
   D. Hysteria over fear of drowning

3. Which of the following techniques might Jung advocate an individual do to process a dream?
   A. Attempt to forget unpleasant aspects of the dream
   B. Analyze the circadian rhythms of his sleep
   C. Summarize the dream into an audio recording device
   D. Wait until an analyst is available to recount the dream

4. Freud and Jung's approach to bring unconscious material to a person's awareness is a major tenet of which branch of psychology?
   A. Humanistic psychology
   B. Psychoanalytic psychology
   C. Cognitive Behavioral psychology
   D. Systems psychology

5. In an experiment of role-taking, a four-year-old is presented with the "Holly scenario": "Holly is an avid 8-year-old tree climber. One day, Holly falls off a tree, but does not hurt herself. Holly's father makes Holly promise that she will stop climbing trees. Later, Holly finds a kitten stuck in a tree, who may fall at any moment." If the child is asked to describe how Holly's father will react if he finds out Holly climbed the tree, what is their most likely response?
   A. "The father will be mad at Holly because she broke her promise."
   B. "The father will not mind the disobedience because he likes kittens and the kitten will make him happy."
   C. "The father will be mad if Holly gets hurt but he will be happy if she saves the kitten."
   D. "The father will understand that saving a kitten is more important to Holly than keeping a promise."

6. A parent wishes to encourage her daughter to complete her homework every night without resorting to extrinsic motivation. Which of the following strategies would be best?
   A. Allow her daughter to set her own homework study schedule, and praise her effectiveness when she sticks to that schedule.
   B. Create an internal sense of competitiveness by fostering a competition between the daughter and the daughter's best friend who is in all of the same classes.
   C. Remind the daughter that getting good grades are their own reward that good grades are the result of hard work doing the homework, and that good grades should generate a sense of accomplishment.
   D. Offer to increase the daughter's allowance if she completes her homework each week.

7. A psychologist conducts an experiment in which a dog is trained to roll over. The dog has a small device strapped to its back. Rolling over depresses a button on the device. If the dog rolls over in time, the button is pressed and the device does not shock the dog. This form of conditioning would best be described as using:
   A. negative reinforcement through escape.
   B. negative punishment.
   C. negative reinforcement through avoidance.
   D. positive reinforcement.

Practice Passage Explanations

Both Freud and Jung believed in the usefulness of analyzing dreams to understand the unconscious. Both viewed the unconscious as expressing itself in the forms and images of the dream. However, they disagreed about the form and function of dreams and how to interpret them.

Key terms: Freud, Jung, dreams

Contrast: Freud, Jung disagree on nature of dreams and their interpretation

Freud viewed dreams as a disguised representation of a person's wishes. He stated that the dream is disguised because if the wish was presented in its natural form, it would be too disturbing for the person. Jung viewed dreams as a direct representation of the dreamer's mental state, represented in symbols. Jung believed that dreams represent the objective and subjective reality, both the events that happen and the person's interpretation of them. This contrasted with Freud, who viewed dreams as only representing individual's wishes.

Contrast: Freud = dreams only represent the desires of the dreamer; Jung = dreams show both facts and desires

Cause and effect: Freud - disturbing desires → disguise desires in dreams

Jung viewed the dream as having a compensatory function, in which the dream represents an aspect of the person that is perceived as lacking. For example, a person who feels stifled may dream of flying. Freud viewed the dream as presenting both manifest and latent content. The manifest content consists mainly of "day residue," which is experiences that the person had during the day. The latent content is the unconscious wishes that the person has, which is disguised in the manifest content, often through condensation, or several aspects of the unconscious representing itself in similar forms.

Key terms: condensation, day residue

Contrast: Freud = dreams present manifest and latent content, Jung = dreams present compensations for the shortcomings

In the method of interpreting dreams, Freud advocated for using free association to interpret, in which the patient talks about the dream and in so doing the significance of the dream comes to be realized only with the help of an analyst. Jung posited that one can interpret their own dreams, and encouraged patients to immediately record their dreams in a dream journal upon waking. This is not to say that Jung did not value the associations a person made with the dream, which he termed amplifications. Rather, Jung wanted to focus more on the dream, while free associations could lead thoughts to almost infinite destinations.

Key terms: amplifications

Contrast: Freud vs. Jung; Freud interprets dreams through free association, requiring a therapist but Jung lets people interpret their own dreams and uses symbols and dream journals.

1. A is correct. As stated in the passage, both Jung and Freud desired to make a person aware of their unconscious, as expressed in the dream. This awareness is known as consciousness.

2. C is correct. According to Freud, the latent content of a dream is the dream's disguised meaning and Freud asserted that dreams represented the wishes of the dreamer. A dream of a lake might represent a wish to return to a favorite family vacation place.

3. C is correct. Jung advocated that an individual attempt to understand his own dream. He also encouraged a person to record his dream immediately after waking in a dream journal. An audio recording could be one form of a dream journal.

4. B is correct. Both Freud and Jung were pioneers in psychoanalytic psychology. In addition, psychoanalytic psychology emphasizes focus on unconscious material.

5. B is correct. Role-taking theory posits that children develop an ability to understand the perspectives and feelings of others as they mature. This ability starts with a child unable to distinguish between his own desires and the desires of others, moves to an ability to understand that others have different desires, to ultimately being able to predict the behaviors of others based on an understanding of the motivations of others. A four year old child would still be in the first stage of development, egocentric role-taking, in which the child cannot understand that others have a different perspective than his own. The child is unable to separate his own fondness for kittens from either Holly or the father's perspectives.
   A, C: These statements reflect the next stage of development, subjective role-taking, in which a child can understand that others have different points of view and that those perspectives can different from the child's own point of view. subjective role-taking begins around age 7-8.
   D. This statement reflects either self-reflective role-taking or the subsequent stage, mutual role-taking, because now the child is able to understand that the points of view of other people can relate to each other, both outside of the child's own view.

6. A is correct. Intrinsic motivation is generated by an enjoyment of the activity itself, rather than by external rewards. It can be fostered when a person has a sense of their own autonomy over an action and when they believe they can be effective in meeting their own goals. Choice A describes a way to foster that sort of motivation.
   B. Competition is inherently extrinsic, since the goal is to win rather than enjoy the task itself.
   C. Completing homework in order to get good grades is extrinsic—the grades are outside the act of doing the homework itself.
   D. Doing an activity for money is extrinsic motivation—the money is outside the activity itself.

7. C is correct. Here the question is testing our knowledge of operant conditioning. When a subject is presented with the removal of a negative stimulus, the subject is experiencing negative reinforcement. Remember reinforcement is used to encourage or increase a behavior. Here, the researcher is reinforcing the behavior of rolling over. This is negative reinforcement because the rolling over behavior is being reinforced through the removal of a negative stimulus.
   A. Escape requires that the subject actually experience the noxious stimulus and the correct behavior then removes the noxious stimulus. For example, the dog would receive a mild shock and the shock would stop upon rolling over.
   B. Punishment is used to stop a behavior. Here we are trying to encourage the behavior of rolling over.
   D. Positive reinforcement is providing a positive stimulus to encourage a behavior. Here, the dog is not receiving any positive stimulus: instead it is merely avoiding a negative one.

Independent Questions

1. Individuals who suffer from narcolepsy have an uncontrollable tendency to fall asleep during the day. During these sleep episodes, they immediately experience cataplexy, or the partial or total loss of muscle control. What stage of sleep do these individuals enter when they fall asleep?
   A. Stage 1
   B. Stage 2
   C. Stage 4
   D. REM sleep

2. The electroencephalogram (EEG) of a patient in stage 2 sleep would most likely be marked by:
   A. quick eye movements.
   B. a complete lack of eye movement.
   C. sleep spindles.
   D. prominent delta waves.

3. Peter has been suffering from insomnia due to his anxiety. His physician prescribed him medication to help him relax before bed. Although the drug did aid him in relaxation, he also experienced tiredness, confusion, slurred speech, and a slowed heartbeat. What category of drug was Peter most likely prescribed?
   A. A depressant
   B. A stimulant
   C. A hallucinogen
   D. An antipsychotic

4. Drug addiction is characterized by either psychological or physiological dependence, or both. Which of the following best describes the mechanism of addiction reinforcement?
   A. Serotonin is released in neural circuits in the prefrontal cortex.
   B. Serotonin is released in neural circuits in the nucleus accumbens.
   C. Dopamine is released in neural circuits in the prefrontal cortex.
   D. Dopamine is released in neural circuits in the nucleus accumbens.

5. Mindfulness-based stress reduction (MBSR) is a program to help assist patients with pain, life challenges, or stress. A key component of MBSR is meditation. Recent controlled clinical research has shown that meditation has all of the following benefits EXCEPT:
   A. lowering of acute stress.
   B. a reduced risk of developing somatic diseases.
   C. increased relaxation.
   D. quality-of-life improvements.

6. Which of the following classes of drug is most likely to result in short-term memory loss?
   A. Stimulants
   B. Barbiturates
   C. Amphetamines
   D. Psilocybin

7. A patient is in your office for a substance abuse evaluation for an illicit drug. She states that she does not use the substance every day, but she often thinks about the next time she would like to use it. She has not experienced symptoms of withdrawal, but she becomes anxious if she has not used for more than a day. Currently, she meets clinical standards for PTSD, and she states that she will use whenever "she starts remembering." Which of the following best describes this patient?
   A. The patient does not have a substance abuse problem.
   B. The patient has a psychological dependence.
   C. The patient has a physiological dependence.
   D. The patient has a psychological and physiological dependence.

8. Night terrors generally occur during the transition between stage 3 and stage 4 sleep. Which of the following statements does NOT correctly describe night terrors?
   A. Night terrors are usually not remembered the next day.
   B. Night terrors are categorized as a parasomnia.
   C. Night terrors are associated with frequent beta waves.
   D. Night terrors in children can be outgrown by adolescence.

Independent Question Explanations

1. D is correct. REM (rapid eye movement) sleep is characterized by paralysis (which was described in the question stem), swift eye movements, and dreaming. Patients with narcolepsy skip the other stages of sleep and enter REM sleep directly.

2. C is correct. Sleep spindles, or high-frequency oscillations, would be found on the EEG of a patient in stage 2 sleep. Delta waves are characteristic of slow-wave sleep (stages 3 and 4), not stage 2 sleep (eliminate choice D). Eye movements would not be observed on an EEG, which measures brain activity, although they would be observed on an electrooculogram (EOG) (eliminate choices A & B).

3. A is correct. The question stem indicates that Peter was prescribed a barbiturate (also known as a tranquilizer) or a benzodiazepine. These drugs are part of the larger category of depressants. After taking a depressant, Peter would be expected to experience a decreased level of consciousness, a slowed heartbeat, slurred speech, and muscle weakness. Choice A can be eliminated because a stimulant would increase activity of the central nervous system, and would not lead to increased relaxation or a lowered heartbeat. Choice C can be eliminated because there is no evidence in this question stem that Peter is experiencing hallucinations, the hallmark side-effect of hallucinogens. Choice D can be eliminated because the purpose of an antipsychotic is to treat hallucinations, delusions, and paranoia, and there is no evidence from this question stem that Peter is suffering from those symptoms here.

4. D is correct. Drug addiction is reinforced by dopamine release in the nucleus accumbens circuit, also known as the pleasure center of the brain.

5. B is correct. Meditation is useful for incorporating mindfulness. Logically, it could conceivably lower acute stress and promote relaxation, both of which constitute quality-of-life improvements. No evidence shows that meditation directly reduces the risk of disease incidence or cures disease. Even if you were not aware of this fact, note that the question stem relates more to psychological issues than somatic disease.

6. B is correct. Depressants are a class of drug that may result in short-term memory loss. This category includes opiates, alcohol, barbiturates (choice B), and benzodiazepines. The other answer choices are less likely than depressants to promote memory loss. Note also that amphetamines are a sub-class of stimulants, making choices A and C virtually interchangeable.

7. B is correct. This patient is described as thinking about the drug often and becoming anxious if she has not used recently. These are characteristic of psychological dependence. There is no indication that this patient has a physiological dependence, as she has no physical symptoms of withdrawal.

8. C is correct. Even if you are uncertain about the other choices, option C should stand out immediately, as beta waves are characteristic of awake individuals, not those in slow-wave (stage 3 and 4) sleep. The remaining options are accurate. Night terrors occur during deep sleep and are typically not remembered the next morning. This condition is an example of a parasomnia, or condition involving abnormal perceptions, behaviors, or movements during sleep. Finally, most children who have night terrors later outgrow them.

This page left intentionally blank.

Cognition and Language

CHAPTER 4

0. Introduction

Cognition is the process by which our brains acquire knowledge and understanding of that knowledge through experience, sensations, and thought. Though it is not limited to human brains, cognition is most advanced and complex in our species. **Language** is the primary method of human communication, written, spoken, and signed, and makes community possible. Essentially, it is a means through which the brain's cognitive ability can extend outward into the world.

1. Cognitive Development

Cognitive development refers to the development of thinking and problem solving abilities from early childhood into adulthood.

I. Piaget's Stages of Cognitive Development

The Swiss developmental psychologist and philosopher Jean Piaget insisted that there are substantial differences in cognitive ability between children and adults, opposing the then commonly held notion that children were like miniature adults when it came to thinking. Piaget's approach to cognitive development centered around **schemas**, patterns of thought that served to organize information into categories, like a mental scaffolding or framework. According to Piaget, when we encounter new experiences, we either **assimilate** those experiences into our existing schemas or we **accommodate** to them by adjusting our existing schemas.

Piaget came up with four different stages of cognitive development:

Sensorimotor Stage: In this first stage, which lasts from birth up to age two, we experience the world exclusively through sensing our environment and crudely moving trough it. In this stage we develop **object permanence**, the understanding that objects continue to exist even though we are not looking at or touching them.

Preoperational Stage: In the second stage, which roughly extends from age two to age seven, we develop **symbolic thinking**, meaning we learn that things and ideas can be represented through symbols such as words, gestures, or pictures. Symbolic thinking is what allowed us to pretend and to play out imaginary situations as children. During this stage, children tend to focus on a single aspect of a thing or experience, a phenomenon called **centration**. This is directly linked with an inability to comprehend the notion of **conservation**, which holds that a quantity remains the same despite a change in shape. For example, water from a large pot is poured into a tall, thin test tube and it still has the same volume. During the Preoperational Stage, children are not able to conceive that both the pot and the test tube contain the same amount of water. Children in this stage are **egocentric**, meaning they do not understand that other people have thoughts or perspectives different from their own.

MCAT STRATEGY > > >

Learning psychology content means tons of memorization. Make a study sheet (discussed in the Next Step Verbal and Quantitative book) for Piaget's Stages (and Erikson's Stages, Maslow's Hierarchy, etc.).

Concrete Operational Stage: In the third stage, which roughly extends from ages 7 to 11, children develop an understanding of conservation, which brings with it an ability to begin to grasp mathematics, and also become less egocentric, gaining the ability to consider that other people have different perspectives. In the third stage, children can think logically about concrete events and objects, but they still have not developed a full capacity for abstract thought.

Formal Operational Stage: In the fourth and final stage, which roughly extends from age 12 into adulthood, people develop the abilities of abstract and moral reasoning. At this point, the human brain can logically consider and comprehend abstract ideas.

II. Cognitive Changes in Late Adulthood

Until roughly the age of 60, cognitive abilities either remain the same or increase. After 60, however, cognitive ability does decline. In elderly people **recall,** which is the ability to retrieve information from memory without any clues, and **recognition**, the same, but with clues, both decline. Time-based activities, like something that is done three times a day, like eating meals, become more difficult for elderly people. In general, the ability to process information slows down in elderly people, slowing down reaction times, speech, and problem solving ability.

III. Cultural Influences on Cognitive Development

Different cultures obviously have different values, and those values are in part responsible for how people develop cognitively. The Soviet psychologist **Lev Vygotsky** actually proposed that the most important driver of cognitive development was how a child internalizes the values of his or her culture. Some cultures value social learning (tradition, societal roles, etc.) while some value the pursuit of pure knowledge, and many cultures exist on a spectrum between these two poles.

IV. Hereditary and Environmental Influences on Cognitive Development

Genetics are responsible for our biological, neurological dispositions, but sociological and cultural factors help to shape those dispositions and point them in certain directions. Though in some sense we are born with our intellectual capabilities, the quality of a child's schooling, and of the intellectual richness of his or her environment, has been proven to have an influence in performances on cognitive functioning tests. And so one's genetics and one's environment both play a significant role in cognitive development.

Certain cognitive developmental issues, such as Down's syndrome, are the result of heredity. Additionally, chemical exposures can cause disabilities, like Fetal Alcohol Syndrome, which occurs when a mother drinks alcohol while pregnant, slowing cognitive development in the child.

V. Biological Influences on Cognitive Development

The development of the brain goes hand in hand with cognitive development. The development of the frontal lobe allows us to plan, organize, and think on our toes. The development of the amygdala and the rest of limbic systems make emotional arousal possible, which helps to motivate us to complete tasks. These elements of the brain, and so many more, have a complex interplay that allows us our cognitive abilities.

2. Problem-Solving and Decision-Making

Our cognitive abilities allow us to deal with the multitude of problems we face every day. First, we frame the problem, basically laying out a blue print of the problem and its component elements. Then, come up with possible solutions and test them out, choosing the best, most efficient one. Often these potential solutions are drawn from a **mental set**, a similar framework for thinking about problems and solutions that can be used again and again. We are, after all, creatures of habit.

I. Types of Problem-Solving

Trial and Error is most effective when there are relatively few solutions to a problem. Basically, various solutions are tried until one works.

An **algorithm** is a step-by-step procedure for solving a problem. Algorithms are often mathematical, and can be designed to automatically find solutions to problems (as they do in computers).

Deductive reasoning is the process of solving a problem by beginning with a set of rules and drawing conclusions and solutions from those rules. For this reason, it is also known as top-down reasoning.

Inversely**, inductive reasoning** begins with particular instances or information and draws conclusions and solutions from them. It is also known as bottom-up reasoning.

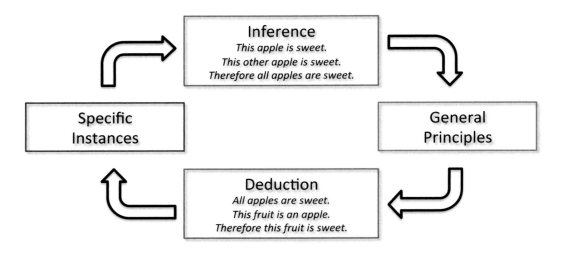

Figure 1. A Simple Chart for Differentiating Deductive and Inductive Reasoning.

II. Heuristics, Biases, Intuition, and Emotion

Heuristics are simply mental shortcuts or simplified iterations of principles that can help us make decisions, but can also lead to poor judgment. In common parlance, they may be referred to as rules of thumb.

The **representativeness heuristic** is the tendency to make decisions about actions or events based upon our standard representations of those events.

MCAT STRATEGY > > >

Heuristics are good (make decisions quickly) and bad (sacrifice accuracy for speed). This trade-off is something we have to do every day. Even a simple trip to the grocery store would take years if we had to carefully evaluate every possible piece of information about every possible product for sale.

The **availability heuristic** is the tendency to make decisions about how likely an action or event is based upon how readily available similar information is in our memories.

A **belief bias** is a tendency that people have to judge things based not upon sound logic, but upon already held beliefs.

A **confirmation bias** is a tendency that people have to focus on information that is in agreement with the beliefs they already have, rather than the information that is contrary to those beliefs. This can contribute to overconfidence, which we'll touch on below.

Overconfidence is the term for when a person overestimates the accuracy and validity of their judgments and knowledge. It can be the result of heuristics and biases. Overconfidence can contribute to **belief perseverance**, the human tendency to stick with one's initial beliefs about something even after receiving new information that disproves or nullifies that initial belief.

Intuition is the ability, developed by experience, to make choices or decisions based on ideas or perceptions that are not evident based on available information. One way of describing intuition is the **recognition-primed decision model**, which holds that the brain, in the face of a problem, can sort through a vast amount of information in order to find a proper solution. This can happen with or without a person being aware of it.

Emotion is the instinctive state of mind a person has based upon mood, circumstances, and relationships, and it can often influence a person's problem solving and decision-making.

3. Intellectual Functioning

Intelligence is, in a broad sense, the ability to acquire knowledge and skills, and then to apply them. Intelligence is hard to define, and scientists have developed several models for studying it.

I. Multiple Intelligences

The American developmental psychologist Howard Gardner developed a theory of **multiple intelligences**, accounting for seven distinct types of intelligence: bodily-kinesthetic, interpersonal, intrapersonal, linguistic, logical-mathematical, musical, and visual-spatial. The most valued of these intelligences varies from culture to culture; Gardner believed that linguistic and logical-mathematical were most valued by western cultures.

II. Intelligence Quotient

Tests for finding intelligence quotient, meant to measure a person's intellectual ability, were spearheaded by the French psychologist Alfred Binet in the early 1900s. Later, a professor at Standard University incorporated Binet's early work into creating the **Stanford-Binet IQ test**, which was for a while the standard method for testing IQ.

III. Variation in Intelligence

Variations in IQ, or any other measure of intelligence, reflect a confluence of heredity, environment, and education. As far as heredity goes, intelligence seems to be passed genetically from parents to their children. Environment, nutrition, socioeconomic status, and parental expectations have been shown to affect IQ. Schooling also has a role in IQ, with early intervention in childhood (Pre-Kindergarten and Kindergarten) improving IQ, especially for children who live in environments that are less than ideal (i.e. impoverished or abusive).

E. Language Development

Language is one of the single most defining characteristic of human beings, distinguishing us from all other animals. And yet, despite all that is known about it, scientists continue to debate what exactly language is and how it develops.

When studying the development of language from an early age, psychologists use the term **language acquisition**, referring not to the process of learning a language in school, but rather, to the way that infants rapidly develop a capacity for their native tongue.

I. The Learning Theory

The **learning theory** (or behaviorist theory), developed by the American psychologist B. F. Skinner, posits that, because language use is a form of behavior, language acquisition is a direct result of operant conditioning. Within this theory, language acquisition results from an infant behaving in a particular way and its parents providing positive reinforcement, compelling the infant to continue behaving in that particular way.

For example, imagine a father playing with his infant daughter. He is pointing at his face, repeating the word, "daddy." Meanwhile, the infant is babbling nonsense, an activity that begins in almost all children within their first year. After awhile of playing in this way, the infant, by random chance, babbles a noise that sounds something like "da-da." The elated father responds with a smile and says, "Very good!" Then, of course, he goes to find the mother and they both shower their infant with praise and affection.

This is positive reinforcement, and it has two primary affects: first of all, it conditions the infant to make the same "da-da" sounds when she encounters the same stimulus, her father's face. Secondly, and more importantly, it encourages the toddler to continue this kind of imitative behavior, to copy the sounds her parent makes. When the infant says a real word, she is rewarded, but when she says something nonsensical, she is not, and therefore, the nonsensical utterance is abandoned. At least in early childhood, all subsequent words learned following that first "da-da" are the result of positive reinforcement.

II. The Nativist Theory

The American linguist and philosopher Noam Chomsky found Skinner's behaviorist model to be somewhat flawed, and proposed an alternative, the **nativist theory** (or biological theory). This theory centers around what Chomsky called the "**language acquisition device**," an innate element of the human brain that allows people to gain a mastery of language simply through limited exposure during sensitive developmental years, from two years old up until puberty.

Chomsky was known for his study of transformational grammar, or changes in word order that don't change the meaning of a sentence. For example, "I ate an apple" and "An apple was eaten by me" have the same meaning. Chomsky noted that children developed a capacity for transformational grammar from an early age, and therefore believed that the ability is innate and is an effect of the language acquisition device.

Because he provided no anatomical evidence for the existence of the language acquisition device, Chomsky's theory was theoretical. However, researchers studying the phenomenon do use empirical evidence, studying actual languages and actual cases of language acquisition.

One such case gave credence to Chomsky's notion of a sensitive period during which language mastery must be developed: a girl, subjected to horrific child abuse, was isolated from all human contact from the ages of two to thirteen, at which point she was discovered and rescued by the authorities. Given exposure to language, the girl was not able to master many of the rules of language, though she did pick up some basic aspects of syntax. Unfortunately, her case proved that full language mastery requires exposure during the so-called sensitive period.

III. The Social Interactionist Theory

The social interactionist theory, maintains that language develops from the relationship between biological and social phenomena. In this way, a child's language acquisition is motivated by the child's desire to communicate and behave socially. Brain development is central to this theory in that the biological capacity for language develops hand in hand with the child's first exposure to language. As the brain develops, it organizes together sounds and meanings from the word's the child is exposed to. As this child interacts socially, proper brain circuits for language are reinforced where others are not, and therefore, they atrophy.

4. Language and Cognition

Most linguists agree that language, to at least some degree, affects cognition, though there are different views as to how and to what extent this is so.

One theory, the **linguistic relativity hypothesis**, was conceptualized by the American linguist Benjamin Whorf. The theory, also known as the Whorfian hypothesis, holds that our perception of reality is dependent upon the content of the language that we speak. Whorf believed that language affects cognition more than cognition affects language.

Physiologically, things are a little clearer.

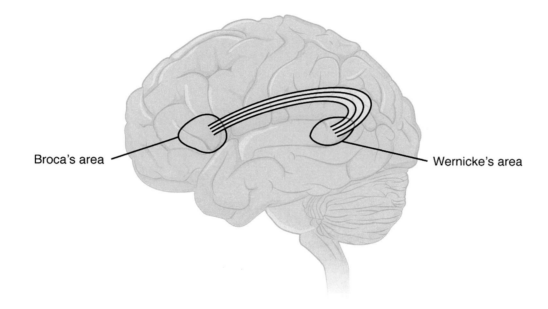

Figure 2. The Areas of the Brain Primarily Responsible for Speech.

Broca's area, located in the left hemisphere of the frontal lobe, controls the physical production of speech. **Broca's aphasia** occurs with damage to the Broca's area, weakening the physical ability to speak.

Wernicke's area, located in the back of the temporal lobe, controls the comprehension of speech and written language. **Wernicke's aphasia** is a result of damage to Wernicke's area, causing the loss of speech comprehension. Patients with this disease can still speak and often do so at great length, but their words are nonsensical.

Practice Passage

Analysis of national special education programs shows there is an overrepresentation of English-language learning (ELL) students. Differences in students' educational experiences in their home country may create difficulties in learning with methods utilized in American schools. In other cases, difficulty in learning English leads to misdiagnosis and improper assignment to special education programs.

However, there is evidence that children who have difficulty learning another language may do so because they have an underlying reading disability (RD). Working memory (WM) deficits are also more common in ELL students diagnosed with a RD. WM assists in rehearsing skills that are involved in phonological processing, a key component of reading and language acquisition. Modern studies reveal that WM deficits are associated with lower levels of vocabulary knowledge and increase the risk of developing RD among both ELL students and English as a first language (EFL) students.

Table 1 shows the findings of a program which taught first language literacy skills to struggling ELL students. The average reading grade level of fifth grade students who received the instruction were measured and compared to students not in the program.

Table 1. Effects of Literacy Program

	Students in literacy program	Control students
Pre-program	2.1	2.2
Post-program	4.3	3.8

(Note: Repeated-measures ANOVA was used to compare the pre/post scores, p = 0.00078)

A follow up study also revealed that first language literacy skills are correlated with the efficiency of second language acquisition (R = 0.79, p = 0.034). In addition to this skill, there are cultural factors involved in language acquisition, such as understanding shared cultural topics, cultural communication, and understanding social contexts.

1. All of the following are possible explanations for ELL students struggling to learn English and NOT having an RD, EXCEPT:
   A. differences in learning styles.
   B. lack of exposure to cultural issues.
   C. misdiagnosis.
   D. difficulty with working memory.

2. If, during the study, all the students knew if they were in the reading instruction group or in the control group, what could be a confounding factor that biased the results?
   A. Placebo effect
   B. Inclusive fitness
   C. Fundamental attribution error
   D. Cultural factors

3. Students with strong first language skills would likely do well with reading and pronouncing what type of word compared to students with weak first language skills?
   A. A sight word that is not pronounced phonetically
   B. A phonetic word that can be pronounced according to phonetic rules
   C. A word that they have first heard pronounced by another person
   D. A word that sounds similar to a word in their first language

4. Why is having a pre-program score for each group important for the research design?
   A. To acclimatize the students to the task
   B. To assess for RD
   C. To control for differences between the two groups
   D. To improve the reliability of the findings

5. A struggling ELL student, without an RD, would likely have trouble understanding what type of reading passage?
   A. A passage with metaphors unique to English
   B. A passage with many phonetic words
   C. A passage that is first read aloud to him
   D. A passage with a number of short words

6. Children are most likely to first understand and empathize with the difficulty their ELL peers face with language during which stage of cognitive development?
   A. Sensorimotor
   B. Preoperational
   C. Concrete operational
   D. Formal operational

7. A proponent of the innatist theory of language would most likely propose which conclusion regarding 2nd language development?
   A. If the second language is too dissimilar from their first, acquisition is not possible.
   B. All immigrant children utilize a language acquisition device to master the second language.
   C. No matter the age, a child will be able to acquire a 2nd language with ease.
   D. The desire to communicate with newfound friends is the primary driver of 2nd language acquisition.

Practice Passage Explanations

Analysis of national special education programs shows there is an overrepresentation of English-language learning (ELL) students. Differences in students' educational experiences in their home country may create difficulties in learning with methods utilized in American schools. In other cases, difficulty in learning English leads to misdiagnosis and improper assignment to special education programs.

Key terms: English Language Learners

Cause and effect: ELL special ed overrepresentation is due to misdiagnosis

However, there is evidence that children who have difficulty learning another language may do so because they have an underlying reading disability (RD). Working memory (WM) deficits are also more common in ELL students diagnosed with a RD. WM assists in rehearsing skills that are involved in phonological processing, a key component of reading and language acquisition. Modern studies reveal that WM deficits are associated with lower levels of vocabulary knowledge and increase the risk of developing RD among both ELL students and English as a first language (EFL) students.

Key terms: RD, WM, EFL

Cause and effect: problems with working memory → smaller vocabulary, reading disabilities, difficulties learning a new language

Table 1 shows the findings of a program which taught first language literacy skills to struggling ELL students. The average reading grade level of fifth grade students who received the instruction were measured and compared to students not in the program.

Cause and effect: a study was done to assess a general reading program on language skills

Table 1. Effects of Literacy Program

Students in literacy program		Control students
Pre-program	2.1	2.2
Post-program	4.3	3.8

(Note: Repeated-measures ANOVA was used to compare the pre/post scores, $p = 0.00078$)

Table 1 shows that all students in the study were reading below grade (5) but the students in the literacy program were brought up nearly to grade level

A follow up study also revealed that first language literacy skills are correlated with the efficiency of second language acquisition ($R = 0.79$, $p = 0.034$). In addition to this skill, there are cultural factors involved in language acquisition, such as understanding shared cultural topics, cultural communication, and understanding social contexts.

Key terms: cultural factors

Cause and effect: 1ˢᵗ language skill ~ 2ⁿᵈ language acquisition; culture matters in language, but RD and ELL are still probably related

1. D is correct. There have been findings of working memory deficits among those struggling with RD and struggling to learn English. The other factors are cultural causes for struggling.

2. A is correct. If students knew they were getting instruction but the other group was not, they might have expected to do better and had better performance as a result, with the opposite effect for the control group. A difference in results being attributable to expectations is the placebo effect.

3. B is correct. According to the passage, phonetic decoding skills have been found to be transferable to another language. Sight words would not be able to be decoded by any student until they have received direct instruction in it. Having a word pronounced first and being similar to a word in the first language would likely benefit both groups of students equally.

4. C is correct. By comparing the change from the initial reading level to the reading level at post-program any differences between students' initial reading level is controlled for.

5. A is correct. A struggling ELL, without an RD, would likely have trouble understanding the meaning of metaphors.

6. C is correct. The children are able to empathize and understand that their peers may not have the same language experience as themselves. This is most akin to the concrete operational stage of Piaget's development (ages 7-11 years). During this stage, the child's thinking becomes less egocentric and they are increasingly aware of external events. They begin to realize that one's own thoughts and feelings are unique and may not be shared by others.

7. B is correct. The innatist, or nativist theory is a biologically based theory, which argues that humans are pre-programmed with the innate ability to develop language, utilizing what is known as the language acquisition device, in their brain.
   A. Nativist theory posits that all languages have similar grammar and/or structural elements.
   C. Nativists believe there is a critical period of language acquisition where language learning will be easiest or most effective.
   D. This would be the view of a learning theorist (Vygotsky).

Independent Questions

1. Patrick recently suffered from food poisoning after consuming improperly prepared chicken. The following week, his friend was not feeling well, and Patrick assumed that his friend must have had food poisoning as well. What type of problem solving did Patrick use?
   A. The representativeness heuristic
   B. The availability heuristic
   C. Belief bias
   D. A stereotype

2. All of the following are approaches to problem solving EXCEPT:
   A. trial and error.
   B. an algorithm.
   C. fixation.
   D. deductive reasoning.

3. Which of the following choices is one of the seven intelligences proposed by Howard Gardner in his theory of multiple intelligences?
   A. Fluid intelligence
   B. Crystallized intelligence
   C. Musical intelligence
   D. General intelligence

4. Sarah just turned six years old. According to Piaget's stages of cognitive development, what characterizes her cognition at this age?
   A. She is egocentric and does not understand the perspectives of others.
   B. She is learning the principle of conservation.
   C. She is beginning to understand complex moral debates.
   D. She is capable of abstract reasoning.

5. Which of the following theories of language development hypothesizes that language is innate for human beings?
   A. The learning theory
   B. The nativist theory
   C. The interactionist theory
   D. The Whorfian hypothesis

6. A patient was involved in a motor vehicle accident, suffering a traumatic brain injury. When he woke up, he was unable to comprehend language, but he could still speak long strings of nonsense words. Which brain area was most likely damaged, and where is it located?
   A. Broca's area, which is in the temporal lobe
   B. Broca's area, which is in the frontal lobe
   C. Wernicke's area, which is in the temporal lobe
   D. Wernicke's area, which is in the frontal lobe

7. The nativist theory of language development focuses in large part on the existence of which of the following?
   A. A zone of proximal development
   B. The role played by operant conditioning
   C. The concept of linguistic relativity
   D. A language acquisition device

8. A child notices that a cat who lives on his street does not like to have its stomach rubbed. When the child later gets a cat of his own, he notes that it also does not like stomach rubs. The child concludes that no cats like to have their stomach rubbed. What form of cognition does this exemplify?
   A. Inductive reasoning
   B. Deductive reasoning
   C. Top-down reasoning
   D. The affect heuristic

Independent Question Explanations

1. B is correct. The availability heuristic is the tendency to believe something due to immediate examples or readily obtainable memory. Since Patrick recently had food poisoning, the example of being sick due to food poisoning was fresh in his mind, and he used this available information to explain his friend's situation. Note that the representativeness heuristic would not apply here because it is when we compare information and make decisions based on an average or prototype (eliminate choice A). We can also eliminate answer choices C and D here because belief bias refers to accepting new information that is aligned with our current belief system and denying information that is not aligned with our current belief systems, and a stereotype refers to a generalized idea about a person or thing.

2. C is correct. Fixation is a barrier to effective problem solving. This concept has its roots in Freudian psychoanalysis. Freud believed that individuals who did not properly progress through the stages of psychosexual development could become "fixated" on one particular stage. Now, fixation refers more broadly to habits or ideas that persist for extended periods. In contrast, trial and error, algorithms, and deductive reasoning are all approaches to problem solving.

3. C is correct. Musical intelligence is one of Gardner's seven intelligences; the others are bodily-kinesthetic, interpersonal, intrapersonal, visual-spatial, logical-mathematical, and linguistic intelligence. Choices A and B were proposed by Raymond Cattell, not Howard Gardner, and are not included in the theory of multiple intelligences. The concept of a single general intelligence is, in a way, the opposite of Gardner's theory, although Charles Spearman did propose the idea in his concept of the "g factor," a general form of intelligence.

4. A is correct. As a six-year-old, Sarah is in the preoperational stage of Piaget's model. Children in this stage are egocentric, meaning that they have difficulty understanding the perspectives of people other than themselves. Choice B relates to the concrete operational stage, while choices C and D are characteristic of the formal operational stage.

5. B is correct. The nativist theory, developed by Noam Chomsky, is the perspective that language is innate to all human beings. This is supported by some evidence, such as the fact that virtually all humans who grow up under typical circumstances are able to speak fluently by the age of 5. The other answer choices are theories related to language, but they do not stipulate that language development is innate.

6. C is correct. Wernicke's area is located in the temporal lobe, and it is responsible for language comprehension. If damaged, the individual will have trouble understanding language or speaking sentences that make logical sense. However, their ability to produce words will still be intact. Note that Broca's area, found in the frontal lobe, plays a major role in language production. Here, Broca's area was unlikely to have been damaged, as the patient could produce words.

7. D is correct. The nativist theory was proposed by linguist Noam Chomsky. A central facet of this theory is that an element of the human brain exists that provides for the mastery of language. This element, termed a "language acquisition device," is the theory's explanation for the fact that nearly all typical humans learn language at a young age. The zone of proximal development was proposed by Lev Vygotsky and relates to learning in general, not language specifically. Operant conditioning is involved in the learning theory of language development, and linguistic relativity is an alternative term for the Whorfian hypothesis.

8. A is correct. Inductive reasoning is the act of beginning with specific observations or examples, finding patterns between them, and finally using those patterns to draw larger conclusions. Here, the child begins with the specific instances of the two cats, then draws a conclusion from their observed patterns. Deductive reasoning and top-down reasoning are two terms for the same concept, meaning that both can be eliminated. The affect heuristic involves making decisions based on emotion and is not relevant here.

This page left intentionally blank.

Emotion and Stress

CHAPTER 5

0. Introduction

As was mentioned briefly in Chapter 4, **emotion** is the instinctive state of mind a person has based upon mood, circumstances, and relationships, and it can often influence a person's problem solving and decision-making. Related to emotion, **stress** is a psychological and physiological state of emotional or mental strain which results from having to face a difficult circumstance.

1. Components of Emotion and Universal Emotions

The three components of emotion are behavioral (action), which includes body language and facial expression, cognitive (mind), which is the brain's subjective interpretation of the feeling, and physiological (body), which accounts for arousal of the sympathetic nervous system, causing changes to blood pressure, heart rate, respiration, skin temperature, and more.

The famous naturalist Charles Darwin believed that human emotions are biologically based, and therefore a result of mankind's evolution. As such, he wrote that regardless of their culture or society, people all over the world have the same set of basic emotions.

According to Darwin's thinking, emotions are the result of evolutionary adaptations that increased our sexual fitness, making humans more likely to successfully reproduce. Therefore, the way we feel in emotional situations is the result of thousands of years of evolution: our feelings are created by highly specialized programs in our brain, designed to deal with the problems that we encounter.

The American psychologist Paul Ekman ran with Darwin's universal emotions concept, developing his theory of seven basic, human emotions, including anger, contempt, disgust, fear, happiness, sadness, and surprise. The image below accounts for these seven emotions:

It makes me disgusted how sad the fear of contempt and anger surprise people.

Figure 1. Ekman's Seven Universal Emotions. (Top row: Happiness, sadness, contempt; second row: fear, disgust, anger; off to the side: surprise)

Happiness and contempt fear disgust anger surprise

2. Theories of Emotion

I. James-Lange Theory

According to **James-Lange Theory**, an emotional experience is the result of behavioral and physiological actions, meaning that physiological and behavioral responses to a stimulus will lead to the cognitive, subjective element of emotion. Within this theory, we feel happy because we laugh, sad because we cry, and afraid because we cringe or run away.

tony 1st think after

There is some truth to the theory: particular ways of breathing can produce particular emotions, and smiling can increase feelings of happiness. However, because it assumes every emotion originates from a particular physiological states, and because it assumes every physiological state can be labeled specifically and accurately (which has shown to be not true), James-Lange Theory alone cannot account entirely for why we feel emotions.

Figure 2. A Simple Diagram of James-Lange Theory.

II. Cannon-Bard Theory *Bombarded*

The **Cannon-Bard Theory** holds that cognitive and physiological responses to a stimulus occur concurrently and independently of one another, with a behavioral response following them. With this theory, scientists can explain why there is so much overlap between certain physiological states (like fear and sexual arousal), because the cognitive element of emotion is completely separate from the physiological. However, under this theory, phenomena like smiling increasing feelings of happiness are not explained.

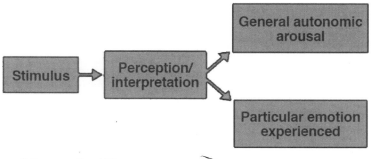

Figure 3. A Simple Diagram of Cannon-Bard Theory.

III. Schachter-Singer Theory

According to the **Schachter-Singer Theory**, once we experience physiological arousal based on a stimulus, the cognitive aspect is conscious: we interpret our circumstances and identify the emotion we are experiencing. In this way, Schachter-Singer Theory is like James-Lange Theory, proposing that emotional experiences are based in physiological reactions, but different in that the cognitive aspect of emotion comes not from a direct correlation to a physiological experience, but from the circumstances and stimuli being experienced. Like Cannon-Bard theory, this allows for similar

> **MCAT STRATEGY > > >**
>
> The MCAT will focus on the differences in causality between the three theories of emotion. James-Lange and Schachter-Singer are similar, but Schachter-Singer inserts an additional step (interpretation) in the causal chain.

physiological states to be interpreted differently on the cognitive level. However, this theory also cannot explain why behavior can affect physiology and cognition, why smiling might increase feelings of happiness.

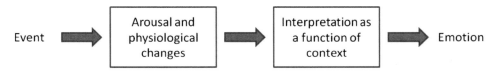

Figure 4. A Simple Diagram of Schachter-Singer Theory.

3. Nature of Stress

Feelings of stress are indicative of the relationship between psychological and physiological experiences: stressful experiences can cause us mental anxiety while the body develops symptoms. This being said, stress is not the result of a simple relationship between stimulus and response: it is a complicated process in which the subjective perception of stimuli can affect the degree of stress experienced.

I. Appraisal

Appraisal is the term used for how an event and its level of stressfulness are interpreted by an individual. People appraise different stressors in different ways: one person may consider an event to be threatening while another considers it to be motivating (think of the soldier-drill sergeant relationship). An event may seem to be uncontrollable to some people while to others its controllable. The former evokes a greater stress response than the latter.

II. Types of Stressors

At the most basic level, stressors are divided into two camps, either causing **distress**, the result of an unpleasant stressor, or **eustress**, the result of a more positive stressor.

Stressors are further divided into three types: daily hassles, catastrophes, and significant life changes.

Daily hassles are the mundane experiences like bad traffic and bills that can be taken in stride or can add up, little by little, to a lot of stress.

Catastrophes are large-scale events that cannot be predicted, effecting a large amount of people. Natural disasters and wartime events are catastrophes that can affect people in different ways (anxiety, depression, PTSD, and etc.).

Significant life changes are major events that happen in our lifetimes, like losing a job, getting married, the death of a loved one, and so on, that can lead to significant stress.

Frustration, degree of predictability, control over a situation, pressure to make decisions, and conflict between multiple decisions are also forms of stress.

III. Effects of Stress

In extreme cases, stress can cause fatigue, irritability, and a decreased ability to concentrate. When paired with a perception that the stressor cannot be controlled, **learned helplessness**, an overwhelming sense that a goal cannot be accomplished, can develop. However, if kept to a moderate degree, stress can be helpful by providing motivation to complete a task.

4. Responses to Stress

I. Physiological and Cognitive Responses

The first response to stress, the "fight-or-flight" response, is physiological and is produced via a stimulation of the sympathetic nervous system, causing the adrenal glands to release the hormones epinephrine (adrenaline) and norepinephrine (noradrenaline). Physiologically, this causes the increased heart rate and respiration characteristic of stressful encounters. Additionally, it directs blood flow away from the digestive system and to the skeletal-muscular system, as well as it dulls pain.

The second response is cognitive, initiating when the hypothalamus releases corticotropin-releasing hormone, which stimulates the pituitary gland to produce adrenocorticotropic hormone, which in turn stimulates the release of **cortisol** from the adrenal glands. Cortisol helps the body to maintain the continuous supply of blood sugar needed to sustain a stress response by shifting the body from using glucose as an energy source to using fat, thus making more glucose available. This is necessary for proper brain function during times of stress because the brain's only energy source is glucose.

corticotropin → adrenocorticotropic hormone (ACTH) → cortisol → ↑ bs

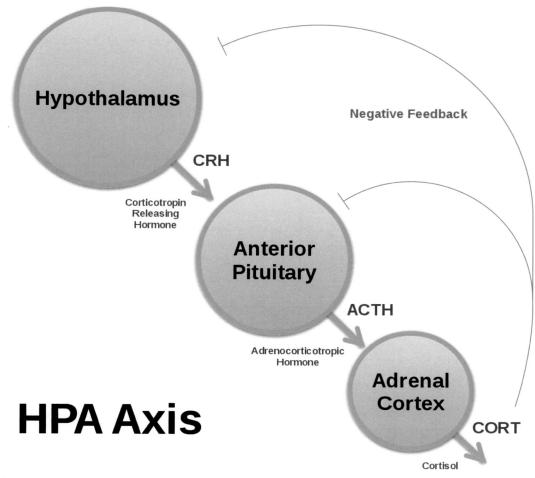

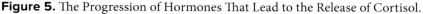

Figure 5. The Progression of Hormones That Lead to the Release of Cortisol.

If cortisol release continues for too long a period, the healthy functioning of white blood cells can be inhibited, making the immune system weaker and thus the body more susceptible to illness and infection.

II. Emotional and Behavioral Responses

Irritability, moodiness, tenseness, and feelings of helplessness are some of the emotional responses that result from elevated stress. Behaviorally, stress can cause people to have difficulties at work or school, to withdraw from others and regular activities, to abuse drugs, and in very bad cases, to commit suicide. Chronic stress can also lead to anxiety, depression, and other issues of mental health.

5. Managing Stress

There are two general kinds of strategies for dealing with stress: problem-focused strategies that people use to help them overcome a stressor, and emotionally focused strategies that help people to change their feelings about particular stressors.

MCAT STRATEGY > > >

Next Step strongly encourages students to set up study groups. The academic and social support they provide offer both problem-focused and emotionally-focused strategies for dealing with the stress of the MCAT. Find your study group today at forum.nextstepmcat.com.

Problem-focused strategies include reaching out for social support from family and friends, confronting the issue head-on, and the creation of systematic plan for overcoming or solving the problem the stressor poses.

Emotionally focused strategies include reappraising a situation and attempting to find positive aspects of the stressor, distancing oneself from or avoiding the issue, and using self control to deal with the stress.

Another excellent means for dealing with stress is exercise, which releases endorphins, physiologically helping us feel good. Of course, exercise also helps us maintain optimal health, which in itself can promote a less stressed life. Less vigorous but still effective, relaxation techniques like mediation and simple deep breathing can contribute to stress management.

Moreover, research has shown that practicing religion or spirituality can help people to manage stressors in their lives.

This page left intentionally blank.

Practice Passage

Culture has a large impact on how death is viewed by an individual. A culture's death ethos can be inferred from observing artistic or traditional rituals that are related to death. The view of death's desirability, whether it is considered sacred or profane, or welcome or unwanted, can have a strong impact on acceptance. In the West, the meaning of death has fluctuated, with death viewed primarily as an end of life during the scientific-minded Renaissance Age. However, during the Romantic Age (1800s), death was glorified and there was an emphasis on achieving a noble death. In the 20th century, death came to be something to be avoided, and saw a surge in medical methods designed to prolong life.

Kubler-Ross conceptualized the five stages of dying. In stage 1, the individual experiences denial upon realizing he will soon die. In stage 2 the individual understands that he will die, but feels cheated out of remaining life. This feeling leads to the third stage, bargaining, in which the individual attempts to negotiate prolonged life with God or whatever other entity the individual feels is responsible. Stage 4 brings with it depression, in which the death is recognized as being inevitable, with a sense of loss felt from unrealized experiences. The final stage is acceptance, wherein the individual comes to realize that death is a natural process. Acceptance often provides comfort and relief.

Bereavement is the process individuals experience as they process the death of a loved one. To study bereavement, researchers assessed levels of depression, via a depression inventory. Subjects were assessed before they became widowed and at 6 and 13 months after they became widowed. The researchers found patterns in bereavement among the individuals that they studied, which they classified into four styles of bereavement.

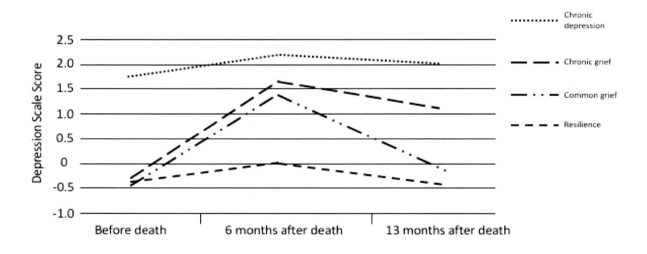

Figure 1. Bereavement styles and depression

The conceptualization of dying in this process lends to the formulation of interventions to assist the dying individual through the process. Kubler-Ross emphasized that the dying person should be allowed to talk openly through the process with caring persons and health care professionals. The emotions that become prominent during each stage should be allowed to be expressed in order for the individual to fully address the themes of each stage. Individuals may proceed through the stages in varying manners, skipping some stages or going through others in different sequences.

1. Which of the following bereavement styles might be most common in a culture which views death as a natural phenomenon?
   A. Chronic depression
   B. Chronic grief
   C. Resilience
   D. Culture will not impact bereavement

2. Individuals who have successfully resolved Erikson's ego integrity v. despair stage are more likely to have achieved what stage in the 5 stage model of dying?
   A. Anger
   B. Bargaining
   C. Depression
   D. Acceptance

3. Psychologists following the Kubler-Ross dying model are most likely to support which approach in bereaving patients?
   A. Encourage bereaving individuals to talk about their experiences
   B. Encourage bereaving individuals to proceed through the 5 step model in sequence
   C. Encourage bereaving individuals to achieve ego integrity about the deceased individual
   D. Recognize that individuals with chronic depression are likely still in the depression stage

4. Individuals fearing death because they can easily recount sensational media accounts of disturbing deaths illustrate what process of conceptualizing information?
   A. Availability heuristic
   B. Fundamental attribution error
   C. Intuition
   D. Anchoring heuristic

5. All of the following are examples of key emotional components EXCEPT:
   A. differentiating between feelings of anger and embarrassment.
   B. crying during Stage 4 of the Kubler-Ross model.
   C. increased heart rate, sweating during Stage 2 of the Kubler-Ross model.
   D. increased amygdala activity during Stage 3 of the Kubler-Ross model.

6. A group of adolescent males, who usually wear earth tones or other similar colors, snicker at and tease a group member who wears light purple shirts. Eventually, the group member switches to a more earth-toned wardrobe. What best describes this situation?
   A. Diversity as a cause of evolving norms and rituals.
   B. The use of peer pressure and stigma to induce a change in deviant behavior.
   C. The role of class as a factor that contributes to prejudice.
   D. The effect of dramaturgical inclinations affecting behavior in different situations.

7. While unknowingly attending a funeral for the first time, a child looks around the room, spots the body of a loved one lying in the coffin in the room, and begins to cry. This example most closely represents what sort of sensory processing?
   A. Unimodal stimuli and top-down processing
   B. Unimodal stimuli and bottom-up processing
   C. Multimodal stimuli and top-down processing
   D. Multimodal stimuli and bottom-up processing

Practice Passage Explanations

Culture has a large impact on how death is viewed by an individual. A culture's death ethos can be inferred from observing artistic or traditional rituals that are related to death. The view of death's desirability, whether it is considered sacred or profane, or welcome or unwanted, can have a strong impact on acceptance. In the West, the meaning of death has fluctuated, with death viewed primarily as an end of life during the scientific-minded Renaissance Age. However, during the Romantic Age (1800s), death was glorified and there was an emphasis on achieving a noble death. In the 20th century, death came to be something to be avoided, and saw a surge in medical methods designed to prolong life.

Key terms: culture, death ethos, Renaissance age, Romantic age, 20th century

Contrast: view of death changes with culture and time; detached, glorified, feared

Kubler-Ross conceptualized the five stages of dying. In stage 1, the individual experiences denial upon realizing he will soon die. In stage 2 the individual understands that he will die, but feels cheated out of remaining life. This feeling leads to the third stage, bargaining, in which the individual attempts to negotiate prolonged life with God or whatever other entity the individual feels is responsible. Stage 4 brings with it depression, in which the death is recognized as being inevitable, with a sense of loss felt from unrealized experiences. The final stage is acceptance, wherein the individual comes to realize that death is a natural process. Acceptance often provides comfort and relief.

Key terms: Kubler-Ross, five stages

Opinion: KR = denial → anger → bargaining → depression → acceptance (comfort/relief)

Bereavement is the process individuals experience as they process the death of a loved one. To study bereavement, researchers assessed levels of depression, via a depression inventory. Subjects were assessed before they became widowed and at 6 and 13 months after they became widowed. The researchers found patterns in bereavement among the individuals that they studied, which they classified into four styles of bereavement.

Key terms: bereavement, depression inventory

Opinion: bereavement style influences depression levels after loss of spouse

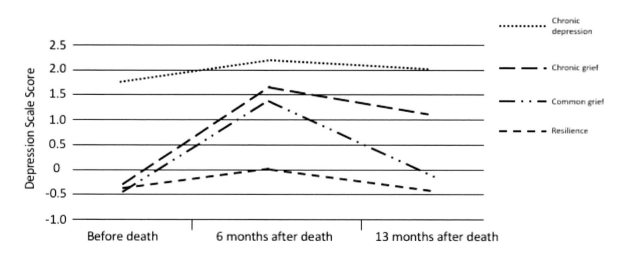

Figure 1. Bereavement styles and depression

Figure 1 shows us resilience led to the lowest levels, while chronic depression led to the highest

The conceptualization of dying in this process lends to the formulation of interventions to assist the dying individual through the process. Kubler-Ross emphasized that the dying person should be allowed to talk openly through the process with caring persons and health care professionals. The emotions that become prominent during each stage should be allowed to be expressed in order for the individual to fully address the themes of each stage. Individuals may proceed through the stages in varying manners, skipping some stages or going through others in different sequences.

Key terms: interventions, emotions, skipping stages

Opinion: KR—dying should express emotions; people can move through the KR stages differently

1. C is correct. In a culture in which dying is considered to be a natural process it is less likely that a death would lead to prolonged feelings of grief.

2. D is correct. Those who have achieved ego integrity have reviewed their life and have found that they have lived a fulfilled life. These individuals have likely come to accept their own death.

3. A is correct. The KR dying model is intended to be used as a framework for processing the experiences and emotions individuals have about dying.

4. A is correct. The availability heuristic refers to people more easily recalling information that is more prominent, such as if it has been sensationalized in media.

5. D is correct. Typically, psychologists have studied emotions in terms of three components-the physical, the cognitive, and the behavioral. The physical component is the physiological arousal that accompanies the emotion (C), the cognitive component determines the specific emotion we feel (A), and the behavioral component of emotions is the outward expression of the emotions (B).

6. B is correct. In the presented situation, the deviant behavior in question—wearing a differently colored shirt than is the norm—is discouraged by the actions of the teen's peer group, specifically peer pressure to conform, and the creation of a stigma against the light purple-colored shirt.
   A. The group's norms remain in place, and they eventually cause conformity in behavior, which is the opposite of diverse behavior.
   C. This is not correct because the prompt contains no information about whether or not the group members belong to different social or economic classes.
   D. Dramaturgical inclinations would cause a difference between front-stage and back-stage behavior—essentially, different behaviors for different audiences. Here, though, the "audience" remains the same, so dramaturgical theory does not apply.

7. B is correct. In this example, the child is using just their visual system (one sense = unimodal), the coffin/body catches their eye, and triggers an emotional response. Bottom-up process occurs when something unexpected is noticed by the senses and catches your attention. This causes you to look over and react. The signal causing this chain of events originated in the environment, at the "bottom" of the sensory processing stream. Top-down processing would be in the child entered the room with an internal, high-level goal (such as knowing they are at a funeral with a dead loved one), which determines where they look next. The child is looking "for" something, so higher-level brain areas prime the low level visual areas to detect that pattern.

Independent Questions

1. All of the following are universal emotions except:
   A. anger.
   B. disgust.
   C. shame.
   D. surprise.

2. As part of a study, subjects were required to give a speech in front of an audience while researchers monitored their physiological stress responses. It was found that subjects given an oral beta-adrenergic antagonist one hour before the speech showed significantly reduced changes in heart rate and skin conductivity compared to subjects who did not receive the medication. However, all subjects reported similar subjective feelings of anxiety. This is consistent with:
   A. the Yerkes-Dodson law.
   B. the Schachter-Singer theory.
   C. the Cannon-Bard theory.
   D. the James-Lange theory.

3. Which of the following hormones would most likely NOT be present in elevated concentrations in the serum of chronically stressed animals?
   A. Cortisol
   B. Epinephrine
   C. Growth hormone
   D. Glucagon

4. All of the following are parts of the stress response outlined by the theory of the general adaptation syndrome EXCEPT:
   A. alarm.
   B. exhaustion.
   C. resistance.
   D. association.

5. Chronic stress has been linked to the development of numerous medical conditions, including hypertension and diabetes mellitus. Which of the following individuals is most likely at risk of developing hypertension as a result of stress?
   A. An individual with an imminent deadline for a major company project
   B. An individual who has spent months training intensely for a marathon
   C. An individual who was recently involved in a verbal argument with a family member
   D. An individual who provides care on a daily basis for a parent with Alzheimer's disease

6. Post-traumatic stress disorder (PTSD) develops following extremely stressful experiences and is often characterized by flashbacks brought on by triggers related to the experience. These flashbacks are frequently accompanied by an intense physiological response, which includes tachycardia, sweating, and elevated blood pressure. Changes in neuroanatomy have been found to accompany PTSD. Affected structures most likely include the:
   A. parietal lobe.
   B. amygdala.
   C. hypothalamus.
   D. cerebellum.

7. After feeling ill for several days, a fifty-year-old man presents to the emergency department with a severe, intractable headache and vision changes. After a battery of tests, he receives a diagnosis of terminal brain cancer. Which of the three main types of stressors most accurately describes this event?
   A. Catastrophe
   B. Significant life change
   C. Traumatic disaster
   D. Daily hassle

8. Which of the following is a maladaptive response to stress?
   A. Alcohol consumption
   B. Pursuing a new hobby
   C. Starting an exercise routine
   D. Joining a religious congregation

Independent Question Explanations

1. C is correct. The six universal emotions, which are expressed similarly across all cultures, are happiness, fear, surprise, disgust, anger, and sadness.

2. C is correct. Although the beta blocker successfully dampened the physiological fight-or-flight response in the subjects who received it, this reduction in physiological response had no effect on their emotional state. Such a finding suggests that subjective emotional state and physiological response to a stimulus develop independently of one another. This is consistent with the Cannon-Bard theory of emotion. Both the James-Lange and Schachter-Singer theories depict emotion as a downstream consequence of a physiological response. Note that answer choice A, the Yerkes-Dodson Law refers to the relationship between stress and performance, where better performance is correlated with medium levels of stress.

3. C is correct. Stress induces the release of corticosteroids and catecholamines. Stress also induces the release of glucagon, which facilitates the elevation of blood glucose to provide readily available energy. Secretion of growth hormone is not a component of the stress response. In fact, chronically stressed children exhibit reduced growth hormone secretion and smaller stature.

4. D is correct. General adaptation syndrome defines a sequence of stages that occur following exposure to a stressor. The initial alarm stage is followed by a resistance stage, which is followed either by exhaustion or recovery. The final stages reflect either the depletion of the organism's resources or successful physiological adaptation to the stressor, respectively.

5. D is correct. According to the question stem, chronic stressors are associated with the development of health problems. Deadlines and arguments are acute stressors, while acting as a primary caregiver for a dependent family member is a chronic stressor that could potentially lead to the development of health problems, including hypertension. Daily exercise reduces the chances of developing hypertension and may aid in effective stress management.

6. B is correct. The amygdala plays a central role in the activation of the fear response, including its physiological manifestations. In fact, PTSD has been found to be linked to changes in the hippocampus and the amygdala. The cerebellum is responsible for motor coordination, the hypothalamus has a primarily endocrine role, and the parietal lobe is involved in somatosensory functions.

7. B is correct. The three main types of stressors are catastrophes, significant life changes, and daily hassles (eliminate choice C). Catastrophes are events that significantly disrupt the lives of a large number of people. Examples include natural disasters and pandemics. Daily hassles are day-to-day problems such as deadlines and relationship conflicts. Daily hassles generally do not pose a significant risk to one's health or well-being unless they become frequent and overwhelming. Significant life changes include serious illness, death of a loved one, or loss of livelihood.

8. A is correct. Hobbies and regular exercise have been shown to increase one's capacity to handle stress. Some research has also suggested that having strong ties to one's community may also help facilitate emotional well-being. Consumption of alcohol is generally considered a maladaptive response to stress, since it has multiple potential negative health effects.

This page left intentionally blank.

Memory and Learning

CHAPTER 6

0. Introduction

When they study memory, scientists investigate how exactly we acquire and maintain the knowledge that we gain from experiences throughout our lives. This chapter will present the three major processes that make memory possible, encoding, storage, and retrieval, as well as the loss of memory.

Learning is the acquisition of new knowledge or skills through education or experience. The most basic way of thinking about learning is the relationship between a stimulus or stimuli and our responses to them.

1. Encoding

Encoding is the process the brain uses to transfer new sensory information into memory. There are two general ways this happens: automatic processing and controlled processing.

I. Types of Encoding

Automatic processing refers to information that is processed into memory without any effort. For example, you move to a neighborhood and walk around, exploring the streets and landmarks around. Without any effort, you are able to remember those streets and landmarks the next time you go out.

Controlled processing refers to a more effortful process of creating memories. For example, studying for a test on complicated subject matter (like the MCAT) or learning a language both require a lot of time, effort, and focus. However, after enough practice, controlled processing can become automatic.

> **MCAT STRATEGY > > >**
>
> You can think of neural impulses as the "computer code" for your brain. Encoding, then, is turning physical stimuli (e.g. waves of air compression for sound) into the code your brain can understand.

When it comes to controlled, effortful processing, we can encode information either with visual encoding, acoustic encoding, or semantic encoding. With **visual encoding** we visualize new information to be stored in memory. This is the weakest form of encoding. With **acoustic encoding** we concentrate and memorize the way something sounds. With **semantic encoding**, we put new information into the context of information we already have committed to memory. This is the strongest form of encoding. Semantic encoding is perhaps most effective when we put new information into the context of our lives, which accounts for the **self-reference effect**, the human tendency to most readily recall information that pertains directly to our lives and our selves.

II. Methods for Aiding Encoding

A **mnemonic** is a device or technique that can help encourage the encoding of information to memory. An example of a simple mnemonic is using the acronym ROYGBIV (pronounced Roy-Gee-Biv) to remember the order of the colors in the visual spectrum of light.

One such mnemonic is **maintenance rehearsal**, or repeating a phrase over and over again until you've memorized it (think of the Pledge of Allegiance in elementary school).

Another is **chunking**, in which a person groups information into separate chunks, like you might memorize the digits of a phone number in groups of three.

Establishing **hierarchies** of information, or grouping that information to ordered groups, can also be useful in assisting memory encoding.

According to the **dual coding hypothesis**, it is easier to memorize words that are paired with a specific image than to memorize either an individual word or image. With both a word and image paired together, information may be processed at a more connected, deeper level. Indeed, there is some evidence that the **depth of processing** is an important factor in how likely information is to be encoded into memory: the deeper the processing of a memory, the more likely we are to remember it. For example, it is easier to remember the general plot of a movie than specific, individual lines.

Because of the dual coding hypothesis, imagery is one of the more effective mnemonic devices. One way of using imagery is the **method of loci**, in which a person associates an item to be memorized at points along a memorized route. For example, if you were trying to memorize the organs of the digestive system in order, you might envision cartoon representations of those organs in different parts of your house, in the order that you walk through it.

2. Storage

After information is encoded, it must be stored in one of four general ways, as sensory memory, short-term memory, working memory, or long-term memory.

I. Sensory Memory

Sensory memory is the initial recording of encoded sensory information, and is therefore the most fleeting form of memory storage. In fact, it is so fleeting that it typically lasts no more than one second and will be lost unless further attended to. There are two main types of sensory memory: **iconic memory**, responsible for visual information and lasting only for a few tenths of a second, and **echoic memory**, responsible for auditory information and lasting for 3 to 4 seconds. In order for sensory memories to not decay, they must be passed through Broadbent's filter (mentioned in Chapter 3), to the short-term memory.

II. Short-Term Memory

Like sensory memories, but lasting closer to 30 seconds without repetition, short-term memories will fade without further attention. Moreover, the **short-term memory** can typically only handle about seven pieces of information at once. Short-term memory can be bolstered by the mnemonic devices previously mentioned.

Working memory is the element of short-term memory that allows us to consciously process and manipulate a few pieces of information. For example, working memory allows us to do basic math in our heads without a calculator or pen and paper. Working memory is representative of an interplay between short-term memory, attention, and the executive function of the brain.

> **MCAT STRATEGY > > >**
>
> Remember, the "short-term" part of short-term memory means *really* short—under a minute!

III. Long-Term Memory

Through **elaborative rehearsal** and other more intensive processes, information can proceed all the way from sensory, to short-term, to **long-term memory**, which is currently believed to have an infinite capacity. Elaborative rehearsal is more complex than maintenance rehearsal, requiring incoming information to be associated with information that has already made its way through into long-term memory. *have to know someone already there to get in*

Long-term memory is divided into implicit memory, also known as nondeclarative memory, and explicit memory, also known as declarative memory.

Implicit (nondeclarative) memory accounts for acquired skills and conditioned responses to circumstances and stimuli. This also includes **procedural memory**, which accounts for motor skills and specific physical actions. The cerebellum plays a primary role in encoding implicit memories.

Explicit (declarative) memory accounts for memories that we must consciously recall with effort and focus. A further division within explicit memory is between **episodic memory**, which accounts for our experiences, and **semantic memory**, which accounts for facts and concepts that we know. The hippocampus plays a primary role in encoding explicit memories.

long term
explicit
episodic experience *semantic facts*
implicit stimuli/responses procedural
don't retrieve actively

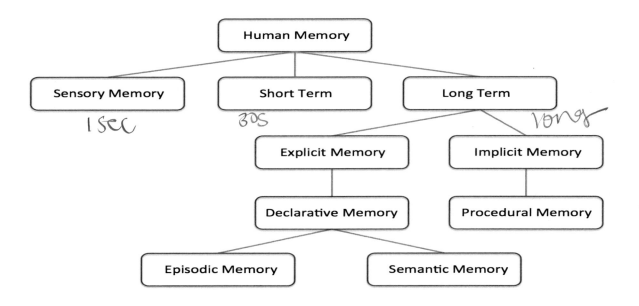

Figure 1. Divisions of Human Memory.

3. Retrieval

Once all those memories are stored, they must be found: **retrieval** is the process the brain uses to find information stored in long-term memory.

I. Recall, Recognition, and Relearning

Recall is simply the ability to retrieve stored information. **Free recall** is when you retrieve this stored information without any further information, while **cued recall** is when you retrieve this information after being provided with a cue, or some other information to help find that stored memory.

Much easier than recall, **recognition** is the ability to identify specific information that has already been learned and set to memory. For examples, recognition is used on a multiple-choice test while recall is used for writing an essay.

Relearning is, as its name suggests, the process of learning information that we have already learned. If you have learned and forgotten something, the second time you set out to learn it, the easier it is to memorize. Moreover, the greater the amounts of time between learning and relearning and more relearning, the more likely the information is to be retained. This phenomenon, first observed by the German psychologist Hermann Ebbinghaus, is known as the **spacing effect**.

II. Organization

We retain a lot of information in our long-term memory, so much so that it all must be organized effectively for it to be of any use to us. Therefore, long-term memories are organized into **semantic networks**, with individual ideas called **nodes**, and the connections between those nodes called **associations**. Some associations are stronger than others, and some nodes have more associations connecting to them than others. These variations depend upon one's environment and experiences. For example, a person that grew up in the Northeast may associate the word "pizza" more closely with the idea of comfort food than someone who grew up in the deep South, who may more closely associate the word "biscuits" to the same idea.

Any given node, like any other neural connection, must be activated by an electrical signal, and that signal must surpass the **response threshold** in order to activate the node. Once a node is activated, it consequently activates adjacent nodes, causing a pattern of further activation, called **spreading activation**, as more nodes activate more nodes. Within the terms of spreading activation, when we attempt to retrieve information from our long-term memory, we activate a single node that then initiates a spreading activation, meaning we do not choose which nodes are activated next. Finally, once the proper node is activated, we have found our information.

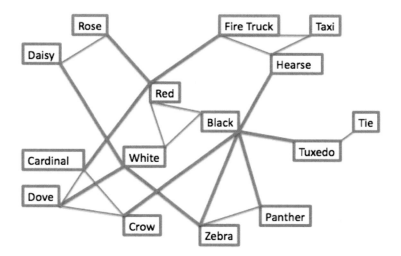

Figure 2. An Illustration of Spreading Activation: the Word "Tie" Represents the Initial Node.

III. Retrieval Cues

Spreading activation accounts for retrieval cues such as **priming**, which allows us to recall a specific piece of information after being presented with a word, phrase, or idea that is neurologically close to the desired piece of information.

Another retrieval cue, **context effects**, aids the process of finding a specific piece of information when we are in the physical location where the memory was originally encoded. For example, if you were studying for the biology section of the MCAT on a trampoline, with a friend quizzing you while you bounced, being on or around a trampoline later on might help you remember a particular fact tested on the MCAT.

State-dependent memory, another retrieval cue, accounts for the fact that someone who learns a new fact or skill while drunk will better remember that fact or skill when they are drunk than when they are sober. Likewise, **mood-dependent memory** means that a person can more readily recall a fact or skill they learned while in a particular mood when they are again in that particular mood. Moreover, the recall of that fact while in that mood will make that mood more persistent. So, say you learn how to bake a cake while you are sad. You will better remember how to make a cake when you are sad, and by remembering, you will continue to be sad. That would be a very sad cake.

Another retrieval cue, most apparent when memorizing lists, is the **serial position effect**. Typically, when a person works on memorizing the items on a list, that person has a tendency to remember the first and last items most clearly, called the **primacy effect** and **recency effect**, respectively. Moreover, after a long period of time, the first items are remembered more than the last items.

4. Memory Loss

Though scientists have posited that the capacity for long-term memory is infinite, there are several events and processes that can cause memory loss.

I. Aging

Though a person's memory can decline as the person reaches old age, aging does not necessarily lead to major memory loss. Moreover, because of a lifetime of memories and connections between them, older people have larger semantic networks. In a big semantic network, important, meaningful information is remembered more readily than less significant details. In fact, when people in their 70s and 80s are asked to remember the highlights of their lives, they often remember events from their adolescence and young adulthood (giving evidence that the brain's encoding of memories is strongest in our teens and 20s).

Because of larger semantic networks, recall of memories can prove to be more challenging for elderly people: the older you are, the more information you have to sort through. One type of recall that is affected is **prospective memory**, which is the ability to remember to perform a task at some point in the future. Without visual cues, elderly people can struggle with prospective memory, and can essentially forget to remember to perform a task. For example, if an old man needs to take a certain series of pills and vitamins, if he does not see them in a day, he may forget to take them for that day. Along with prospective memory, remembering time-based activities, like taking those pills and vitamins at 9am and 9pm, also becomes more difficult for older people.

II. Brain Disorders

Because memory has a neurological basis, damage to different parts of the brain can cause memory failure. Because the hippocampus is primarily responsible for encoding new, explicit memories, damage to it can cause **anterograde amnesia**, an inability to create new memories, as well as **retrograde amnesia**, an inability to recall memories. Such damage to the hippocampus can be caused by stroke, major trauma to the head, alcoholism, or tumor growth. Both kinds of amnesia can also be caused by a thiamine deficiency in the brain, called **Korsakoff's syndrome**. Beyond anterograde and retrograde amnesia, another symptom of Korsakoff's syndrome is that patients develop a propensity for **confabulation**, the creation of vivid but entirely fabricated memories. Scientists consider confabulation an attempt by the brain to fill in neural space left void by actual memories that have been lost.

Alzheimer's disease is the most common and culturally recognized disease that can cause memory loss. Though it is still not fully understood, at this point Alzheimer's is believed to be the result of diminished production of the neurotransmitter acetylcholine, which is important for proper function of the hippocampus. Without it, the neurons of the hippocampus begin to die. Alzheimer's most marked symptoms are memory loss, atrophy of the brain, and **dementia**, which refers to the loss of cognitive abilities. All of these symptoms become progressively worse and worse in an Alzheimer's sufferer. For the most part, memory loss is retrograde, beginning with the most recent memories of the patient before deeper, long-term memories are lost as well. Below, Figure 6.3 illustrates the brain atrophy that Alzheimer's disease can cause.

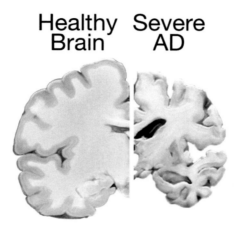

Healthy Brain   Severe AD

Figure 3. The Physical Effect of Alzheimer's Disease on the Human Brain.

Another disorder that causes memory loss, **agnosia** is an inability to recognize objects, people, or sounds, though thankfully it is typically only one of the three. Agnosia is caused by damage to the brain from strokes or other neurological issues or disorders.

III. Decay

Even without disorders or damage of the brain, memories can be lost and forgotten. And as Hermann Ebbinghaus found (mentioned above as the man who demonstrated the spacing effect), memories are lost not in a linear fashion, but along a so-called "curve of forgetting." On such a curve, recall of new information falls the most sharply just after learning it, but tapers off after more time.

> **MCAT STRATEGY > > >**
>
> Review MCAT content again and again. Don't let those memories decay!

Moreover, the more you review new information, the less sharply recall ability falls and the longer the ability to recall the information lasts. See the diagram below for an illustration:

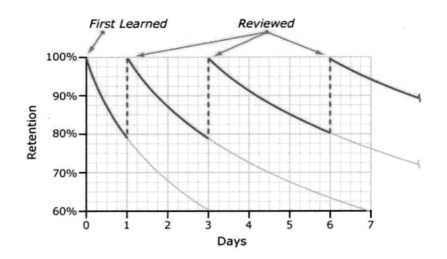

Figure 4. Ebbinghaus' Curve of Forgetting.

IV. Interference

Interference is an error in memory retrieval caused by newer information interfering with older information, or vice versa. Moreover, interference is particularly likely when old and new information are similar.

Retroactive interference is when more recently learned information blocks recall of information learned in the past. For example, say you are a student studying abroad for a year, first in Spain, then in France. After studying in France and gaining proficiency with the language, you head to Spain and find the language easy to master because of its similarity to French. However, some of your French friends come into town and you struggle to speak in French with them, occasionally reverting to Spanish.

Proactive interference, on the other hand, is when older information interferes with new information that you are trying to learn. For example, think back to a time when you got a new phone number: the new number may have been more difficult to remember than the last one because you had become so used to the old one.

5. Habituation

Habituation is a decrease in response to a stimulus after repeated, continuous exposure to that stimulus. Habituation is a form of **nonassociative learning**, which involves exposure only to a single event. Say you are new to the Army and are training for airborne combat operations and the first time you make a parachute jump, you are scared. After repeatedly jumping and safely landing, you are less bothered by the prospect of jumping out of a high-speed object, 30,000 feet above the ground.

Dishabituation, another form of nonassociative learning, is the opposite of habituation: it is the recovery of a particular response to a stimulus after habituation has lessened that response. Say you are playing a game of peek-a-boo with a baby, covering your face and then revealing it. At first, the baby laughs with delight, but after a while, through habituation, loses interest. Then, you replace your face with a favorite stuffed animal. The baby again responds with laughter. After this new stimulus is introduced, you return to showing your own face, and the baby laughs again. That stuffed animal caused dishabituation and gave the baby a new interest in your face. Importantly, dishabituation refers to changes in response to an old stimulus and not a new one.

6. Classical Conditioning

Classical conditioning is one of two primary types of **associative learning**, which refers to the creation of an association between either a behavior and a response or between two stimuli (we'll get to the other type, operant conditioning, in a moment). Classical conditioning is the creation of an association between two unrelated stimuli through instinctual responses to those stimuli.

In classical conditioning, an **unconditioned stimulus** and the subsequent **unconditioned response** to it are used to turn a **neutral stimulus** into a **conditioned stimulus** which causes a **conditioned response**.

Let's break that down with the famous experiment the Russian physiologist Ivan Pavlov conducted on dogs:

Pavlov's unconditioned stimulus was meat and the dogs' unconditioned response to it was to salivate: without any conditioning, this stimulus causes an instinctive response in the subjects. Pavlov then introduced a neutral stimulus, which initially caused no response from the dogs. However, when he began ringing the bell before feeding meat to the dogs, the dogs began to associate the ringing of the bell with receiving meat. Therefore, the ringing of the bell actually made the dogs salivate. The neutral stimulus (the ringing of the bell), through association with the unconditioned stimulus (the meat), had become a conditioned stimulus that caused a conditioned response (salivating). The whole process is simply illustrated in Figure 7.1 below:

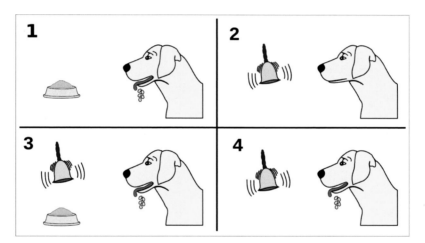

Figure 5. The Classical Conditioning of Pavlov's Dogs.

Just like long-term memories, conditioned responses are not necessarily permanent. If Pavlov rang the bell enough times without providing any meat to his dogs, the dogs would become habituated to the conditioned stimulus and no longer have a conditioned response to it. This process if called **extinction**. Sometimes, however, after habituation has occurred and time has passed, an extinct conditioned stimulus can again cause a conditioned response, albeit a weaker one. This is called **spontaneous recovery**.

Conditioned responses can be modified by both generalization and discrimination.

Generalization is the process through which additional stimuli can come to elicit the same conditioned response as the initial conditioned stimulus. For another famous example, a young boy, referred to as Little Albert for the experiment, was conditioned to be afraid of a white rat (neutral and then conditioned stimulus) with the simultaneous playing of a loud noise (unconditioned stimulus). This conditioning underwent generalization to the point that Albert was also afraid, in the same way that he was of the white rat, of a white stuffed rabbit and a man with a big, white beard.

Discrimination is the exact opposite of generalization, making a conditioned response more specific when a subject learns to discriminate between two similar stimuli. For example, say Pavlov used bells with different tones in his experiments, and only gave meat to the dogs after ringing the bell with the higher pitch. The dogs would begin to discriminate and would only salivate upon hearing the higher pitched bell.

7. Operant Conditioning

While classical conditioning uses unconditioned stimuli and responses to create conditioned responses out of previously neutral stimuli, **operant conditioning** uses both punishment and reinforcement to shape behavior.

MCAT STRATEGY > > >

If you find yourself mixing up operant and classical conditioning, stay focused on a single question: does the animal's behavior have consequences? If so, that's operant conditioning. By contrast, in classical conditioning, the animal's behavior doesn't result in any rewards or punishments—if one of Pavlov's dogs salivates, the salivation isn't "rewarded" with food.

The study of operant conditioning was spearheaded by B.F. Skinner, who was mentioned earlier for his learning theory (or behaviorist theory) of language acquisition. Skinner conducted famous experiments with a so-called operant conditioning chamber (colloquially known as a "Skinner box"), in which he subjected rats to different tests. In one such experiment, the box was fitted with electrical wires that would deliver a shock until the rat pulled a lever. With the shock initiated, the rat ran around until it accidentally hit the lever, stopping the shock and the pain it caused. As such, the rat learned to pull the lever anytime the shock began again. In another experiment, Skinner placed a hungry rat in the box and wired the lever to deliver a pellet of food when pulled. After a while, the rat learned to pull the lever when it was hungry.

[handwritten notes: Pavlov = classical, dogs; Skinner = operant]

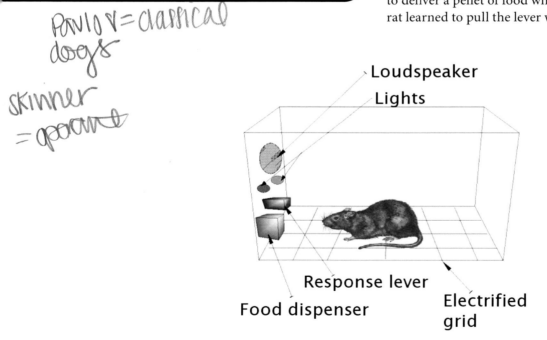

Figure 6. An Operant Conditioning Chamber (or "Skinner Box").

I. Reinforcement

Both experiments relied upon **reinforcement**, which is doing anything to increase the likelihood that a certain behavior will be repeated. There are two primary types of reinforcement: **positive reinforcement** is adding a positive stimulus directly after a behavior (like adding a food pellet after the pull of a lever), and **negative reinforcement** is subtracting a negative stimulus (electric shock) directly after a behavior (pulling the lever). Negative reinforcement can be divided into **escape learning**, in which a behavior is used to avoid a currently unpleasant thing, and **avoidance leaning**, in which a behavior is used to avoid a unpleasant thing that has not happened yet.

Reinforcers, the things doing the reinforcement, can be divided into primary and secondary reinforcers.

Primary reinforcers (or unconditional reinforcers), including things like food and water which are necessary for daily survival, are innately desirable. Food is a primary positive reinforcer. Inversely, avoiding pain is a primary negative reinforcer because pain is innately undesirable.

Secondary reinforcers (or conditioned reinforcers) are not innately desirable, but are paired with primary reinforcers and are learned to be reinforcers. A great example of a secondary reinforcer is money. Money can be used to reinforce behaviors because money allows us to acquire primary reinforcers, like food and water, shelter, clothing, sex, and etc.

II. Punishment

On the flip side of reinforcement is **punishment**, which is divided into positive and negative as well. **Positive punishment** is making an unpleasant response to a certain behavior in order to reduce that behavior. For example, a coach making an unruly soccer player run six laps for goofing off during practice, with the intention of making the player goof off less. Conversely, **negative punishment** is removing a stimulus in order to reduce a certain behavior. For example, if a child misbehaves in public, his parents take his video game privileges away. The idea is to take away a desired stimulus (video games) in order to reduce an undesired behavior (misbehaving in public).

In both reinforcement and punishment, positive means adding something and negative means taking something away.

III. Reinforcement Schedules

Desired behaviors can be acquired through the reinforcement or punishment of operant conditioning at variable rates. A **reinforcement schedule** is basically a tool for controlling the timing and frequency of reinforcement or punishment while trying to elicit a particular behavior from a subject. A reinforcement schedule can be either continuous or intermittent, fixed or variable, and it can be based either on an interval or a ratio.

With a **continuous** reinforcement schedule, every single occurrence of a behavior is reinforced whereas with a **intermittent** reinforcement schedule, occurrences are sometimes reinforced and are sometimes not. Continuous reinforcement will allow for a behavior to be learned faster, but it will fade faster. Intermittent reinforcement typically takes longer, so a behavior will be learned more slowly, but also, the learned behavior will be retained for longer. These two methods can be paired, with continuous reinforcement used at first then intermittent reinforcement used to maintain the behavior. For example, a parent could give their child a small toy every time they got all A's on a report card. After time, they could give a reward for only some all A report cards.

With a **fixed-ratio schedule**, reinforcement of a particular behavior is given after a set amount of times that behavior is performed. For example, in a Skinner Box experiment, the rat will be given the food pellet after every fourth pull of the lever.

With a **variable-ratio schedule**, reinforcement of a particular behavior is given after an unpredictable amount of times the behavior is performed. A basic example of a variable-ratio schedule is gambling: winnings (the reinforcements) are unpredictable and possibly rare, but the hope of winnings, and occasional actual winnings, will continue to motivate the behavior.

With a **fixed-interval schedule**, reinforcement of a behavior is given after a set period of time that does not change. For example, imagine a 10 year-old boy who is always home before his parents on weekdays. He is not allowed to watch TV on the weekdays and he doesn't risk it because he never knows when his parents will come home, and the TV is in the basement, so he can't tell when they are coming. They reward him with praise for not watching TV on weekdays. However, he begins to realize that his parents come home at the exact same time on different days (5pm on Thursday, 6pm on Friday, and etc.). As such, he learns that he can watch TV up until those times, when he turns it off and pretends to have been studying and they praise him again for not watching TV on weekdays.

MCAT STRATEGY > > >

Variable ratio is how slot machines pay out at casinos. Casino owners want people to keep playing as long as possible.

With a **variable-interval schedule**, reinforcement of a behavior is given after a period of time that is not constant. Extending the previous example, now the boys parents return home at random times of day, so he doesn't know exactly when they'll be coming home. He becomes much more cautious with his TV watching, if he continues it at all (depends how much his parents punish him for disobeying).

The following diagram depicts how the four major reinforcement schedules work, with variable-ratio working the fastest. The hatch marks on each line represent iterations of a reinforcement.

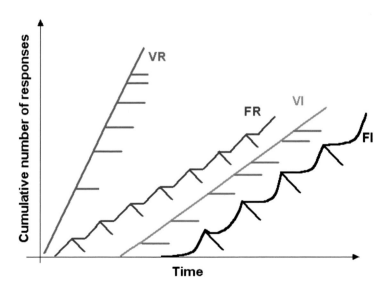

Figure 7. Types of Reinforcement Schedules (VR: Variable-Ratio; FR: Fixed-Ratio; VI: Variable Interval; FI: Fixed-Interval).

Some behaviors are too complicated to be learned directly through operant conditioning. Rather, some behaviors must be shaped through reinforcement of several, smaller behaviors that will in turn lead to the bigger, more complex behavior. An example of this is a toddler walking. Babies cannot one day just stand up and start walking and be praised for it. Instead, every step along the way is reinforced, shaping the baby's path to eventually walking on its own two legs.

8. Observational Learning

Observational learning, also sometimes referred to as social or vicarious learning, is the process of learning though watching others and imitating their behavior.

Neurologically, **mirror neurons**, located in the frontal and parietal lobes, have a major role in observational learning: they fire when we perform an action but also when we observe someone else performing that same action. Mirror neurons function for physical actions as well as emotions, playing a role in human empathy.

Perhaps the most notorious demonstration of observational learning was the so-called "Bobo doll" experiment, conducted by the Canadian-American psychologist Albert Bandura between 1961 and 1963. In the experiment, children watched from the outside of an enclosed room as an adult punched and kicked an inflatable, five foot-tall Bobo doll. Later, when the children were allowed to play in the room, many of the children ignored the other toys in the room and beat up Bobo as the adult had done before them.

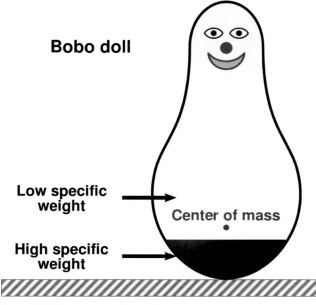

Figure 8. A Diagram of the "Bobo Doll" Used in Bandura's Experiment.

Beyond neurology, one of the most basic phenomena behind observational learning is **modeling**, in which a person (or animal) observes another conducting some kind of behavior, and later, with that observed person or animal in mind, **imitates** the behavior. The common phrase "actions speak louder than words" has some basis in this phenomenon: though some parents may adopt a policy of "Do as I say, not as I do" while raising their children, research has shown that children more often imitate actions than what they are verbally told to do. This is why many of the best leaders, and not just parents, lead by example.

9. Behavior and Attitude Change

An **attitude** is a way of thinking and feeling about a person, place, or thing that is usually reflected by a person's behavior. **Social cognition** is the study of how exactly our attitudes affect our behavior.

The three primary aspects of an attitude are the affective component, the behavioral component, and the cognitive component. The **affective component** is emotional: it's the way a person feels about something (for example, a person saying "I love oatmeal"). The **behavioral component** is the way that a person acts in relation to something (for example, avoiding places with cold weather during the winter). The **cognitive component** is the way a person thinks about something (for example, knowing how cold a Northern city can be during the winter, and perhaps remembering a dismal experience in cold weather from one's childhood).

There are several theories of attitude that scientists use to study social cognition, with four of the most important being learning theory, functional attitudes theory, the elaboration likelihood model, and social cognitive theory.

I. Learning Theory

Simply put, according to **learning theory**, we develop attitudes through the various forms of learning that were covered earlier in this chapter, including classical conditioning, operant conditioning, and observational learning. Attitudes can also be learned through direct interaction with something or someone: for example, eating a delicious food for the first time creates a positive attitude towards that food and other people who eat that food. Another way we can learn an attitude is from direct instruction: if two parents tell their child to stay out of a particular neighborhood, that child may develop a negative attitude about the neighborhood, as well as the people that live in it.

II. Functional Attitudes Theory

Within **functional attitudes theory**, attitudes are classified by their function and are divided into four types: adaptation, ego defense, ego expression, and knowledge.

An **adaptive attitude** is one that is widely held and will make the person holding the attitude socially accepted. In a specific social circle or group, an adaptive attitude is one that will most likely be accepted within that group. For example, if you are an up-and-coming sports journalist and you want to be socially accepted in a particular circle of sports journalists, you will adapt the attitude of that circle on a particular matter, say, that the San Francisco Giants are the best baseball team, in order to be accepted by that circle.

An **ego-defensive attitude** can be used to justify actions that we know are wrong in order that we may protect our ego or self-esteem. For example, if you try to fly a remote control airplane and end up crashing it again and again, you might develop a negative attitude about remote control airplanes, essentially shielding yourself from your own failure.

An **ego-expressive attitude** is one that can communicate to other people how a person identifies her or his self. For example, a huge Giants fan might wear a Giants hat and a Giants t-shirt to communicate her self-identification.

A **knowledge-based attitude** is one based on the knowledge of something and can be helpful in predicting the behavior of other people. For example, it can be predicted with at least some likelihood that an older man who obviously cares more about financial and economic issues than social issues will vote Republican.

III. Elaboration Likelihood Model

The **elaboration likelihood model** involves persuasion and how different people process persuasive information differently. The model is a continuum, with those who think deeply and critically (i.e. they **elaborate** extensively) about persuasive information on one extreme, and on the other extreme, those who do not elaborate extensively, focusing more on less substantial, superficial information. A person closer to the first extreme use **central route processing** when considering persuasive information, while the person closer to the second extreme uses **peripheral route processing**. Consider the famous presidential debates of 1960, with Kennedy vs. Nixon. Those who listened on the radio thought Nixon won, while those who watched on television thought that Kennedy won. Peripheral route processing may have played a role in the latter, with Kennedy being better looking, better dressed, and not sweating like Nixon was. In general, people fall in the middle of the elaboration spectrum.

IV. Social Cognitive Theory

Social cognitive theory holds that our attitudes and behaviors are the result of observation of the attitudes and behaviors of others. According to this theory, we do not learn how to behave through trial-and-error or even conditioning, but rather, through direct emulation of the other people and things that populate our environment.

Albert Bandura, mentioned above for his "Bobo doll" experiment, worked with the notion of triadic reciprocal causation, in which behavior, personal factors, and environment all influence our attitudes. The interaction between these three factors is called **reciprocal determinism**.

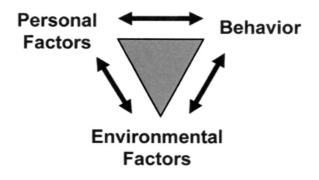

Figure 9. Bandura's Triadic Reciprocal Causation.

Furthermore, there are three general ways that individuals interact with their environments through these factors.

First, people can choose the environment they live in and then the environment shapes them in a particular way.

Second, a person's distinct personality shapes how he or she interacts with his or her environment.

Third, a person's distinct personality affects a certain situation which that person in turn must react to. This aspect of reciprocal determinism accounts for the fact that the way a person treats another person will in turn influence how the second person treats the first person.

For an example of social cognitive theory in action, imagine a 10th grade biology class. The study habits of the students are influenced, to at least some degree, by how hard all the other students study, the previously held attitudes the students have had about biology and studying in general, as well as their home and school environments and the systems in place to encourage studying. Study habits are behavioral, previously held attitudes are personal, and systems at home and school are environmental.

Practice Passage

To better remember names, it is important to pay attention and hear the name being spoken. Many people forget names because they are not truly processing due to distraction. Focusing on internal feelings and thoughts at the time, concern over how one appears to the other party are all distractions. Maintain focus on the other person, and when the name is spoken, repeat the name three times, and maintain eye contact.

To integrate your sense of vision, try to imagine that you see the person's name written on his forehead, and written in your favorite color. This will make the name stand out more. Touch can also be incorporated to assist memory. Imagine writing out the name, feel the pencil and the paper. You can even gently move finger micro-muscles as you are imagining writing. If you are meeting a group of people and are trying to remember several names, a good strategy is to remember them in groups. For example, you might group together the names of couples or group the names in the order in which you heard them. Finally, it can be helpful to use a mnemonic device for remembering names, such as grouping their names with an object that begins with the same letter.

In a study, participants were instructed to use one of the techniques discussed when being introduced to 20 people over the course of 10 minutes. Next, participants were given an unrelated counting task that they were to perform for 30 seconds. Upon completing the task, the participants were given 1 minute and asked to write down as many names as they could recall.

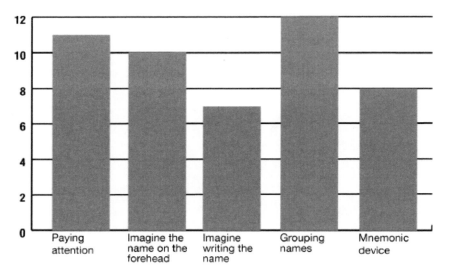

Figure 1. Names recalled

1. What flaw in the research design of the study would cause there to be serious doubts of the validity of the results?
   A. Having the participants use all techniques in the same order
   B. Having different participants use different techniques
   C. Having a control group
   D. Recording participant demographic characteristics

2. Participants were queried a month after the study about names they recalled. This type of memory primarily involves what part of the brain?
   A. Brain stem
   B. Corpus callosum
   C. Hippocampus
   D. Orbitofrontal cortex

3. In a follow-up study participants were brought back two days later and either asked to simply recall as many names as possible (group 1) or presented with a list of 50 names and asked to select names from the list that had been among the original 20 names presented (group 2). Which of the following is most likely true about this follow-up study?
   A. Both groups will correctly identify approximately the same number of names as in the original study since the memory techniques discussed improve both long-term and short-term memory.
   B. To have any external validity the participants must be required to perform the same twenty second intervening task at the start of this second recall attempt.
   C. Both groups will correctly identify fewer names two days later, with group 1 performing better.
   D. While long-term memory is likely to involve some forgetting for both groups, group 2 will correctly identify more names.

4. Using all of the memory techniques tested in the study at once is most likely to strengthen memory building through what process?
   A. Multi-tasking
   B. Parallel processing
   C. Long-term potentiation
   D. Neuroplasticity

5. One of the researchers objected to the use of a counting task prior to name recall. They argued that it is only time that will influence the loss of names. This view is in most accordance with which theory of memory?
   A. Interference theory
   B. Decay theory
   C. Displacement theory
   D. Retrieval failure theory

6. If the task time given to complete the memory encoding task were increased, and the subjects allowed multiple sessions to reinforce and practice with the list of names, an increase in recall is most likely due to which synaptic process?
   A. Post-synaptic inhibition
   B. Pre-synaptic activation
   C. Long-term potentiation
   D. Neuroplasticity

7. One of the controls the researchers put in place was to assess the emotional state and mood of each participant immediately prior to testing. If this information is used as an independent variable in follow-up studies, the researchers are most likely controlling for:
   A. context cues.
   B. state-dependent retrieval.
   C. confirmation bias.
   D. attributional bias.

Practice Passage Explanations

To better remember names, it is important to pay attention and hear the name being spoken. Many people forget names because they are not truly processing due to distraction. Focusing on internal feelings and thoughts at the time, concern over how one appears to the other party are all distractions. Maintain focus on the other person, and when the name is spoken, repeat the name three times, and maintain eye contact.

Key terms: better remember names

Opinion: distractions hurt recall; focus and repetition → better name recall

To integrate your sense of vision, try to imagine that you see the person's name written on his forehead, and written in your favorite color. This will make the name stand out more. Touch can also be incorporated to assist memory. Imagine writing out the name, feel the pencil and the paper. You can even gently move finger micro-muscles as you are imagining writing. If you are meeting a group of people and are trying to remember several names, a good strategy is to remember them in groups. For example, you might group together the names of couples or group the names in the order in which you heard them. Finally, it can be helpful to use a mnemonic device for remembering names, such as grouping their names with an object that begins with the same letter.

Key terms: vision, touch, groups, mnemonic

Cause and effect: vision/touch/mnemonics can improve recall; mnemonics work with groups

In a study, participants were instructed to use one of the techniques discussed when being introduced to 20 people over the course of 10 minutes. Next, participants were given an unrelated counting task that they were to perform for 30 seconds. Upon completing the task, the participants were given 1 minute and asked to write down as many names as they could recall.

Key terms: study, name recall

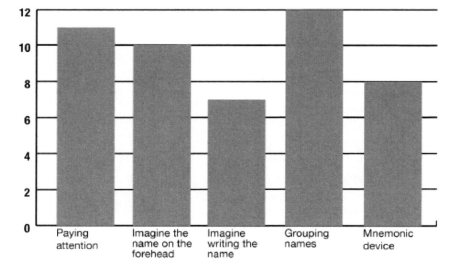

Figure 1. Names recalled

Figure 1 shows that name grouping worked best, imagining writing worst

1. A is correct. Having participants use the techniques in the same order would lead to ordering effects as there would likely be some benefit from using previous techniques when being assessed for later techniques.

2. C is correct. The area of the brain primarily associated with memory retrieval and encoding is the hippocampus.

3. D is correct. Recognition is typically much easier than recall, so the group that simply had to pick the correct names out of the list would be much more likely to correctly identify more names. Both groups, however, will recall fewer names since all types of memory degrade over time (often called the "curve of forgetting").

4. D is correct. Neuroplasticity refers to the brain's ability to form multiple synaptic connections in regards to information. Using all of the senses will form multiple connections to the information to be memorized through neuroplasticity. Choice C, LTP, is a specific type of neuroplasticity, but we not not have enough information to conclude LTP is occurring.

5. B is correct. According to the trace decay theory of forgetting, the events between learning and recall have no effect on recall. It is the length of time the information has to be retained that is important. The longer the time, the more the memory trace decays and as a consequence more information is forgotten.

6. C is correct. With repeated training (cells that fire together, wire together), the pre-synaptic neuron sends signals to a specific post-synaptic neuron over and over, which results in the neuron getting better at sending those signals, and membrane channels will become more responsive. If this increase in synaptic "strength" is retained, it is called long term potentiation.

7. B is correct. The basic idea behind state-dependent retrieval is that memory will be best when an individual's physical or psychological state is similar at encoding and retrieval.
   A. Context cues, or external cues, are memory retrieval cues based on context (i.e. the setting or situation in which information is encoded and retrieved). Examples include a particular room, time of year, or time of day.
   C. Confirmation bias is the tendency to seek out and interpret new evidence as confirmation of one's existing beliefs or theories, avoiding or ignoring conflicting evidence.
   D. Attributional bias is a cognitive bias that refers to the systematic errors made when people evaluate or try to find reasons for their own and others' behaviors.

Independent Questions

1. Suppose you are taking an exam and trying to remember the names of the bones in the wrist. While staring at your hand, you recall that fingernails are composed of keratin, which is also a component of human hair. You remember that you have a haircut tomorrow. This situation is an example of:
   A. short-term memory.
   B. spreading activation.
   C. recognition.
   D. plasticity.

2. Anterograde amnesia is best exemplified by which of the following scenarios?
   A. After a car accident, a young woman is initially unable to form new memories of her day-to-day activities.
   B. A middle-aged man suffers a head trauma and, as a result, cannot remember his experiences from college.
   C. An alcoholic suffering from a nutritional deficiency often thinks he remembers events that never truly happened.
   D. A student typically forgets a significant amount of material soon after studying it.

3. During his testimony, a witness states that he saw a mugging committed by a man wearing a purple sweatshirt. After the trial, the witness realizes that he had actually seen the purple sweatshirt on a man depicted on a billboard near the crime scene. This situation describes faulty:
   A. self-reference effect.
   B. priming.
   C. prospective memory.
   D. source monitoring.

4. Consider an experiment that tests the possible effects of a certain medication on learning in mice. As part of the test, the mouse is placed in an enclosure with an electrified floor, which shocks the mouse until it pulls a lever. In this setup, the deactivation of the electrified floor would be considered:
   A. positive punishment.
   B. positive reinforcement.
   C. negative reinforcement.
   D. negative punishment.

5. The behaviorist approach has been used to suggest that language is acquired by observing others speak. Small children then replicate this behavior with increasing frequency when praised by their parents. This perspective implies that language is learned largely via:
   A. classical conditioning.
   B. operant conditioning.
   C. universal grammar.
   D. insight learning.

6. The proposed role of mirror neurons is most closely associated with which of the following?
   A. Biofeedback
   B. Latent learning
   C. Observational learning
   D. Associative learning

7. Which of the following is NOT consistent with the typical course of age-related cognitive decline?
   A. An elderly person takes longer than a younger person to calculate the tip when paying for dinner.
   B. An elderly person has a hard time remembering how to lace their shoes.
   C. An elderly person is unable to remember the name of a politician they saw on television the day before.
   D. An elderly person is interrupted while composing a letter and forgets to finish writing it.

8. Which of the following is considered a form of implicit memory?
   A. Episodic memory
   B. Semantic memory
   C. Declarative memory
   D. Procedural memory

Independent Question Explanations

1. B is correct. Spreading activation is a theory of memory that proposes that concepts and ideas exist as a nodal network. Each node, when activated, activates neighboring nodes. This implies that the individual has limited control over which specific nodes are activated, which can lead to recall of several different concepts in addition to the one originally desired. In this situation, your activation of the node related to fingernails and keratin in turn activates a node that holds your memory of your upcoming haircut.

2. A is correct. Anterograde amnesia is the inability to form new memories, often stemming from some kind of trauma. In choice A, the young woman is unable to form at least some new memories after her accident, making this option a good answer here. Choice B better relates to retrograde amnesia, since the middle-aged man is unable to recall events from his past. Option C describes Korsakoff's syndrome, and option D is a normal occurrence, as illustrated by Ebbinghaus' curve of forgetting.

3. D is correct. Source monitoring is the ability to attribute information to its source. In this case, the witness truly did see a man wearing a purple sweatshirt, but he mistakenly attributed this piece of information to the perpetrator of the mugging. Thus, the memory was not entirely confabulated, but the witness associated it with the wrong source. The self-reference effect describes people having better memory for information that is personally relevant (eliminate choice A). Priming is how exposure to one stimuli can effect the interpretation of other stimuli (eliminate choice B). Prospective memory describes the memory of task that needs to happen in the future (eliminate choice C).

4. C is correct. Negative reinforcement occurs when an unpleasant or aversive stimulus is removed if the subject performs the desired behavior. This is occurring here, as the electrified floor is deactivated if the mouse pulls the lever. Positive reinforcement (choice B) happens when a desirable stimulus is provided if the subject performs the desired behavior. Negative punishment (choice D) is the confiscation of a desirable stimulus, while positive punishment (choice A) is the application of an aversive stimulus.

5. B is correct. Operant conditioning involves the pairing of reinforcement with a learned behavior. In this case, the reinforcement is praise and the behavior is speaking. Universal grammar (choice C) is an alternative theory of language acquisition that suggests that some aspect of language is innate, which would explain how humans are able to acquire such an enormous amount of language-related information in such a short period during the formative years. This choice, however, is not related to the question stem. Classical conditioning does not fit here because it involves associative learning, where a stimulus is taught to be paired with a specific behavior versus a reward paired with a behavior (eliminate choice A). Finally, insight learning describes a process where learning happens suddenly without trial and error (a "eureka!" moment) (eliminate choice D).

6. C is correct. Mirror neurons are activated in a similar manner regardless of whether a subject is personally performing a task or simply watching another individual perform the task. For this reason, it has been proposed that observational learning may be facilitated, at least in part, by mirror neuron activity.

7. B is correct. The nature of age-related cognitive decline is still debated, but it is generally accepted that some level of cognitive dysfunction is a normal consequence of aging and does not indicate a state of disease. Such deficits often include impairments in processing speed, semantic memory, and prospective memory. Procedural memory is minimally affected, so it would be unusual for a healthy elderly person to forget how to tie their shoes.

8. D is correct. Implicit memory occurs without conscious recall and includes procedural memory. Explicit memory (also called declarative memory) occurs with conscious recall and includes semantic and episodic memory.

This page left intentionally blank.

Motivation, Attitude, Identity and Personality

CHAPTER 7

0. Introduction

Motivation refers to the driving force or reasoning behind our particular actions and behaviors. Motivation can be broadly divided into two types: **extrinsic motivations** are created by external forces and **intrinsic motivations** are created by internal forces.

Attitude is also related to our behaviors: an attitude is a way of thinking or feeling about people, places or things that is reflected in our actions and our behaviors.

Broadly speaking, a discussion of identity and personality can begin with three basic terms.

Personality refers to the amalgamation of characteristics and qualities that come together to comprise a person's character.

Self-concept, or self-identity, is our understanding of ourselves and our personalities. Note that this is different from self-consciousness, which is simply an awareness of oneself as an individual. **Self-discrepancy theory** holds that every person actually has three conceptions of self: our **actual self**, how we see ourselves at the current moment, our **ideal self**, how we would like to see ourselves, and our **ought self**, how we think other people would like to see us.

Identity may seem synonymous with self-concept, but when sociologists use the term, they are referring to the relationship of one's self-concept with the social groups that one belongs to. There are many types of identity, including gender identity, ethnic identity, national identity, class identity, and so on and so forth.

> ### MCAT STRATEGY > > >
>
> While it's a point we make frequently, it bears repeating: the terminology in the psych/soc section can seem like a jumble of terms that all sound similar or that sound like normal conversational English words. They aren't! Learn the technical definitions!

1. Factors Affecting Motivation

I. Instincts

An **instinct** is an innate, unlearned, and usually fixed pattern of behavior that is, in general, present in all members of a species. One example found in humans is the instinct to suckle: babies do not need to be taught how to suckle milk from their mothers or bottles.

II. Drives

A **drive** is an urge that results from an urge to reach a goal or satisfy a need. Basic drives stem from states of physiological need like hunger or thirst. In these basic cases, the drive would be to eat or drink.

Drives typically work through **negative feedback**, the process by which a biological system produces a product or an effect that actually counteracts or diminishes that biological system in order to maintain the product or effect. Basically, an effect is diminished by its own influence on the system that originally gave rise to it. For a basic example, when there is a high concentration of a particular hormone in the blood stream, this may inhibit further secretion of the hormone.

Basic drives like hunger and thirst, referred to as **primary drives**, work by alerting the body to the fact that it is out of homeostasis, or out of equilibrium: it needs more blood sugar (hunger) or water (thirst) to return to homeostasis. The purpose of a negative feedback system is to maintain homeostasis.

Secondary drives are those that are not based in a biological need and actually stem from learning and experiences. Secondary drives can include feelings such as love and aggression.

III. Arousal

Even when all basic instincts and drives are fulfilled, people are still motivated to do things, sometimes out of boredom, sometimes out of curiosity: some behaviors are motivated by a desire to achieve an optimal level of arousal, the physiological state of being reactive to stimuli. If a person is not stimulated enough and is below their optimal level of arousal, their desire for arousal may motivate an action, decision, or behavior. On the flip side, if someone is above their optimal level of arousal, their desire to lower the stimulation they are experiencing will motivate their behavior (for example, getting off an overly crowded subway car before reaching one's destination).

IV. Needs

Needs go beyond the previous three factors affecting motivation, and are less rooted in biological or physiological phenomena, but in higher-level desires. For example, a young person may aspire to be a great artist not to satisfy any biological urge, but to reach spiritual fulfillment and make the world a better place.

2. Motivation and Behavior

I. Instinct Theory

The **instinct theory** of motivation, originally inspired by Charles Darwin's theory of evolution, claims that people and animals are driven to act or behave in certain ways because of innate instincts that have been programmed into them through the process of evolution.

The American psychologist William James, often considered the father of modern psychology, was one of the first to include human instincts in his study of the science. He wrote that human are motivated by 20 distinct, physical instincts (for example, suckling) and 17 distinct, mental instincts (for example, curiosity). James did believe, however, that these instincts could be overridden by experience. That is, a learned behavior could override an instinctive impulse (for example, waiting for everyone to be seated before you begin eating while you are very hungry and instinctually motivated to begin eating).

Another psychologist, the British William McDougall, proposed 18 instincts that motivated all human behaviors.

II. Drive Reduction Theory

In **drive reduction theory**, a physiological need, such as the need for blood glucose, creates a chemical state in the body, such as a feeling of hunger, that drives a person to engage in a behavior, such as eating, that will reduce the physiological need for glucose, returning the body to homeostasis.

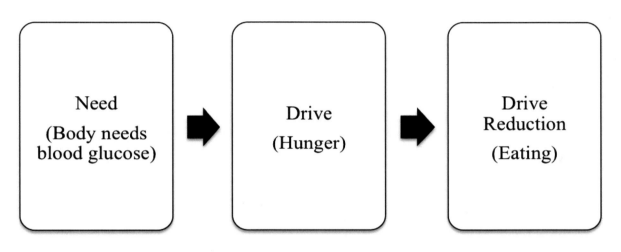

Figure 1. Drive Reduction Theory.

III. Incentive Theory

While the needs behind drive reduction theory are physiological and internal, those behind **incentive theory** are external. Incentive theory holds that actions and behaviors are motivated by a desire to acquire rewards and avoid punishments, both of which are external forces. If working a certain amount of hours during the holiday warrants a holiday bonus, you may be motivated to work more during the holidays. However, if you know your family will be angry with you for doing so, you may be motivated to work less during the holidays. Respectively, these are examples of positive and negative incentives.

IV. Arousal Theory

Arousal theory, as previously mentioned, posits that people behave or act in certain ways to maintain a level of optimal arousal which is variable from person to person. **Yerkes-Dodson law** is an important element of arousal theory, stating that performance of actions or behavior is least efficient at high and low levels of arousal. The optimal level of arousal is somewhere between the two, creating an upside down U-shaped function when arousal is graphed on the x-axis and performance on the y-axis (see Figure 9.2 for an illustration). Too little arousal and you won't be interested in a task, too much, and your efforts may be impaired by anxiety.

Moreover, highly cognitive actions, like playing chess, require lower levels of arousal while less cognitive, more physical actions, like playing basketball, require higher levels of arousal.

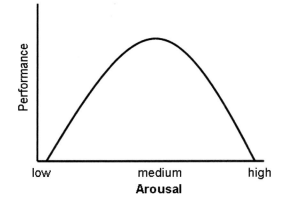

Figure 2. Yerkes-Dodson Law.

V. Need-Based Theories

The American psychologist Abraham Maslow theorized that certain types of needs exerted more influence over human behavior than others. Therefore, Maslow took his idea of a **hierarchy of needs** and constructed a pyramid, divided into five sections, organized from the most base, primal needs on the bottom, to the highest, most abstract needs on the top. From bottom to top, those sections are physiological needs, safety needs, love/belonging needs, esteem needs, and self-actualization needs. Maslow believed that if a lower level of need is not satisfied, motivation to fulfill that need will be strongest. For example, if you are hungry, more motivation will be put behind a desire to eat than a desire to reach self-actualization.

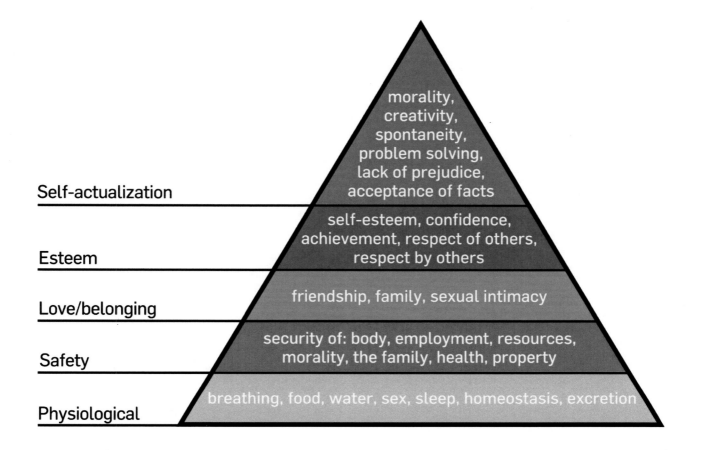

Figure 3. Maslow's Hierarchy of Needs.

Another theory that accounts for need-based motivation, the **self-determination theory**, describes three general needs that must be met for a person to have ideal relationships with other people, her environment, and herself. These are autonomy, the need to be in control of one's actions and destiny, competence, the need to be able to optimally complete tasks and actions, and relatedness, the need to feel accepted by people and in society.

VI. Sexual Motivation

People can be sexually motivated physiologically, cognitively, and culturally.

Physiologically, humans are motivated to pursue and engage in sexual activity in response to the secretion of certain hormones, including, estrogens, progesterone, and androgens, as well as certain odors and pheromones that can heighten sexual desire. Of course, pleasure seeking can also motivate sexual activity.

Cognitively, we can be sexually aroused by certain ideas or images, or else unaroused by ideas of images we find repulsive.

Culturally, we are often motivated and driven by what is seen to be socially acceptable. Cultural values often dictate which sexual acts are appropriate, at what age they are appropriate, and with whom they are appropriate.

VII. Opponent-Process Theory

MCAT STRATEGY > > >

"Opponent-process theory" is a good example of a technical term whose name is misleading. If you haven't memorized it and you encounter it on a test, you may start to think about an "opponent" in the sense of a person working against you. Instead, it refers to a basic physiological process of habituation in which the person does more and more of a maladaptive behavior.

The **opponent-process theory** accounts for the destructive motivations behind drug abuse and addiction. When a certain drug is taken repeatedly, the body will attempt to counteract the chemical effects of that drug with physiological changes. For example, when a person drinks too much, their body increases arousal to counteract the depressive effects of alcohol. This is why alcohol withdrawal can cause jitteriness, anxiety, and restlessness, all effects of increased arousal.

This theory extends beyond drugs to all addictive behaviors. Say a person has an eating problem and eats too much. This person eats a whole pizza, and feels so guilty about it, he eats another whole pizza to cheer himself up. It's a vicious cycle.

VIII. Expectancy-Value Theory

Expectancy-value theory posits that the amount of motivation required to achieve a certain goal is affected both by a person's expectation of reaching a certain goal and how much that person values reaching that goal. So, if someone expects to reach a goal and values reaching that goal highly, she will need less motivation to achieve it, and vice-versa.

3. Sociocultural Motivators of Behavior

Societal and cultural values can have a big impact on the behavior of individuals. Images of models with perfect cheekbones and highly proportional bodies can motivate people to eat less, lose weight, and consider plastic surgery. Likewise, images of larger than life, muscular athletes can motivate people to go to the gym, buy protein supplements, and generally devote themselves to shaping themselves along the lines of that cultural image.

These motivators can be so strong that people ignore the other phenomena motivating them. For example, someone who wanted to emulate a fashion model and become very thin might ignore the physiological drive of hunger.

Naturally, as different communities and nations have different values, sociocultural motivators vary widely from place to place.

4. Components of Attitudes

As previously mentioned in Chapter 7, the three primary components of an attitude are the affective component, the behavioral component, and the cognitive component. The **affective component** is emotional: it's the way a person feels about something (for example, a person saying "I love oatmeal"). The **behavioral component** is the way that a person acts in relation to something (for example, avoiding places with cold weather during the winter). The **cognitive component** is the way a person thinks about something (for example, knowing how cold a Northern city can be during the winter, and perhaps remembering a dismal experience in cold weather from one's childhood).

A helpful mnemonic for these three components of attitudes is the acronym A.B.C. (affective, behavioral, cognitive).

5. Attitudes and Behavior

The relationship between our attitudes and our behaviors is by no means black and white. Sometimes our attitudes hold more influence over our behavior and sometimes the opposite is true.

I. Attitude Influencing Behavior

When a person is given time to reflect on his or her beliefs and attitudes, actions will be more in line with those beliefs and attitudes than if that person were to act impulsively. For example, a man who does not believe in consuming foods or drinks containing high fructose corn syrup is very thirsty. If he is presented with a Coke and nothing else, if he is very thirsty, and if he is not given any time to think it over, he might drink the soda. However, if he has time to think about it, he might delay quenching his thirst until he can find a drink without HFCS.

According to the **principle of aggregation**, attitudes affect the aggregate of a person's behavior, but not every single action. So, a person's attitudes are typically more able to account for general patterns of behavior than specific instances. So, for the man from the previous example, for the most part, his attitude about HFCS will guide his behavior, though he still may drink a Coke or a Sprite every once in a while.

Inversely, specific attitudes are more likely to predict specific actions than general attitudes. Say for example the man from the previous examples believed in living a healthy lifestyle. This general attitude would be less helpful in predicting his behavior regarding soda drinking than the specific attitude he has about not consuming foods and drinks containing HFCS.

Attitudes are more likely to influence behaviors when social influences are lessened or taken away entirely. This is because behavior is more likely to be affected by social pressure than attitudes are.

II. Behavior Influencing Attitude

The effect of making a **public declaration** demonstrates the power that behavior can have over our attitudes. Consider that the man from the previous examples is actually ambivalent about the presence of high fructose corn syrup in the foods and drinks that he consumes. However, he is running for office in a county government, and he knows that the majority of potential voters are not fans of HFCS. He makes his speech, deriding HFCS, foods that contain it, and the major conglomerates that produce it. By simply saying these things, the man may believe them more, but also, add in the fact that now his potential constituency believes he has a strong stance against HFCS. The social pressure from the constituency will make it more likely that the man sides against HFCS than for it, even if he was ambivalent to begin with. This effect can be noticed beyond the political arena, in classrooms, workplaces, and at kitchen tables.

Another way behavior can influence attitudes is through **role-playing**. Perhaps the most famous example of this phenomenon was the prison study that was led by the American psychologist Philip Zimbardo at Stanford University in 1971. For the experiment, Zimbardo randomly assigned a group of students to either be prisoners or guards in a realistic, prison scenario. After a brief time of joking and laughing about it, the students began to seriously engage with their roles, with guards humiliating prisoners and the prisoners either giving up entirely or attempting to foment rebellion. The scenario became so realistic that it had to be stopped early, after six days (it was intended to continue for two weeks). The experiment demonstrated in solid terms how effectively one's role in a society can influence one's behavior. Imagine real life scenarios in which this effect might have played a role, including wars, genocides, and slavery.

Figure 4. Photograph of a Soldier Tormenting Prisoners in Abu Ghraib Prison in Iraq (A Real Life Example of Zimbardo's Findings at Stanford).

Another way of accounting for the effect of behavior on attitude is the notion of **justification of effort**, the tendency that people have to justify the amount of work and energy they have put into reaching a goal by increasing their own estimation of the value of that goal. Imagine a couple whom are both contractors and who have both spent months designing and building their dream house. Once the house is finished, they don't like it as much as they would have hoped to, and they happen to find another house they like better that has already been built. Because of the effort put in to creating that house, the couple might increase their estimation of the dream house and end up living in it despite those initial misgivings upon completing it.

III. Cognitive Dissonance Theory

Cognitive dissonance theory seeks to explain why justification is such a potent influence on attitudes. According to the theory, people have a tendency to seek consistency between their opinions, attitudes, and beliefs, and when there are inconsistencies between these (called dissonance), something must change to make them more consistent. Often times, dissonance will be resolved by a change of opinion or attitude.

For example, a student has been studying for the LSAT and preparing to be a lawyer for his whole life. However, while in his junior year of college, he discovers his talent and passion for acting in theater. He now has a tension between whether he wants to become a lawyer or become an actor. The choice to be a lawyer would perhaps be more safe, dependable, and lucrative. The choice to be an actor would perhaps be more exciting, more undependable, and less lucrative. This dissonance must be resolved, and whichever path the student chooses, he is likely to internalize the values of the decision to justify it. So, if he chooses to continue the path to law school, he might internalize the importance of a dependable and lucrative job, whereas if he chooses to become an actor, he might internalize the importance of excitement, risk, and artistic expression. Either way, this justification helps to alleviate the tension the student will feel for turning down the losing option.

6. Identity Formation

Identity formation, also known as **individuation**, is the process through which we develop our individual identities, which of course rely upon the development of our personalities and self-concepts as well. There are several theories that attempt to account for how we become ourselves through identity formation.

I. Erikson and Psychosocial Development

Psychosocial theory, developed by the American developmental psychologist and psychoanalyst Erik Erikson, is based around 8 crises that people generally encounter during their lives. These crises are all the result of tension between personal needs and social demands. A crisis does not necessarily have to be resolved for the next to become apparent. According to Erikson, an individual's identity forms as he or she deals with these crises.

The first conflict, occurring between the ages of 0 and 1, is **trust vs. mistrust**. A young child can either resolves the conflict and trust the people in its life and its environment, or else learn to mistrust the world. It is possible that such mistrust can last a lifetime.

The second conflict, occurring between 1 and 3 years, is **autonomy vs. shame/doubt**. A toddler either resolves towards autonomy, and therefore develops a feeling of control and self-restraint, or else resolves towards constant doubt, shame, as well as an ongoing external locus of control (more on that in a bit).

The third conflict, occurring between 3 and 6 years, is **initiative vs. guilt**. A child can resolve towards initiative and develop an ability to self-start, as well as a sense of purpose and the ability to enjoy successes, or else resolve towards guilt and develop a propensity for self-restriction and fear of punishment.

The fourth conflict, occurring between 6 and 12 years, is **industry vs. inferiority**. A child can resolve towards industry and develop a feeling of competency and a freedom to do the work he or she wants to do, or else resolve towards feelings of inferiority, incompetency, and low self-esteem.

The fifth conflict, occurring between 12 and 20 years, is **identity vs. role confusion**. A teenager/young adult can resolve towards identity and develop the ability to see herself as a unique, sufficient individual, or else resolve to confusion about her identity, having no set personality.

The sixth conflict, occurring between 20 and 40 years, is **intimacy vs. isolation**. An adult can resolve towards intimacy and develop the ability to be in an intimate, loving relationship, as the ability to commit oneself to people, things, or ideas, or else resolves towards isolation and develop a penchant for avoiding commitment.

The seventh conflict, occurring between 40 and 65 years, is **generativity vs. stagnation**. A middle-aged adult can resolve towards generativity and become capable of productivity and contributing to society, or else resolve towards stagnation and develop self-indulgent, egocentric, and unmotivated qualities.

> **MCAT STRATEGY > > >**
>
> Make a study sheet out of the chart of Erikson's stages!

The eighth and final conflict, above 65 years, is **integrity vs. despair**. A person over 65 can resolve towards integrity and become able to accept that his life has been worth living, and therefore, the notion of death, or else resolve towards despair and develop feelings of worthlessness and a fear of death. Erikson believed that those who resolve for integrity experience wisdom, a detached but sympathetic concern with the very notion of life.

AGE	Stage of Development (Conflict)	Central Question	Positive resolution
Birth to 1	Trust vs. Mistrust	Can the world be trusted?	Hope
1 to 3	Autonomy vs. Shame/Doubt	Is it acceptable for me to be myself?	Will
3 to 6	Initiative vs. Guilt	Is it acceptable for me to take initiative?	Purpose
6 to 12	Industry vs. Inferiority	Do I have a shot at making it in the world?	Competence
12 to 20	Identity vs. Role Confusion	Who am I and what is my potential?	Fidelity
20 to 40	Intimacy vs. Isolation	Am I able to love another person and to commit myself to people and things?	Love
40 to 65	Generativity vs. Stagnation	Am I able to live and work in a way such that my life matters?	Care
65 to Death	Integrity vs. Despair	Did I live a good life?	Wisdom

Table 1. Erikson's 8 Stages (Crises) of Psychosocial Development.

II. Freud and Psychosexual Development

Certainly better known than Erikson, Sigmund Freud, the Austrian neurologist who is commonly considered the father of psychoanalysis, proposed the theory of psychosexual development. For Freud, there were five stages to the development of individual identity, and like Erikson's theory, each stage centers around a conflict with societal pressures. However, in Freud's theory, the tension is between societal pressures and the desire to reduce libidinal tension in a particular part of the body.

A tangent on **libido**: often mistaken to simply mean sex drive, it is actually a more broad term: it is the life instinct we all have, the instinct for survival, growth, procreation, and pleasure. Its foil is the **death instinct**, the instinct to hurt or kill others or ourselves.

In each stage of Freud's theory of psychosexual development, a person can become **fixated** on whatever libidinal energy is prominent in that stage, overindulging or overly frustrated by that libidinal energy. In adulthood, fixation leads to **neurosis**, a functional mental disorder.

The first stage, occurring between 0 and 1 years, is the **oral stage**, in which libidinal energy is most focused in the mouth. In order to reduce libidinal tension and reach gratification, babies put objects in their mouths and suck or bite on them. Fixation in this stage can translate to issues with excessive dependency.

The second stage, occurring between 1 and 3 years, is the **anal stage**, in which libidinal energy is most focused in the anus. In this stage, libidinal tension is relieved through the elimination and retention of excrement. Fixation in the anal stage can lead to anal-retentiveness (an excessive desire for order and control), and on the flip side, a penchant for disorder and sloppiness.

The third stage, occurring between 3 and 5 years, is the **phallic stage** (also known as the **Oedipal stage**). In this stage, libidinal tension resides in the genitals. It is in this stage that boys develop an **Oedipal complex**, an attraction to their mother and a hostile attitude toward their father, and girls develop an **Electra complex**, which is the exact opposite of the Oedipal complex. This is the stage in which girls develop **penis envy**, as they discover they do not have penises like their fathers. During this phase, libidinal tension is resolved through **sublimation**, the process by which socially unacceptable impulses are replaced by socially acceptable behaviors (for example, playing with toys or doing school work).

The fourth stage, continuing from the sublimation of the libido until puberty, is called the **latency stage**. It is a time of relative stability, is far as identity formation is concerned.

The fifth stage, beginning with the onset of puberty and lasting into adulthood, is the **genital stage**. In this stage, sexual themes from earlier in development that were sublimated during latency begin to resurface. It is here that people begin to have sexual relationships. Moreover, the libido now fuels other activities, such as the making of friendships, the creation of art, and the pursuit of a career.

AGE	STAGE	DESCRIPTION
0-1	Oral Stage	Libido centered in mouth
1-3	Anal Stage	Libido centered in anus
3-5	Phallic Stage	Libido centered in genitals
5-Puberty	Latency Stage	Relatively stable, libido sublimated
Puberty-Adulthood	Genital Stage	Normal sexual relationships, given previous stages have been resolved

Table 2. Freud's Five Stages of Psychosexual Development.

III. Moral Reasoning Development

Whereas Erikson and Freud focused on resolving conflicts as the drivers of identity formation, the American psychologist Lawrence Kohlberg focused on the development of moral reasoning.

Kohlberg's understanding of moral thinking was developed from asking test subjects their opinions about hypothetical moral dilemmas, the most famous of which was **the Heinz dilemma**. In this hypothetical situation, a man's wife is near death with a rare form of cancer. Recently a new drug, derived from radium, was developed that could save the man's wife from her imminent death. The new drug costs $200 to produce but the drug maker is charging $2,000 for it. Heinz attempts to haggle with the drug maker, but to no avail. Without any other options, Heinz breaks into the drug maker's laboratory and steals the drug.

Kohlberg's six stages of moral development, divided into three phases, reflect the opinions of subjects when presented moral dilemmas such as Heinz's.

The first phase, which is most typical of preadolescent thinking, is called **preconventional morality**. In this first phase, people are most concerned with the consequences of their choices and actions. Stage 1 is **obedience**, in which a person simply makes decisions based upon avoiding punishment. Stage 2 is **self-interest**, in which a person makes decisions based upon receiving potential rewards.

The second phase, which develops in early adolescence, is **conventional morality**. Upon entering adolescence, people begin to understand themselves within the context of their relationships, and so, the second phase centers around social rules and norms. Stage 3 is **conformity**, in which a person makes decisions based upon the approval of others. Stage 4 is **law and order**, in which a person makes decisions based upon maintaining law and order.

The third phase, which develops in adulthood, if it does at all, is called **postconventional morality** and is based on social values that may in fact oppose the laws on the books. Stage five is the **social contract**, in which a person makes decisions based upon the greater good of society and the rights of individuals. Stage six is **universal human ethics**, in which a person makes decisions based upon abstract ideas such as justice, ethics, and morality.

AGE	PHASE	STAGES
Preadolescence	Preconventional Morality	1. Obedience 2. Self-interest
Adolescence to Adulthood	Conventional Morality	3. Conformity 4. Law and order
Adulthood	Postconventional Morality	5. Social contract 6.Universal human ethics

Table 3. Kohlberg's Three Phases and Six Stages of Moral Development.

IV. Cultural Development

The Soviet psychologist Lev Vygotsky believed that identity development was inextricably tied to cognitive development, and that the main force behind cognitive development was the internalization of culture. So, as a child develops, she internalizes various elements of her culture (laws, language, custom, and etc.) and she develops cognitively, and therefore, her identity develops.

One of Vygotsky's most well known ideas is the **zone of proximal development**. Skills that have not yet been developed fully, but are undergoing development, are said to be in the zone of proximal development. In order for a skill to move from the zone to being fully developed, a developing child typically needs the help of a **more knowledgeable other** (for example, a parent or a teacher).

V. Influences of Other People on Identity Formation

Other theories, such as the idea of the **looking-glass self**, first proposed by the American sociologist Charles Cooley, put more emphasis on the role of other people in the development of our identities. According to the looking glass self theory, all throughout our lives, we develop our self-concept and identities from our interactions with other people. Therefore, our identities are based upon our perception of how others perceive us.

The idea of **social behaviorism**, proposed by another American sociologist, George Herbert Mead, holds that our minds and sense of self fully develop through communicating with others. In the first stage of social behaviorism, the **preparatory stage**, children do not yet understand that different people see the world differently, and therefore, merely imitate their parents, siblings, and other children. In the second stage, the **play stage**, children are now able to take on the roles of others when playing, and therefore begin to learn different perspectives and what is called **theory of mind**, or the ability to perceive how another person thinks. In the third stage, the **game stage**, children can learn and play multiple roles at once. The last development in social behaviorism is the understanding of the behavioral expectations of society, called the **generalized other**.

7. Self-Esteem and Self-Efficacy

Self-esteem is one's own measure of self-worth. High self-esteem is marked by confidence in one's own value or worth, while low self-esteem is marked by doubt and insecurity. Self-discrepancy theory, mentioned earlier, was the theory that divided the self-concept of a person into actual self, ideal self, and ought self. Broadly speaking, the closer these three selves are, the more they accurately reflect each other, the higher a person's self-esteem will be. Self-esteem can obviously be too low, bringing with it anxiety and depression, but it can also be too high as well (high self-esteem can be used to mask deeper problems for overly confident people, including gang members, bullies, extremely wealthy people, and etc.).

Self-efficacy is one's own measure of efficacy or effectiveness. High self-efficacy is marked by a belief in one's own competence, while low self-efficacy is marked by feelings of ineffectiveness or inferiority. According to some studies, self-efficacy can have a real, physical effect on our actual competence to complete tasks and jobs, i.e., if you believe you are a good actor, you will rehearse and perform better than if you believed you were an ineffective actor.

8. Locus of Control

Locus of control refers to the extent to which people believe they have control of their lives and the events that affect them. People with an **internal locus of control** believe that they have control over situations and events, that their actions can contribute to influencing the outcomes. People with an **external locus of control** believe that they have no control over situations and events, that only outside forces contribute to influencing the outcomes. For an example, imagine a rising high school senior who has just received his AP Biology scores back. He got a 3, much lower than he expected. He can either attribute that loss internally and say, "I didn't study enough," or he can attribute it externally and say, "The teacher didn't prepare us well enough, or I was so tired and sick for the test, or maybe they got the score wrong?" By viewing enough of life with an external locus of control, people can stop making decisions and actions in situations, having no confidence that they have control over them. This phenomenon, learned helplessness, was mentioned in an earlier chapter. With the three self-evaluation tactics just mentioned, the happiest person typically, has high self-esteem, high self-efficacy, and an internal locus of control

9. Theories of Personality

Whereas identity refers more to the way we, and society, define ourselves, personality is more like the pattern and range of qualities, from our thoughts and feelings to our specific traits and behaviors, that define us.

I. Psychoanalytic Theories of Personality

Psychoanalytic theories of personality are based upon the idea that our unconscious thoughts, feelings, and memories both determine our personalities and motivate our choices and actions. Certainly the most famous and notable proponent of psychoanalytic theory was Freud, who developed a structural model for studying the three major components of personality.

The **id**, for the most part unconscious, is the element of personality that contains primal instincts and urges (libido and the death instinct included). It is governed by the **pleasure principle**, which guides all actions towards gratification. The id's response to frustration is known as the **primary process**, which seeks immediate gratification through immediate resolution of the frustration (i.e., if you've got an itch, scratch it). Because the id does not actually distinguish physical objects from mental images, the primary process can be fulfilled either by a physical action (itching), or through daydreams and mental images that resolve the frustration. This non-physical process is known as **wish fulfillment**. The id does not rely upon any kind of logic or morality, and is the primary driver of behavior in most young children.

As children develop and begin to learn about the world, they start to understand that wish fulfillment cannot permanently reduce the tension produced by the id. Therefore, the **ego** develops and allows for logic to control aspects of both consciousness and the id. Governed by the **reality principle**, the ego takes reality into account and seeks to hold off the pleasure principle until realistic, acceptable gratification can be had. This is known as the **secondary process**. As the ego continues to negotiate the base desires and urges of the id with the constraints of reality, a person begins to develop their perception of reality, as problem-solving, memory, and thinking are all necessary skills for the ego to successfully bridge the gap between reality and the id.

The **superego**, also for the most part unconscious, is the element of personality that is responsible for inhibiting the primal urges of the id and bolstering the ego to strive for not just realistic, but moral goals. Using moral customs and perspectives that have been gleaned from our parents, the superego is the part of us that can be said to be behind our sense of "higher purpose." It can be divided into two distinct elements, the **conscience**, which is essentially a database of actions and behaviors that warrant punishment, and the **ego-ideal**, which is the same, but for ideal or appropriate actions and behaviors that warrant rewards. As a person develops, punishments and rewards are refined into a sense of wrong and right, respectively.

Our access to these elements of personality are divided into three general sectors: the **conscious** contains thoughts that we are currently aware of, the **preconscious** contains thoughts were are not currently aware of, and the **unconscious** contains thoughts that have been repressed. The unconscious element of our personalities is by far the largest.

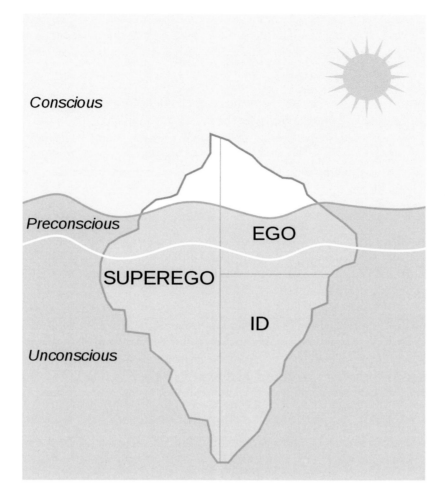

Figure 5. Freud's Structural Model, Illustrated as an Iceberg.

When dealing with the tension and anxiety caused by the constant push and pull of the super ego and the id, the ego employs one or more of eight **ego defense mechanisms** to unconsciously distort reality.

Repression is the process the ego uses to pushing undesired or unacceptable thoughts an urges down into the unconscious.

The conscious, deliberate form of this is known as **suppression** or **denial**, and is typically used to willfully forget an emotionally painful experience or event.

Regression is the process of reverting back to behaviors that are less sophisticated and often associated with children (sucking one's thumb, wetting the bed).

Reaction formation is the process of repressing a feeling by outwardly expressing the exact opposite of it. For example, if you really hate a person, you would pretend to really like them.

Projection is the process of attributing one's own undesired thoughts or feelings onto another person. For example, if you have a serious problem with your roommate, you will believe that your roommate has a serious problem with you. The **Rorschach inkblot test**, in which patients or subjects identify what they believe is being depicted by amorphous shapes, relies upon the projection.

Displacement is the process of redirecting violent, sexual, or otherwise unseemly impulses from being directed at one person or thing to another. For example, if a teacher having a huge amount of trouble with a problem student begins to feel aggressive urges towards him, the teacher might displace those aggressive feelings towards their spouse when arriving at home.

Rationalization is the process of justifying one's behaviors, which might be socially unacceptable and impulsive, with intellectual explanations that are more acceptable. For example, you might explain your vandalism of a public wall with spray paint by saying, "Well, so many other people do it, look how many walls have graffiti on them."

Sublimation is the process of transferring unacceptable urges or impulses into acceptable and perhaps laudatory behaviors. For example, if a man has undesirable and unrequited sexual desire for a woman, he might sublimate those urges and write a poem or song about her.

Carl Jung was another major contributor to psychoanalytic theory, differing from Freud in some crucial ways, yet still maintaining the basic idea that unconscious forces shape conscious thoughts and actions. First of all, for Jung, libidinal energy referred not only to energy geared towards life, creativity, and procreation, but all psychic energy (including what Freud called the death instinct).

Second of all, Jung's structure of personality is a bit different: the conscious part of the mind is referred to as the ego, and the unconscious is divided into the **personal unconscious**, which is mostly in line with Freud's concept, and the **collective unconscious**, completely distinct from the former, which is the part of the unconscious derived from a shared history and experience, common to all human beings. The collective unconscious contains images, or as Jung referred to them, **archetypes**, of common experiences such as child-rearing, having family, and living in communities.

For Jung, the point at which the three elements of personality, the conscious, the personal unconscious, and the collective unconscious, meet is the self.

Furthermore, Jung described three primary conflicts of personality that further define a person: extraversion vs. introversion, sensing vs. intuiting, and thinking vs. feeling. Most people do not fall squarely on one side or the other, but rather, are somewhere along a spectrum between the dichotomies. The **Myers Briggs Type Inventory**, a commonly used personality test, uses these three contrasts, as well as another, judging vs. perceiving, to label a person's personality with a four variable combination.

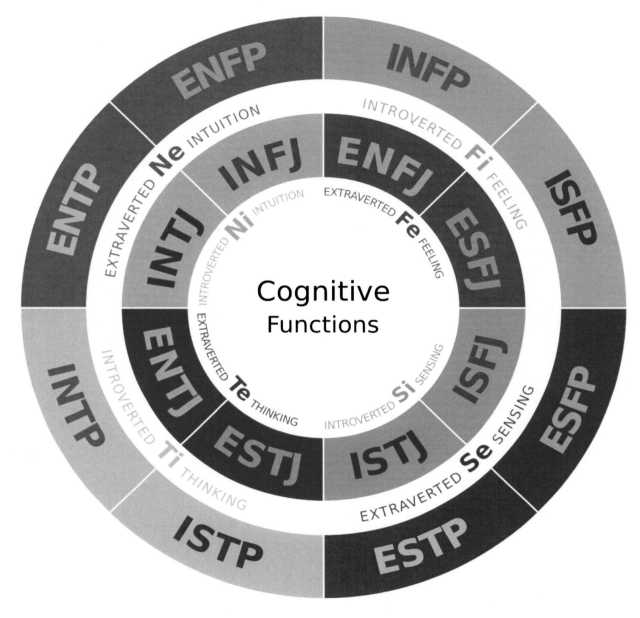

Figure 6. A Diagram Depicting the Cognitive Functions of Each Type Characterized by the Myers Briggs Type Indicator.

Besides the heavyweights Freud and Jung, other notable contributors to the field of psychoanalysis include Karen Horney, Alfred Adler, and Erik Erikson, mentioned earlier for his theory of psychosocial identity formation.

Alfred Adler conceived of the **inferiority complex**, which is the sense of incompleteness or inferiority that motivates a person to strive for superiority. Adler also conceived the notion of **fictional finalism**, the idea that a person is more motivated by his or her expectations of the future than his or her past experiences.

One of the underlying principle of Karen Horney's take on psychoanalysis is **basic anxiety**, the vulnerability and learned helplessness that can result from inadequate parenting and cause **basic hostility** in a person. Both basic anxiety and hostility are overcome in one of three ways, by moving towards people to guarantee their goodwill, by moving against people to obtain a position of power over them, or by moving away from people to avoid them all together.

Unifying almost all threads of thought on psychoanalysis is the notion of **psychoanalytic therapy**, which is the typically one-on-one process between a psychiatrist or psychologist and a patient in which the doctor attempts to help the patient become more aware of his or her unconscious. Furthermore, therapy aims to empower patients to make conscious decisions based on reality rather than the primal, base urges that inhabit the unconscious.

II. Humanistic Theories of Personality

The focus of **humanistic theory** is on the healthy development of personality, and moreover, it ascribes free will to people rather than the constraints of early relationships that Freud espoused. Within the humanistic context, the most pressing driver of human behavior is the so-called **actualizing tendency**, that is, the tendency to not only maintain one's health and vitality, but also to improve oneself. Without the intervention of obstacles, people progress towards a full realization of their potential, known as **self-actualization**.

The American psychologist Carl Rogers introduced what is called **client-centered** or **person-centered** psychotherapy, in which the person being treated is not called a patient, but rather, a client, implying that person's sound mental health. Part of this technique is **unconditional positive regard**, which holds that the therapist accept the client unconditionally and empathize with him or her, no matter what. Rogers spearheaded the ideas of the real and ideal self, which were touched on earlier. The point of psychotherapy is to help the client sort through issues and make positive decisions regarding them, rather than make a diagnosis or provide a concrete solution for the problem underlying it.

With his **force field theory**, the German-American psychologist Kurt Lewin focused very little on a person's past, but almost entirely on the present, with specific focus on the sum of the influences (or force field) affecting a person at any given time. Within the larger context of humanistic theory, the influences on a person can be drawn into two general categories: they can either assist in self-actualization, or else obstruct the path to our realization of potential.

The American psychologist George Kelly developed the notion of **personal construct psychology**, which holds that people act like scientists by observing the behavior of significant people in their lives, and then test their theories about that behavior through their own behavior. In this way, people construct what Kelly called a scheme of anticipation about how these other people will behave in certain circumstances. Within this context, the person who suffers from anxiety is simply struggling to understand the variables at play in his life and environment. Therapy based on this idea sets out to allow clients to develop new ways of thinking about their environment and troubling, potentially anxiety-inducing events, that will help them overcome their anxieties.

Another American psychologist, Abraham Maslow, studied the lives of people typically considered to be great geniuses (i.e. Einstein and Beethoven), and examined how they were atypically strong at actualizing themselves. Maslow believed that people like this, characterized by creativity, a sense of humor, and spontaneity, among other qualities, were more likely to have **peak experiences**, those being the profound, rare moments that lend richness and depth to life.

III. Type Theories of Personality

Type theory, which has been in around far longer than Freudian psychosexual theory, attempts to identify a variety of set personality types. A very example of this is the idea of bodily humors, wherein four types of bodily humors (yellow bile, black bile, phlegm, and blood) were said to correlate to certain elements (fire, earth, water, and air). Any imbalance in these humors would cause personality disorders. This early iteration of type theory has obviously been outdated.

A more modern type theory was that developed by the American psychologist William Sheldon, in which somatotypes, or particular body types, are used to classify peoples' personalities. For example, tall people are high-strung, short people are excessively jolly, and people in the middle are typically well adjusted.

Perhaps the most common and referred to version of type theory is the conception of Type A and Type B personalities, with Type A people more compulsive and Type B people more relaxed.

IV. Trait Theories of Personality

Trait theory relies upon the notion of **personality traits**, which are predispositions to certain behaviors. Many trait theorists distinguish traits as either **surface traits**, those which are outwardly apparent from a person's behavior (i.e. even tempered, down-to-earth, lazy, and etc.) and **source traits**, those that are less apparent and more abstract (extroversion/introversion, agreeableness, and etc.).

The American psychologists Paul Costa and Robert McRae developed the most widely recognized trait theory of personality, the **Five-Factor Model**, which includes the **Big Five** factors, which are openness to change, conscientiousness, extroversion, agreeableness, and neuroticism (the helpful mnemonic is the acronym O.C.E.A.N). For each of these a polar opposite is also implied, and a person falls somewhere between those two poles.

Each one of the Big Five source traits have corresponding surface traits. For example, Conscientiousness corresponds to lazy v. hardworking, aimless vs. ambitious, quitting vs. perseverance, easy-going vs. efficient, and careless vs. organized.

Before Costa and McRae, another psychologist, the British American Raymond Cattell, proposed a similar organization that identified five **global factors**, comparable to the source traits of McCrae and Costa's theory. Those global factors include receptivity, self-control, extroversion, accommodation, and anxiety. Moreover, instead of surface traits, Cattell categorized 16 **primary factors**, including spectrums between reserved and warm, shy and bold, and dominant and deferential.

Five-Factor Model (McCrae & Costa)		Global Factors Model (Cattell)	
Source Traits	**Surface Traits**	**Global Factors**	**Primary Factors**
Openness to experience	-Cautious vs. Curious -Consistent vs. Inventive -Down-to-earth vs. Imaginative -Prefers routine vs. Prefers Variety -Uncreative vs. Original	Receptivity	-Abstract vs. Practical (1) -Reserved vs. Warm (2) -Traditional vs. Open to Change (3) -Unsentimental vs. Sensitive (4)
Conscientiousness	-Aimless vs. Ambitious -Careless vs. Organized -Easy-going vs. Efficient -Lazy vs. Hardworking -Quitting vs. Perseverant	Self-control	-Abstract vs. Practical (1) -Expedient vs. Rule-conscious (5) -Lively vs. Serious (6) -Tolerant of Disorder vs. Perfectionist (7)

Extroversion	-Internal Stimuli vs. External -Loner vs. Joiner -Reserved vs. Affectionate -Quiet vs. Talkative	Extroversion	-Forthright vs. Private (8) -Lively vs. Serious (6) -Self-reliant vs. Group-reliant (9) -Shy vs. Bold (10) -Reserved vs. Warm (2)
Agreeableness	-Antagonistic vs. Cooperative -Cold vs. Friendly -Not pleasing to others vs. Pleasing to others -Ruthless vs. Merciful -Suspicious vs. Trusting	Accommodation	-Dominant vs. Deferential (11) -Traditional vs. Open to Change (3) -Trusting vs. Vigilant (12) -Shy vs. Bold (10)
Neuroticism	-Calm vs. Worrying -Confident vs. Nervous -Emotionally Stable vs. Unstable -Even-tempered vs. Emotional -Secure vs. Sensitive	Anxiety	-Assured vs. Apprehensive (13) -Emotionally Stable vs. Reactive (14) -Relaxed vs. Tense (15) -Trusting vs. Vigilant (13)
			-Problem Solving (16)

Table 4. Five-Factor Model and Global Factors Model of Personality Traits (Cattell's Primary Factors are Followed By Numbers to Demonstrate Overlap Between Global Factors).

Before Costa McRae and Cattell, another American psychologist, Gordon Allport used a different model, with three basic types of traits. **Cardinal traits** were there one's around which people organized their entire lives. For example, Steve Jobs' lifelong passion for bringing creativity and technology together fueled all of his work at Apple and Pixar. **Central traits** were those that were defining characteristics of a person, and were easy to infer from a person's behavior. For example, Steve Jobs was short-tempered, brutally honest, and emotional. **Secondary traits** are those that only occur sometimes, particularly when a person is in a certain social situation, For example, Steve Jobs had a penchant for theatricality and showmanship when he was talking about an Apple product, or introducing it to the world onstage.

V. Biological Perspective on Personality

The basis for biological perspectives on personality comes from two basic scientific findings: that basic personality traits have been shown to be at least somewhat hereditary, and that brain structure and function has been shown to have at least some connection to personality. According to proponents of biological perspectives on personality, the innate biological differences between people are at least somewhat responsible for our distinct personalities.

For an example, the German-born, British scientist Hans Eysenck, proposed that differences in the reticular formation, the part of the brain stem that helps control arousal and consciousness and that receives visual and auditory information before relaying onward, can account for how extroverted or introverted a person is. His reasoning was that extroverts are comfortable in very stimulating situations, whereas introverts are not, and that their reticular formations actually cannot handle as much stimulation as can those of extroverts.

VI. Behaviorist Perspective on Personality

B.F. Skinner, previously mentioned for his behaviorist theory of language acquisition, as well as his work with operant conditioning (the "Skinner box"), was a major proponent of the behaviorist perspective on personality, which holds that a person's personality is a reflection of the behaviors that person has learned, from other people and the environment, over time. Naturally, Skinner believed operant conditioning was one of the primary drivers behind behaviors, and in turn, personality.

VII. Social Cognitive Perspective on Personality

The social cognitive perspective on personality stresses not just our environment's effects on us, but our effects on it. Central to this perspective is Bandura's notion of reciprocal determinism, that our actions in any given situation are determined by an interplay of behavior, personal factors (thoughts, feelings, preferences), and our environment. The idea of locus of control, mentioned earlier in this chapter, also plays into the social cognitive perspective: the amount of influence you perceive yourself to have over your own actions and environment reflects whether you have an internal (you have control) or external (you have no control) locus of control.

10. Situational Effects on Personality

Say you go with a friend to a Halloween party. When you show up, you find that the music is far too loud and many of the costumes being worn are offensive and even violent. You are fine with this, but after a few minutes, you get a text from your friend, telling you he left the party. The question is, which was more responsible for his quick departure: his introverted personality, or the situation itself?

The controversy between scientists about which of these answers is more true is known as the **person-situation debate**. It breaks down to traits, which are internal, stable, and constant aspects of a personality, versus states, which are variable, temporary reactions to external events. In the example above, the trait was introversion and the state was stress or nervousness.

Both sides seems to have truth to them: our traits are constant, yet our behavior can sometimes be more reflective of our reactions to a specific environment. For example, a person who is usually an extrovert might become quite quiet and introverted in a situation that is new to her. She is still an extroverted person, but her behavior has been modified as a reflection of her new, unfamiliar environment.

Practice Passage

As an explanation to why the framing of offers impacts the choices people make, prospect theory offers that people see expected gains or losses in terms of their departure from an assumed expected amount. People tend to consider in terms of relative departure, rather than absolute departure. For example, an individual making $100,000 will value a $10,000 raise more than a person making $1,000,000.

Within this principle, whether a person is gaining or losing money is an important factor, with those gaining money tending to be more risk-averse and those losing money tending to be more favorable to risk. For individuals who start with $0, any gain is a substantial increase, making them more aversive to risk and happy to take the guaranteed amount. For individuals who start with $20, a greater loss may not seem as drastic, as they are starting with an amount of money, leaving them more inclined to court risk.

In an experiment to measure situational dependence on risk-averse decision making, researchers recruited 200 lottery-playing subjects and told each that they could choose to receive either: 1) a guaranteed $15 or 2) have a 50% chance of receiving either $10 or $20, respectively. Most participants (160) choose option 1, despite the expected gains being similar.

Prospect theory can be applied to public health promotion. For example, loss-framed public health is evident in the campaigns that warn if you don't stop smoking, you might get lung cancer. Gain-framed approaches are rarer, as telling individuals that smoking cessation makes one healthier is not as effective. Health treatments and recommended procedures can be framed in terms of detection of a physical disease (e.g. examination) or prevention of the disease (e.g. exercise). Detection of a disease is generally perceived as riskier than prevention.

To determine how well participants responded to messages that were either gain-framed or loss-framed a study was conducted and applied to health behaviors that either involved detection or prevention. Table 1 shows the average rate of participant compliance with the message.

Table 1. Patient Compliance

	Loss-framed Message	Gain-framed Message
Detection Behavior	67%	48%
Prevention Behavior	51%	68%

1. Based on the results of the study, which message would likely lead to the greatest rate of compliance of encouraging people to eat healthily every day?
   A. Not eating healthy can lead to a number of diseases
   B. Eating healthy can help you feel your best
   C. Eating junk food leaves you feeling like junk
   D. Obesity is at an all-time high in the United States

2. According to the experiments conducted, with which desired behavior would the message, "Heart disease is the number one killer in the U.S.," be most likely to induce compliance?
   A. Encouraging annual cholesterol checks
   B. Encouraging low-fat diets
   C. Encouraging people to exercise daily
   D. Encouraging people to reduce stress

3. Despite numerical evidence to the contrary, many rank homicide as a greater threat to their health than heart disease because it murder covered in the media much more often. These people are exhibiting which line of erroneous reasoning?
    A. Fundamental attribution error
    B. Stereotype threat
    C. Availability heuristic
    D. Belief perseverance

4. If a man receives a $1,000 bonus, how might comparing his bonus to his co-workers make his mood more negative?
    A. If his co-workers received the same amount as he did
    B. If his co-workers received less than he did
    C. If his co-workers received more than he did
    D. If he cannot compare his bonus to his co-workers' bonuses.

5. If the motivations for the study participants were judged to be instinctive, which of the following characteristics would apply to these motivations?
    I. Irresistible
    II. Variable
    III. Unlearned
    A. I only
    B. II only
    C. I and II only
    D. I and III only

6. In a follow-up questionnaire, some participants were asked to describe their motivations for playing the lottery. Which of the following explanations would best exemplify the fantasy factor in intrinsic motivation?
    A. "I wonder what it would be like to have that much money."
    B. "I can finally buy that big, beautiful house over on Maple St."
    C. "It's the only way to have a car as nice as my sister's."
    D. "It is my money, and I can spend it any way I choose."

7. The example of reward valuation differences in the first paragraph is most directly an example of which aspect of Expectancy theory?
    A. Valence
    B. Instrumentality
    C. Motivational force
    D. Self-efficacy

Practice Passage Explanations

As an explanation to why the framing of offers impacts the choices people make, prospect theory offers that people see expected gains or losses in terms of their departure from an assumed expected amount. People tend to consider in terms of relative departure, rather than absolute departure. For example, an individual making $100,000 will value a $10,000 raise more than a person making $1,000,000.

Key terms: prospect theory, relative departure

Cause and effect: PT = people view gains and losses relative to expectations

Within this principle, whether a person is gaining or losing money is an important factor, with those gaining money tending to be more risk-averse and those losing money tending to be more favorable to risk. For individuals who start with $0, any gain is a substantial increase, making them more aversive to risk and happy to take the guaranteed amount. For individuals who start with $20, a greater loss may not seem as drastic, as they are starting with an amount of money, leaving them more inclined to court risk.

Key terms: risk averse, gain/lose $

Cause and effect: seeking gain → less risky; avoiding loss → more risky

In an experiment to measure situational dependence on risk-averse decision making, researchers recruited 200 lottery-playing subjects and told each that they could choose to receive either: 1) a guaranteed $15 or 2) have a 50% chance of receiving either $10 or $20, respectively. Most participants (160) choose option 1, despite the expected gains being similar.

Key terms: situational dependence, guaranteed $, potential $

Cause and effect: given a choice in obtaining $, most choose the "less-risky option"; option 1 = 100% change of receiving $15, option 2 = 50% chance $10 and 50% chance of receiving $20; expected gain is $15 for both

Prospect theory can be applied to public health promotion. For example, loss-framed public health is evident in the campaigns that warn if you don't stop smoking, you might get lung cancer. Gain-framed approaches are rarer, as telling individuals that smoking cessation makes one healthier is not as effective. Health treatments and recommended procedures can be framed in terms of detection of a physical disease (e.g. examination) or prevention of the disease (e.g. exercise). Detection of a disease is generally perceived as riskier than prevention.

Key terms: public health promotion, loss-framed, gain-framed, detection, prevention

Contrast: loss = warnings; gain = positive; detection (risky) vs. prevention (less-risky)

To determine how well participants responded to messages that were either gain-framed or loss-framed a study was conducted and applied to health behaviors that either involved detection or prevention. Table 1 shows the average rate of participant compliance with the message.

Key terms: rate of compliance

Table 1. Patient Compliance

	Loss-framed Message	Gain-framed Message
Detection Behavior	67%	48%
Prevention Behavior	51%	68%

Table 1 shows us that when phrased as a potential loss → ↑compliance with detection; phrased as a potential gain → ↑compliance with prevention

1. B is correct. Encouraging people to eat healthily is a prevention behavior; thus people should be most receptive to a gain framed message.

2. A is correct. This message is a loss-framed message. Examining Table 1, we see that a detection behavior is the best match for this type of message. Diagnostics and annual check-ups would be a good example of detection.

3. C is correct. The availability heuristic describes an individual using information that is more readily available than other information to form their opinions. The constant news coverage is not an accurate measure of risk, but it is what the person consider first and foremost in their decision making.

4. C is correct. By framing the bonus as being less than what his co-workers received the man is now less happy about his bonus.

5. D is correct. The Instinct Theory of motivation views biological programming as the cause of motivation. This theory posits that all humans have the same motivations due to our similar biological programming. These motivations are generally unlearned, uniform in expression, universal in the species, unmodifiable, irresistible, automatic, and do not require training.

6. B is correct. Intrinsic motivation does not involve working on activities for the sake on an external reward; rather, it involves the feeling of inner pleasure in the activity itself. Fantasy is a factor that which typically manifests as mental images that stimulate the person to behave to achieve the fantasy. For instance, the subjects sees himself with a new house, new material goods, and a better life after winning the lottery.
    A. This would be curiosity as a motivator.
    C. This would be competition as a motivator.
    D. This would be control as a motivator.

7. A is correct. The example in the first paragraph was of relative valuation. The money meant more to the person with a lower salary. Valence refers to the value that a person sets on the reinforcements or rewards. These values are usually based on an individual's values, needs, goals and intrinsic or extrinsic sources of motivation.
    B. Instrumentality refers to the notion that a person will get a reward upon the successful completion of the expected performance.
    C. Motivational force is the product of the other three expectancy theory variables: expectancy, valence, and instrumentality.
    D. Self efficacy is an individual's belief regarding his own ability to perform a specific behavior.

Independent Questions

1. A consultant goes to work early in the morning because he hopes to make more money. This urge to increase his personal income is best described as a(n):
   A. basic need.
   B. primary drive.
   C. secondary drive.
   D. instinct.

2. Which of the following scenarios best exemplifies drive reduction theory?
   A. A man eats a large meal and, even though he is no longer hungry, also drinks a milkshake because he feels driven to do so.
   B. While trying to lose weight, a woman mentally congratulates herself when she skips a meal. Over time, she skips meals more and more often.
   C. A teenage girl at the movies is not hungry, but she eats popcorn anyway to reduce the social pressure from her friends to eat.
   D. After not eating all day, a boy's blood sugar is low; he becomes hungry and eats a sandwich, which increases his blood sugar back to normal.

3. Of the options below, which places the needs in order from most urgent (most basic) to most abstract, according to Maslow's hierarchy?
   A. Physiological needs, safety needs, love and belonging, esteem, self-actualization
   B. Self-actualization, love and belonging, esteem, safety needs, physiological needs
   C. Safety needs, physiological needs, esteem, love and belonging, self-actualization
   D. Physiological needs, love and belonging, safety needs, esteem, self-actualization

4. Which of the following theories of motivation has been most commonly used to describe the motivations behind addictive behavior?
   A. The Yerkes-Dodson theory
   B. The opponent-process theory
   C. Expectancy-value theory
   D. Incentive theory

5. The three primary components of an attitude are:
   A. the cognitive component, the affective component, and the behavioral component.
   B. the cognitive component, the behavioral component, and the emotional component.
   C. the behavioral component, the emotional component, and the logical component.
   D. the logical component, the affective component, and the cognitive component.

6. Which of the following behaviors can influence attitude?
   I. Justification of effort, when a person decides to start working toward a goal even when it will require hard work, because the goal makes this work worthwhile
   II. A public declaration, when making a public statement consistent with an attitude causes the individual who made the statement to align more strongly with the attitude
   III. Role-playing, when an individual takes on attitudes consistent with the role he or she is playing
   A. III only
   B. I and III only
   C. II and III only
   D. I, II, and III

7. A teenager takes an online personality test and is told that his personality type is INFP. This personality test most likely:
   A. was a Myers-Briggs Type Indicator, and is based on the work of Sigmund Freud.
   B. was a Myers-Briggs Type Indicator, and is based on the work of Carl Jung.
   C. evaluated the teenager based on trait theory, and is based on the work of Sigmund Freud.
   D. evaluated the teenager based on trait theory, and is based on the work of Carl Jung.

8. The five-factor model of personality can be used to evaluate an individual's personality along five scales, known as the "Big Five" traits. All of the following are examples of Big Five traits EXCEPT:
   A. extraversion.
   B. neuroticism.
   C. confidence.
   D. agreeableness.

Independent Question Explanations

1. C is correct. A drive is an urge to reach some sort of goal. Primary drives are urges to fulfill basic human needs, such as being fed and hydrated. Money is not a basic need (eliminate choices A and B). Secondary drives are those which are learned, often through conditioning; the urge to obtain money is a classic example of a secondary drive. Note that instincts are biologically innate, or present from birth; this term does not apply here.

2. D is correct. Drive reduction theory is a theory of motivation that is centered around our need for homeostasis (a stable internal physical state). This theory postulates that we feel drives, or urges to act in a certain way, in response to disturbances in homeostasis. We then act to reduce these drives and return our bodies to a stable state. In choice D, low blood sugar represents a disturbance in homeostasis. The boy feels a drive (hunger) in response to this, and he eats to reduce this uncomfortable drive. Consuming the sandwich returns his blood glucose to normal. The other options do not describe returning to biological homeostasis.

3. A is correct. We are asked to order Maslow's needs from lowest on the hierarchical pyramid (most basic) to highest on the pyramid (most abstract). According to Maslow, the most basic needs are physiological ones, such as the need to eat and drink. These will be fulfilled first, followed by safety-related needs, the need for love and belonging, the need for self-esteem and the esteem of others, and the need for self-actualization, or self-fulfillment.

4. B is correct. The opponent-process theory of motivation states that at least some processes (actions) promote opposite physiological responses. For example, a drug user may consume a stimulant, which speeds up his heart rate and keeps him awake. In response, his body will attempt to slow down his heart rate and promote sedative processes. Over time, this opponent process becomes stronger, causing the individual to need to consume more of the drug to counter its effects. In fact, drug and alcohol dependency is the most common situation about which the opponent-process theory is cited.

5. A is correct. The three primary components of attitudes can be remembered using the mnemonic "ABC." These are the affective component (emotions connected to the attitude), the behavioral component (actions taken in relation to the attitude), and the cognitive component (how one thinks in relation to the attitude).

6. C is correct. Public declarations and role-playing can both impact attitude, and both are properly described here. This makes Roman numerals II and III correct. The concept of justification of effort can also affect one's attitude, but it is not correctly described. Justification of effort is not a conscious decision to begin an activity if the work required seems worth it. Instead, it is our tendency to justify a decision or behavior if we have already put work and energy into it. For example, let's say you want to build your own computer from parts bought online. Dozens of hours into the task, you are no longer having fun and want to quit, but you convince yourself that you really do want to build a computer because otherwise, you will see your effort as having gone to waste.

7. B is correct. INFP stands for "introverted, intuiting, feeling, and perceiving." These attributes are associated with a Myers-Briggs Type Indicator personality test. While not directly developed by Carl Jung, the Myers-Briggs test was based on his work related to the conflicts that define our personalities. The Myers-Briggs test is not based on trait theory; it and Jung's work are actually more closely associated with type theory, as they aim to define personality types. Note that trait theory describes individuals based on specific traits, such as those described by the "Big Five" personality traits like conscientiousness, openness, neuroticism, agreeableness, and extroversion.

8. C is correct. Confidence is not a Big Five personality trait. These five traits can be remembered using the acronym "O.C.E.A.N.": openness to change, conscientiousness, extraversion, agreeableness, and neuroticism.

This page left intentionally blank.

Psychological Disorders

0. Introduction

A **psychological disorder**, also known as a mental illness, is a behavioral pattern that impairs a person's ability to function in social settings, in the work place, and in his or her personal life. Moreover, the behavioral and psychological symptoms of a psychological disorder defy standardly accepted cultural norms regarding behavior.

Studies estimate that as many as 26% of people over the age of 18 suffer from at least one psychological disorder.

1. Classification

There are two primary systems used for classifying psychological disorders, the biomedical approach and biopsychosocial approach.

The **biomedical approach** is based on the idea that every psychological disorder has its basis in a biomedical phenomenon (i.e., a chemical imbalance in the brain). Within this approach, every disorder has a biomedical solution (i.e., a drug meant to restore chemical balance to the brain). This approach is the narrower of the two, and it fails to account for non-biomedical factors, such as socioeconomic status and environment, that can influence mental illness.

> **MCAT STRATEGY > > >**
>
> While the MCAT generally refrains from making value judgments, be aware that the biopsychosocial approach is generally seen as a superior, more comprehensive model.

The **biopsychosocial approach** is broader, taking sociocultural and psychological influences into account, as well as biomedical influences. This approach can be thought of as a Venn diagram, with the three aspects meeting in the center to account for psychological disorders. Some of the overlaps include drug use, between biomedical and sociocultural influences, and family dynamics, between sociocultural and psychological influences.

The Diagnostic and Statistical Manual of Mental Disorders, commonly referred to as the DSM, is the most important resource used to classify psychological disorders. The current version, DSM-5, was published in May 2013, 13 years after the publication of DSM-IV. The book classifies disorders by symptoms rather than causes or treatments, and it is divided into 20 diagnostic classes of psychological disorder. The book is used not only by doctors and psychologists, but insurance companies, lawyers, and pharmaceutical companies as well, which also have to deal with issues of mental illness.

Figure 1. A Copy of DSM-5 on Top of the Previous Version, DSM-IV-TR,

2. Mood Disorders

A **mood disorder** is characterized by the elevation or lowering of a person's mood beyond the standard range of variation, causing personal distress and making appropriate functioning in social, work, or personal settings difficult or impossible. When talking about mood disorders, the term **mood** refers to a sustained, internal state of feeling or emotion, whereas an **affect** is an emotion that is visible at a specific point in time.

I. Bipolar Disorders

Bipolar disorders are characterized by swings between extremes of mood, between depression and mania.

Bipolar I disorder is marked by manic episodes with or without any depressive episodes. A **manic episode** is characterized by a period of no less than one week in which a person has an irritable or abnormally euphoric mood, is highly distractible, makes poor judgments, is more talkative than usual, has high energy and does not sleep much, of has an inflated, delusional sense of self-esteem. At least three of these characteristics must be present for it to be considered a manic episode. Manic episodes can be severe enough to cause psychosis and an inability to function in social, occupational, and personal capacities.

In **bipolar II disorder**, these manic episodes are less extreme, and are known as **hypomanic episodes**, which are not strong enough to cause serious delusion or psychosis. A person with bipolar II experiences both hypomania and major depressive episodes, which cycle back and forth. A **major depressive episode** is characterized by a person feeling noticeably worse than usual for at least two weeks, with those depressed feelings happening most every day for most of the day.

A **mixed episode** describes a period in which a period has had symptoms of both major depressive episodes and manic episodes every day or almost every day for a week. Like a manic episode, its effects can be debilitating.

II. Major Depressive Disorder

Major depressive disorder is characterized by at least one major depressive episode. Beyond what was said about depressive episodes, at least five of the following symptoms must be present for it to be considered a major depressive episode: decreased energy, sleep disruption, change in appetite, substantial change in weight, feelings of guilt and worthlessness, difficulty thinking of concentrating, loss of interest in activities that were once enjoyable (called **anhedonia**), and thoughts of suicide. At least one of the five symptoms must be depressed mood of anhedonia.

III. Dysthymic Disorder

Less severe than major depressive disorder, **dysthymic disorder** is characterized by a depressed mood that has been mostly persistent for two years, with symptoms never absent for a period longer than two months.

IV. Cyclothymic Disorder

If dysthymic disorder is like a less severe version of major depressive disorder, **cyclothymic disorder** is a less severe version of bipolar II disorder, characterized by hypomanic episodes and depressive episodes that are milder than major depressive episodes. These cyclic moods must be evident for two years, with no disappearance of symptoms for over two months, in order for a diagnosis of cyclothymic disorder.

MCAT STRATEGY > > >

Psychological disorders, and mood disorders in particular, are especially good fodder for making study sheets to quiz yourself. They tend to sound similar, and the MCAT will expect us to know the exact definition.

V. Seasonal Affective Disorder

Seasonal affective disorder (SAD) is officially classified as major depressive disorder with a seasonal onset, most often during the cold, dark winter months. SAD has been correlated to the abnormal metabolism of melatonin as well diminished level of serotonin, both of which can be caused by reduced exposure to sunlight. For this reason, SAD is often treated with **bright light therapy**, in which someone with SAD is exposed to bright light, meant to emulate the sun's effects on hormones, for a certain amount of time each day.

Figure 2. A Light Therapy Lamp for the Treatment of SAD.

VI. Causes of Mood Disorders

Chemically, one of the theories for the causation of mood disorders is the **catecholamine theory of depression** (also known as the **monoamine theory of depression**), which posits that too much serotonin and norepinephrine in the synapses leads to mania while too little of both leads to depression.

Other factors that can lead to depression include unusually high levels of glucocorticoids, unusually high glucose metabolism in the amygdala, and atrophy of the hippocampus.

Also, the effects of certain medications or drugs, as well as withdrawal from them, can often seem to be mood disorders.

3. Anxiety Disorders

An **anxiety disorder** is characterized by a state of excessive uneasiness or apprehension about an imminent event or thing. Anxiety causes a state of heightened physical arousal that can be unpleasant and inhibit regular functioning.

I. Generalized Anxiety Disorder

Generalized anxiety disorder is characterized by undue, persistent worry about many different things for at least six months. This disorder can result in physical symptoms such as trouble sleeping, fatigue, and muscle tension.

II. Social Anxiety Disorder

Social anxiety disorder is characterized by persistent anxiety that is caused specifically by social situations, such as a party, a public space, or a classroom.

III. Specific Phobias

Specific phobias are characterized by an irrational fear and avoidance of one specific thing. These are the most common kind of anxiety disorders. Examples include acrophobia (fear of heights), agoraphobia (fear of a situation in which escape is difficult), claustrophobia (fear of enclosed spaces), and arachnophobia (fear of spiders).

IV. Panic Disorder

Panic disorder is characterized by repeated panic attacks. A **panic attack** is a sudden feeling of disabling anxiety and can cause shortness of breath, rapid heartbeat, sweating, trembling, and a sense of impending doom, which can convince a person they are about to have a nervous breakdown. Panic disorder heavily correlates to agoraphobia, as people with the disorder fear having panic attacks in public and being unable to escape.

V. Obsessive-Compulsive Disorder

Obsessive-compulsive disorder is characterized by **obsessions**, which are repeated, uncontrollable thoughts or impulses that cause anxiety, and **compulsions**, which are repeated behaviors that result from an obsessions and are undertaken in order to reduce anxiety and prevent something from happening. So, an obsession might be an irrational fear of germs and getting sick. Its corresponding compulsion would be a propensity for thorough, constant hand washing.

4. Trauma and Stress-Related Disorders

I. Posttraumatic Stress Disorder

Posttraumatic stress disorder (PTSD) can develop after a person is exposed to an overwhelming traumatic event, such as warfare, sexual assault, or serious injury. It causes recurring and troubling recollections of the original event, as well as nightmares, flashbacks, and a propensity to avoid stimuli that are associated with the event. To be diagnosed with PTSD, a patient must have experienced a traumatic event and must have at least one intrusion symptom (disturbing memories or dreams, feelings of intense psychological distress), one avoidance symptom (avoiding thoughts, memories, activities, people, and places that are associated with or trigger memories of the event), two negative effects on cognition and mood (memory loss for parts of the event, persistent negative emotional state, feeling of detachment, inability to experience positive emotions, and etc.), and two altered arousal and reactivity symptoms (difficulty sleeping, lack of concentration, irritability, heightened startle response, and etc.). All of these symptoms must be present for at least one month for diagnosis.

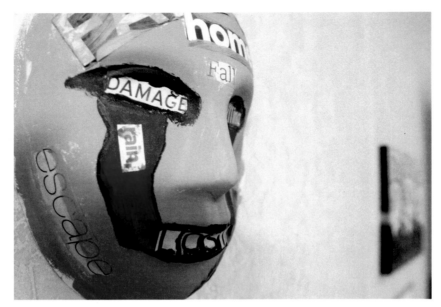

Figure 3. A Mask Made by a U.S. Marine Who Attended Art Therapy for Treatment of PTSD.

II. Acute Stress Disorder

Acute stress disorder (ASD) is essentially a less intense version of PTSD. It is characterized by a brief period of intrusive recollections that develop within four weeks of exposure to a traumatic event. ASD is diagnosed when a patient has 9 of the symptoms characteristic to PTSD but they have lasted for a duration of anywhere from three days to one month.

III. Adjustment Disorders

Adjustment disorders are marked by emotional and behavioral symptoms that occur when a person is unable to cope with an identifiable, specific stressor. These symptoms occur within three months of the onset of the stressor. In order for an adjustment disorder to be diagnosed, distress must be in excess of what would typically be expected from exposure to the stressor, and it must cause significant impairment to social, occupational, and personal functioning.

IV. Reactive Attachment Disorder

Reactive attachment disorder is a condition in which an infant or child does not establish healthy attachments with its parents or caregivers. Symptoms can include withdrawal, sadness, listlessness, no interest in playing games, watching others but not engaging in social interaction with them, and not seeking comfort. In order to be diagnosed, a patient must possess these symptoms and not be diagnosed with autism spectrum disorder.

5. Somatic Disorders

Somatic disorders are unified by somatic symptoms (bodily symptoms) that can cause stress and impairment to a sufferer.

I. Somatic Symptom Disorder

A patient with **somatic symptom disorder** displays at least one symptom of a physical illness or injury that cannot be explained entirely by a general medical condition (though an underlying medical condition can exacerbate it), are not the direct effect of a substance, and are not the effect of another mental disorder. Moreover, the patient devotes a disproportionate amount of time and concern towards worrying about it, causing elevated levels of anxiety. A patient must have recurring somatic complaints for six months to be diagnosed.

II. Illness Anxiety Disorder

Illness anxiety disorder is marked by a preoccupation with and fear of developing a serious medical condition. This preoccupation can be so thorough that a patient's anxiety about developing an illness can impair social, occupational, and personal function. A patient must have recurring illness anxiety, despite reassurance from medical professionals, for six months to be diagnosed.

Illness anxiety disorder is new to the DSM-5. In the DSM-IV-TR, hypochondriasis accounted for patients with both somatic symptom disorder and illness anxiety disorder. Patients with somatic symptoms were diagnosed with the former and those without symptoms with the latter. The term hypochondriasis was dropped because of the pejorative connotation it had acquired.

III. Conversion Disorder

Conversion disorder causes sufferers to develop neurological symptoms such as numbness, blindness, tremors, and paralysis without any organic cause. These symptoms typically begin soon after the sufferer has experienced a traumatic event, or high levels of stress (though in some instances they can begin after some time has passed).

Conversion disorder can only be diagnosed after thorough medical examination has ruled out neurological disorders that might cause the patient's symptoms. Moreover, the symptoms observed in a patient with conversion disorder are not consistent with neurological disease. For example, if a tremor disappears when a patient is distracted, it may be a symptom of conversion disorder.

6. Schizophrenia

Schizophrenia is a **psychotic disorder**, meaning that sufferers experience at least one of the following symptoms: delusions, disorganized thoughts, disorganized behavior, hallucinations, catatonia, and negative symptoms. In order for a diagnosis of schizophrenia, a person must have at least two of those symptoms for at least six months, and one of them must be delusions, disorganized speech, or hallucinations.

Figure 4. Self-Portrait of a Person with Schizophrenia Representing What Schizophrenia Feels Like.

I. Positive Symptoms

In terms of schizophrenia, a **positive symptom** is one that adds something. Examples include delusions, hallucinations, disorganized speech, disorganized behavior, and catatonia.

II. Negative Symptoms

A **negative symptom** is one that takes something away. Examples include reduced motivation to do things, reduced fluency of speech, and an impaired or absent emotional expression.

III. Types of Schizophrenia

The five different types of schizophrenia are categorized by the type of psychosis that each cause.

MCAT STRATEGY > > >

Much like with operant conditioning, remember that 'positive' and 'negative' don't mean good and bad when it comes to psychiatric symptoms. They refer to adding or removing something.

Paranoid-type schizophrenia is characterized by hallucinations and delusions. A **hallucination** is the experience of perceiving something in the absence of any sensory stimuli that might explain it. It should not be confused with an **illusion**, which is a misperception of sensory stimuli that are actually present. A **delusion** is a belief or impression that is not based in reality and is adamantly maintained despite evidence or rational argument against it. Common delusions include delusions of control, grandeur, poverty, persecution, and ill health.

Disorganized-type schizophrenia is characterized by disorganized speech and behavior as well as the negative symptom of flat affectation or expression. With **disorganized speech**, a patient's speech is not dictated by typical language rules and logic, but rather, by free association, rhymes, and the pairing of similar sounds. **Disorganized behavior** is illogical behavior without any goal. Laughing for no reason is an example of this.

Catatonic-type schizophrenia is characterized by catatonic behavior, which can cause either diminished or heightened motor activity. On the heightened side of things, catatonia often involves repetition of words, known as **echolalia**, or repetition of actions, known as **echopraxia**. Catatonia can also be expressed as hyperactive activity that has no purpose, as well as **negativism**, which is resistance to instruction for no reason, **posturing**, which is assuming bizarre postures, and **mannerisms**, which are unnecessary movements made during goal-oriented behaviors.

Inversely, the diminished side to catatonia can bring about **catalepsy**, which causes loss of sensation and consciousness, as well as rigidity of the body. A complete stop in voluntary speech or motion due to catalepsy is known as a stupor.

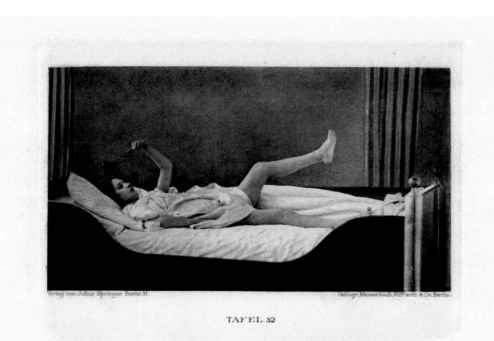

TAFEL 32

Figure 5. An Old Photograph of a Woman Experiencing Catalepsy.

Undifferentiated-type schizophrenia is the term used for a case of schizophrenia that meets all the general requirements of the disorder, but not any of the requirements for the previous three types.

Residual-type schizophrenia is the term used for a case of schizophrenia in which the worst symptoms have resolved and the requirements for diagnosis are no longer met. A person with residual-type schizophrenia can still have mild symptoms of the disorder.

IV. Prodromal Phase

The **prodromal phase** is a precursor to fully symptomatic schizophrenia and is characterized by social withdrawal, unusual behavior, inappropriate or unusual affect, and evidence of psychological deterioration. If this phase is slow and drawn out, the prognosis for the patient is relatively poor, whereas if it is fast and symptoms occur suddenly, prognosis is typically more favorable.

V. Disorders Like Schizophrenia

Brief psychotic disorder refers to when a patient has at least one psychotic symptom for at least a month.

Schizophreniform disorder refers to when a patient has suffered the symptoms of schizophrenia for between one and six months. Nearly half of people diagnosed with this are eventually diagnosed with schizophrenia.

Schizoaffective disorder refers to a comingling of mood symptoms (manic, depressive, or mixed episodes) with psychotic symptoms.

VI. Causes of Schizophrenia

Schizophrenia is passed genetically from generation to generation: studies have shown that is one twin has schizophrenia, the other twin has a 50% chance of also having the disorder.

The **stress-diathesis theory** posits that, although schizophrenia is rooted in biology and is passed genetically, environmental stressors are responsible for the eventual onset of the disorder.

Another theory, the **dopamine hypothesis**, posits that people with schizophrenia have an overactive dopamine pathway in their brains, because of an overabundance of dopamine and the hypersensitivity of receptors. This dopamine overactivity is responsible, at least in part, for the positive symptoms of schizophrenia. Indeed, medications that limit dopamine production and reception have been shown to be at least somewhat effective as antipsychotic medications.

7. Dissociative Disorders

Dissociative disorders involve the disruption or breakdown of perception, identity, memory, or awareness as a tool for avoiding significant stress.

I. Dissociative Identity Disorder

In **dissociative identity disorder**, previously known as multiple personality disorder, a patient has two or more personalities that alternate back and forth. At any given time, one identity is controlling a patient's behavior and interacting with other people. These multiple identities can be quite varied, with different ages, genders, and other traits. Most often DII is the result of severe physical or sexual abuse at some point during childhood.

Figure 6. An Artist's Representation of Dissociative Identity Disorder.

II. Dissociative Amnesia

Dissociative amnesia causes a person to forget important personal information or past experiences and is most often caused by trauma. In order to be diagnosed, it must not be due to a neurological disorder and there must have been at least one episode. Dissociative amnesia is typically localized, meaning that everything that happens during the traumatic time period is forgotten. It can also be generalized, meaning the person's whole life is forgotten, continuous, meaning everything since that time period has been forgotten, or selective, meaning only some events during the particular time period are forgotten. Dissociative amnesia usually ends suddenly and full memory of the forgotten event (and any other forgotten information) is recovered.

III. Dissociative Fugue

Dissociative fugue causes a person to suddenly go on a journey for a few hours or days in which they do not recall their own personal history. Rarely, such a journey can last for months and the person can assume a fully new identity. Typically these journeys end suddenly with the full restoration of personal history and memories.

IV. Depersonalization/Derealization Disorder

Depersonalization/derealization disorder causes a person to either feel detached from his own body and mind (depersonalization) or from his surroundings (derealization). **Depersonalization** can cause out of body experiences while **derealization** can make the world feel unreal or dreamlike. Both can happen simultaneously and can inhibit normal function. Importantly, patients with this disorder do not experience psychotic symptoms.

8. Personality Disorders

Personality disorders are characterized by long lasting, inflexible, maladaptive patterns of behavior that can cause impaired functioning in cognition, emotions, interpersonal behavior and communication, and or impulse control (at least two of the these must be true of a patient for a personality disorder to be diagnosed).

Unlike many of the disorders explained in this chapter, which are **ego-dystonic**, meaning the patient recognizes that the illness is troubling and intrusive, personality disorders are **ego-syntonic**, meaning the patient perceives his or her behavior, which is in part dictated by the disorder, as correct and normal.

Most people will find they have elements of personality disorders in their behavior, which is why for a personality disorder to be diagnosed, the distress or impairment caused by the disorder must be severe, must have been present from adolescence or young adulthood, must affect all or almost all personal and social interactions, and must, as was said before, affect at least two of the factors mentioned above.

Personality disorders are organized into three clusters.

I. Cluster A (Paranoid, Schizotypal, and Schizoid Personality Disorders)

All cluster A disorders are characterized by behavior that is odd in comparison to common expectations of behavior.

Paranoid personality disorder is characterized by a constant mistrust and suspicion of other people and their motives, causing a person to be guarded and self-sufficient. Occasionally, a person with this disorder can be in the prodromal phase of schizophrenia.

Schizotypal personality disorder is characterized by unusual or eccentric patterns of thinking that can inhibit interpersonal functioning and communicating. A person with schizotypal personality disorder might have symptoms of magical and paranoid thinking, odd beliefs and behaviors, odd speech patterns, and unusual affects. This disorder can also develop into schizophrenia.

Schizoid personality disorder is characterized by a pattern of detachment from people, including family members and loved ones, and a limited range of emotional expression. People with this disorder tend to be loners with no interest in social interaction.

II. Cluster B (Antisocial, Borderline, Histrionic, and Narcissistic Personality Disorders)

All cluster B disorders are characterized by behavior that is considered to be overly dramatic, emotional, or unpredictable.

Antisocial personality disorder is characterized by a lack of regard for the rights of others, as well as a pattern of violating those rights. To be diagnosed, a person must have a history of violating the rights of others, including fights, dishonesty, illegal activities, and lack of remorse from the age of 15 onwards. The disorder is also typified by aggression against both people and animals, destruction of property, and serious violations of rules and laws. Males are three times more likely to have this disorder than females.

Borderline personality disorder is characterized by an ongoing inability in ones ability to control one's mood, as well as fluctuation in ones image of one's self and other people. This disorder can cause severe mood swings, reckless behavior, and anger, all of which can make interpersonal relationships very dramatic, intense, and sometimes dangerous. People with this disorder often have an overwhelming fear of abandonment and may develop a propensity for **splitting**, meaning that they view people as either 100% good or 100% bad. Borderline personality disorder is twice as likely to affect women as it is men.

Histrionic personality disorder is characterized by the constant seeking of attention. A person with this disorder may dress in flashy clothing or behave seductively in order to be the center of attention wherever he or she is. A person with this disorder often employs dramatic means to express an emotion, but the emotions themselves are often shallow and transitory.

Narcissistic personality disorder is characterized by feelings of self-importance, self-uniqueness, and entitlement, fantasies of power, beauty, and intelligence, and a need for constant admiration and attention. People with this order have an underdeveloped sense of self-esteem and base their self-worth on how other people see and think of them. Moreover, narcissistic people lack empathy and have a propensity for exploiting others.

III. Cluster C (Avoidant, Dependent, and Obsessive-Compulsive Personality Disorders)

All cluster C disorders are characterized by behavior that is considered to be overly anxious or fearful.

Avoidant personality disorder is characterized by overwhelming shyness and fear of rejection. Though people with this disorder have a strong desire for acceptance, they will often be socially inept and avoid social situations, unless they are certain of being liked by the other people.

Dependent personality disorder is characterized by a need to be taken care of and reassured by others. People with this disorder often cling to one person and submit themselves to that person's will, even enduring abuse, in order to gain support from that person. They are fearful of abandonment and rejection.

Obsessive-compulsive personality disorder is characterized by perfectionism and a need for control in all or most aspects of his or her life. Therefore, people with this disorder struggle to collaborate with others, and often have trouble expressing affection. The disorder often causes sufferers to have a preoccupation with organization and list making, so much so that he or she can struggle to complete tasks.

Cluster	Personality Disorder
A - behavior that is odd in comparison to common expectations	Paranoid Schizoid Schizotypal
B - behavior that is overly dramatic, emotional, and unpredictable	Antisocial Borderline Histrionic Narcissistic
C - behavior that is overly anxious or fearful	Avoidant Dependent Obsessive-Compulsive

Table 1. Personality Disorders.

Practice Passage

The following is a case study of a patient with borderline personality disorder (BPD): John began treatment about 6 months ago. John has a history of failed relationships, trauma, and substance abuse. John described having a series of relationships in which he would become attached to a partner whom he had known for a short time. John would feel overwhelmed by this closeness and soon there would be a fight between John and his partner, resulting in John distancing himself. As a result, John would become despondent and feel abandoned by his partner, and attempt reconciliation. This cycle of attachment and separation continued until John's partner became overwhelmed and terminated the relationship. John would frequently abuse drugs and alcohol, both when he felt overwhelmed and also when he felt abandoned.

John had been physically abused by one of his parents. His parent would behave unpredictably, sometimes abusing John for no discernible reason. This would be followed by the parent trying to reconcile with John. This distance and closeness cycle led to a disorganized style of attachment and seems to have created the template for how John interacts in relationships. For many people who have been raised without a sense of security these feelings are manageable if they are able to understand the relationship between their feelings, actions, and thoughts. This process of being able to think about the relationship of these personal processes is called mentalization.

Mentalization is a process that invokes the prefrontal cortex, the area of the brain that is responsible for executive processes. When mentalizing, humans use their prefrontal cortex to examine how they are thinking and feeling in a situation. However, individuals with a disorganized style of attachment learn to react with arousal. This may happen if frequent feelings of frustration are evoked and paired with needs, resulting in a style of processing information that relies less on mentalization and the prefrontal cortex and more on hyperarousal.

To address these deficits in mentalization, John is undergoing psychotherapy, with the goal of helping John improve in his ability to mentalize. To monitor John's progress, Table 1 charts John's monthly scores (over 6 months), on the BPD-rating scale, an inventory of 10 behaviors characteristic of BPD.

Table 1. Six-month BPD Ratings

Month	January	February	March	April	May	June
BPD Score	8	9	10	10	8	9

1. Which of the following is likely NOT a factor explaining why John's scores on the BPD initially increased?
   A. Attachment based disorders take a long time to treat.
   B. John may have felt distress initially in his relationship with his therapist.
   C. John missed a sensitive period in his life for learning to mentalize.
   D. Mentalizing is a complicated task.

2. If John is put on anti-depressant medication to address his feeling of abandonment, which of the following neurotransmitters is least likely to be targeted by this drug?
   A. Serotonin
   B. Norepinephrine
   C. Dopamine
   D. Acetylcholine

3. Which of the following would be a secondary gain for John if his BPD scores continue to exhibit the changes seen in Table 1?
   A. He will want to improve his mentalization
   B. He will cease wanting to improve his mentalization
   C. He would continue his relationship with his therapist
   D. He continues his previous relationship patterns

4. If a brain scan shows that John's prefrontal cortex becomes more activated in the months following June, what might this suggest about John's emotional reactions?
   A. John will likely have less extreme reactions.
   B. John will likely have more extreme reactions.
   C. John will likely feel more attachment to his caregivers.
   D. John will likely feel less attachment to his caregivers.

5. In one of his psychotherapy sessions, John revealed that he pretends to be a man named Robert, both in public and private, in order to avoid confronting his parents
   A. Somatic symptom disorder
   B. Obsessive-compulsive disorder
   C. Dissociative disorder
   D. Bipolar disorder

6. Why would John not have been diagnosed with BPD or any other personality disorder when he was a youth?
   A. Relationship issues do not begin until adulthood.
   B. Personality disorders may only be diagnosed in adults.
   C. Personality disorders were not diagnoses when John was younger.
   D. Youth relationships typically do not impact adult relationships.

7. If John is further observed for 24 months, and the trend in his BPD behavior continues in a similar manner to what is discussed in the passage, this is most in accordance with which behavioral perspective?
   A. Dispositional theory
   B. Humanistic theory
   C. Social cognitive theory
   D. Intersectionality

Practice Passage Explanations

The following is a case study of a patient with borderline personality disorder (BPD): John began treatment about 6 months ago. John has a history of failed relationships, trauma, and substance abuse. John described having a series of relationships in which he would become attached to a partner whom he had known for a short time. John would feel overwhelmed by this closeness and soon there would be a fight between John and his partner, resulting in John distancing himself. As a result, John would become despondent and feel abandoned by his partner, and attempt reconciliation. This cycle of attachment and separation continued until John's partner became overwhelmed and terminated the relationship. John would frequently abuse drugs and alcohol, both when he felt overwhelmed and also when he felt abandoned.

Key terms: BPD, John, case study

Cause and effect: John experiences cycles of attachment/withdrawal; substance abuse

John had been physically abused by one of his parents. His parent would behave unpredictably, sometimes abusing John for no discernible reason. This would be followed by the parent trying to reconcile with John. This distance and closeness cycle led to a disorganized style of attachment and seems to have created the template for how John interacts in relationships. For many people who have been raised without a sense of security these feelings are manageable if they are able to understand the relationship between their feelings, actions, and thoughts. This process of being able to think about the relationship of these personal processes is called mentalization.

Key terms: mentalization, disorganized attachment, physical abuse

Cause and effect: childhood pattern → disorganized attachment style into adulthood; lack of safety or ability to express needs → frustration; frustration can be managed by understanding (mentalization)

Mentalization is a process that invokes the prefrontal cortex, the area of the brain that is responsible for executive processes. When mentalizing, humans use their prefrontal cortex to examine how they are thinking and feeling in a situation. However, individuals with a disorganized style of attachment learn to react with arousal. This may happen if frequent feelings of frustration are evoked and paired with needs, resulting in a style of processing information that relies less on mentalization and the prefrontal cortex and more on hyperarousal.

Key terms: mentalization, prefrontal cortex, hyperarousal

Cause and effect: disorganized attachment → ↓mentalization/PFC, hyperarousal instead

To address these deficits in mentalization, John is undergoing psychotherapy, with the goal of helping John improve in his ability to mentalize. To monitor John's progress, Table 1 charts John's monthly scores (over 6 months), on the BPD-rating scale, an inventory of 10 behaviors characteristic of BPD.

Opinion: Therapy is helpful for the patient by teaching him to mentalize about his experiences in a safe environment, which he can then transfer outside of the therapy sessions

Table 1. Six-month BPD Ratings

Month	January	February	March	April	May	June
BPD Score	8	9	10	10	8	9

Table 1 shows us that John's progress has remained relatively steady over the 6 months

1. C is correct. According to the information in paragraphs 3 and 4, during therapy clients can develop the capacity to mentalize.

2. D is correct. Depression has been linked to problems or imbalances in the brain with regard to the neurotransmitters serotonin, norepinephrine, and dopamine. The evidence is somewhat indirect on these points because it is very difficult to actually measure the level of neurotransmitter in a person's brain.

3. C is correct. A secondary gain is a benefit a patient incurs from continuing to present with their issues. For John, who may avoid recreating feelings of abandonment, this may allow him to have a continued relationship with the psychologist.

4. A is correct. Prior to June, John's BPD rating scale scores were high, suggesting he was still experiencing symptoms of BPD, which include extreme emotional reactions. If John's prefrontal cortex is more activated, this suggests he is reacting with less hyperarousal and is better able to use mentalization to reflect on his experiences, making him have less extreme reactions.

5. C is correct. The question states that John has formed a new identity to avoid dealing with his childhood trauma. Dissociative disorders are mental disorders that involve experiencing a disconnection and lack of continuity between thoughts, memories and identity. People with dissociative disorders escape reality in ways that are involuntary and unhealthy and cause problems with functioning in everyday life.
   A. Somatic symptom disorder is when the mental disorder manifests as physical symptoms that suggest illness or injury, but which cannot be explained fully by a medical condition, substance, or another mental disorder.

6. B is correct. As youths' personalities are assumed to still be developing until adulthood and personality disorders are seen to be relatively stable disorders, these disorders are not diagnosable until adulthood.

7. A is correct. Table 1 shows that John's BPD behavior remains relatively constant over the 6 months he is assessed. Dispositional theory (aka trait theory) is an approach to the study of human personality, which is primarily interested in the measurement of traits (i.e. habitual patterns of behavior, thought, and emotion). According to this Trait theorists, traits are relatively stable over time, differ across individuals, and influence behavior.
   C. The social cognitive theory explains how people acquire and maintain certain behavioral patterns, while also providing the basis for intervention strategies. Properly gauging behavioral change depends on environment, people and behavior. This theory will also attempt to build a framework for the design, implementation, and evaluation of treatment.

Independent Questions

1. Which of the disease states listed below is driven by pathology involving the substantia nigra, a region of the brain involved in dopamine synthesis?
   A. Huntington's chorea
   B. Vascular dementia
   C. Multiple sclerosis
   D. Parkinson's disease

2. Which of the following conditions tends to affect males more than females?
   A. Major depressive disorder
   B. Migraines
   C. Obsessive-compulsive disorder
   D. Autism

3. Chlorpromazine is a first-generation antipsychotic medication that is known to function as a dopamine antagonist. Such a medication would most likely be used to treat:
   A. Parkinson's disease.
   B. schizophrenia.
   C. generalized anxiety disorder.
   D. post-traumatic stress disorder.

4. All of the following are personality disorders except:
   A. avoidant.
   B. narcissistic.
   C. borderline.
   D. bipolar.

5. Selective serotonin reuptake inhibitors (SSRIs) are a class of medications with a broad range of clinical applications, including the treatment of depressive disorders, anxiety disorders, and obsessive-compulsive disorder. Which of the following is a likely physiological consequence of SSRI treatment?
   A. Delayed clearance of serotonin from the synaptic cleft
   B. Decreased release of serotonin from the presynaptic neuron
   C. Increased serotonin breakdown by the postsynaptic neuron
   D. Increased serotonin production by the adrenal medulla

6. A patient visits his doctor with reports of trouble swallowing and difficulty seeing properly. A battery of medical tests, however, show no physical abnormalities with the patient, and he is later diagnosed with conversion disorder. This psychological condition is classified as:
   A. a mood disorder.
   B. a somatic disorder.
   C. an anxiety disorder.
   D. a form of schizophrenia.

7. Stem-cell therapy is currently employed as a treatment for cancers of the blood, in which healthy cells in the bone marrow are starved for space by rapidly proliferating cancer cells. Stem cells are introduced to repopulate the marrow and restore hematopoiesis. Stem-cell therapy would most likely be an applicable treatment for which of the following?
   A. Major depressive disorder
   B. Multiple sclerosis
   C. Bipolar disorder
   D. Epileptic seizures

8. Delusions are a component of a number of psychiatric disorders, including schizophrenia and bipolar disorder. Which of the following would NOT be considered a delusion?
   A. A person believes his thoughts are being read and his mind controlled.
   B. A person believes she died many years ago and describes herself as a "walking corpse."
   C. A person believes that God spoke directly to him during a religious ceremony.
   D. A person refuses to speak to his mother, believing she is an imposter who kidnapped his real mother.

Independent Question Explanations

1. D is correct. Parkinson's disease is a movement disorder resulting from inadequate production of CNS dopamine, resulting in bradykinesia, tremors, and an unsteady gait. This disease is caused by the death of dopamine-producing neurons in the substantia nigra. Note that multiple sclerosis is a disease characterized by myelin degeneration, Huntington's disease is characterized by cell death of multiple different types of brain cells, not just cells in the substantia nigra, and vascular dementia is dementia caused by problems with blood flow to the brain.

2. D is correct. Autism is roughly five times as common in males than in females. Migraines and major depressive disorder are more common in females. There is no significant difference between rates of OCD in males compared to females.

3. B is correct. Although its underlying etiology has not been fully elucidated, schizophrenia is thought to involve abnormal activation of dopaminergic pathways. Newer antipsychotic medications have largely replaced chlorpromazine, but many of them still function as inhibitors of dopaminergic activity. Parkinson's disease is caused by inadequate dopaminergic activity, making it the reverse of the correct answer; in fact, some antipsychotics have the side effect of causing Parkinsonian movements by antagonizing dopaminergic pathways.

4. D is correct. Bipolar disorder has multiple subtypes, but all are considered mood disorders rather than personality disorders. Other mood disorders include major depressive disorder and seasonal affective disorder. Personality disorders include avoidant, narcissistic, and borderline personality disorders, among others.

5. A is correct. SSRIs inhibit the transport of synaptic serotonin back into the presynaptic neuron, which allows it to remain in the synaptic cleft for an extended period of time and continue to exert its effects on postsynaptic receptors.

6. B is correct. Somatic disorders are psychological disorders characterized by physical symptoms that cause significant stress to the patient, but have no clear physical cause. Conversion disorder is an example of such a condition.

7. B is correct. Research into stem-cell therapy is based on the premise that stem cells might be a viable means of repairing damaged tissue and generating new somatic cells. Multiple sclerosis (MS), a neurodegenerative disorder, is characterized by the loss of cells responsible for CNS myelination and consequent loss of motor function. As the disease progresses, neurons are also lost. Of the given choices, MS would be the most likely target of stem-cell therapy.

8. C is correct. Delusions are immutable convictions held by people despite clear evidence that disproves these convictions. Religious or cultural beliefs are an exception to this definition and are not considered delusions.

This page left intentionally blank.

0. Introduction

Human beings are social animals, and as such, our attitudes, behaviors, and beliefs are strongly influenced by our interactions with others. The human brain has a tendency to categorize things, to help us make sense with all the stimuli and information we encounter daily. Attribution is way that we attempt to understand the actions of others, and it can often be misguided. Prejudice is a way that we attempt to categorize people, places, and things, often without fully understanding them. Discrimination and stereotypes are related to prejudice, but they are markedly different when it comes to the study of human behavior. To borrow from the three components of attitude, if prejudices are affective or emotional, discrimination is behavioral and stereotypes are cognitive.

For better or worse, the way we see the world is often imperfect and does not take into account the full complexity of people and things. There are methods, however, such as cultural relativism, that allow us to counteract this effect.

1. Social Facilitation

Social facilitation is the tendency that people have to perform simple tasks better or more efficiently when in the presence of other people. Inversely, when performing a complex or new task, the presence of others can hinder one's performance. For example, an expert bassoonist may perform better in concert than when he rehearses by himself, while an amateur bassoonist may perform worse in a concert setting.

The Yerkes-Dodson law, mentioned earlier, accounts for social facilitation as well, as the chart below demonstrates:

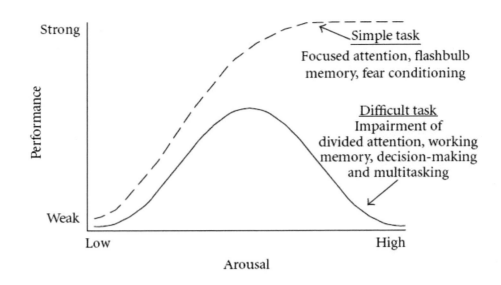

Figure 1. Yerkes-Dodson Law and Social Facilitation's Effect on Simple and Difficult Tasks.

The effect of social facilitation is, at least in part, due to the fact that the presence of other people stimulates arousal. For complicated tasks, there is an optimal amount of arousal between extremes of low and high. According to **Yerkes-Dodson law of social facilitation**, the optimal level of arousal for a simple task is high.

3. Deindividuation

> **MCAT STRATEGY > > >**
>
> Although we tend to focus on the negative impact that the presence of other people has on human behavior, it can be positive as well. Remember that social facilitation makes people perform *better* at some tasks.

Deindividuation is the tendency people have to lose their sense of self-awareness in a large group setting, which provides a high degree of arousal and a low sense of responsibility. It is the process by which people's individual attitudes and beliefs can become separated from their actual behavior in a large group setting.

A violent mob can be explained by deindividuation: in a mob, people act in ways that are far out of line with their normal selves.

The three most important factors that contribute to deindividuation are anonymity ("no one will know what I've done"), diffused responsibility ("I am not responsible for my actions"), and group size, which heightens both anonymity and diffused responsibility.

The people in the image below have undergone at least some degree of deindividuation. It should be noted that, as in this picture, this effect does not necessarily lead to violence.

Figure 2. A Protest Against Scientology, February 10, 2008.

4. Bystander Effect and Social Loafing

The **bystander effect**, sometimes referred to as bystander apathy, is a phenomenon of group psychology in which people do not offer help to a victim if there are other people (bystanders) present. Moreover, the likelihood of responding and helping a victim is inversely related to the number of bystanders: the more bystanders there are, the less likely anyone is to help.

One event in particular, the murder of Kitty Genovese, gave rise to the research that would first develop into an understanding of the bystander effect. Late on March 13, 1964, in the Kew Gardens neighborhood of New York City, Kitty Genovese was stabbed to death. She had cried for help, but no one came to help her. When detectives interviewed the neighbors (in this case, bystanders), they said they had heard her screams, but had done nothing about them because they assumed someone else had called the police.

One of the major factors driving this effect is the diffusion of responsibility that happens in a crowd, where there is no one person that bears total responsibility to help.

Another is rooted in human social behavior: we are less likely to notice a dangerous situation when in a large group than when we are in a smaller group or alone. We take behavior cues from each other: if no one in a large group is responding to a situation, we are far less likely to perceive that situation as dangerous. Social etiquette also plays a role, as it is often considered impolite to pay too much attention to strangers in public.

Of course, sometimes we do respond to someone in need, even if in a large group. If the group is made up of people that are acquainted, a response is more likely than from a group of strangers. Moreover, the more dangerous a situation is, the more likely someone is to help.

Social loafing is the tendency that people have to put in less effort when they are in a group setting, particularly if the group is being evaluated as a whole and not on an individual basis. Imagine you are one of six people carrying a heavy log. You are exerting yourself and it is getting too heavy, so you decrease your effort, but the log is still being carried. You diffused some of the effort you had to exert to others. Social loafing can also apply to mental tasks that require thinking and initiative, like group projects, and social situations, like a theatre performance with 500 people in the audience where you can clap less than you would if there were only five audience members.

Social loafing and social facilitation can be viewed as being two sides of one coin. When the fact that you belong to a group decreases your concern of being evaluated individually, social loafing can occur. When the fact that you belong to a group increases your concern of being evaluated individually, social facilitation can occur.

5. Group Polarization and Groupthink

Group polarization is the tendency that groups have to make decisions that are notably more extreme than the initial, individual opinions of its members. For example, think about the American political system: say that Republican senators are meeting to discuss the Affordable Care Act. Some may feel more moderate on the topic, but by the end of their discussion, they've decided as a group to gut the program.

There are two major reasons for this effect, informational influence and normative influence. **Informational influence** refers to how the most common ideas to emerge out of a group discussion are the ones that are most in line with the dominant, or majority, viewpoint. As they are most common, these ideas encourage more moderate members of the group to take a stronger stance, as they are also a part of the group.

Normative influence refers to the pull we feel of being socially desired, accepted, admired, or just liked. If you want to be recognized by a group as a strong and likable member, you may take a stronger stance on an issue than you did initially.

Groupthink refers to when a group of people has such a strong desire for harmony and individual conformity that the group makes irrational decisions. The American research psychologist Irving Janis was the first to research this effect, focusing on eight specific factors that indicate groupthink is happening, illustrated on the chart below:

Janis' Eight Factors of Groupthink	Practical Definition
Collective rationalization	Group members ignore warnings and do not reconsider their actions, assumptions, or beliefs.
Excessive stereotyping	Negative views of outside or dissenting opinions render effective responses to conflict unnecessary.
Illusion of invulnerability	An unjustified and excessive sense of optimism encourages risk-taking.
Illusion of morality	Member of the group believe in the moral rightness of their cause and therefore ignore the consequences of their actions.

Illusion of unanimity	The majority views of the group are assumed to be unanimous.
Mindguards	Members of the group protect the group's cohesiveness by filtering out information that would be problematic.
Pressure on dissenters	Members are constantly under pressure to not express views or beliefs that are against those of the group.
Self-censorship	Members who do hold dissenting opinions do not share them.

Table 1. Irving Janis' Eight Factors of Groupthink.

6. Social Norms and Deviance

I. Norms

Social norms are the rules, spoken or unspoken, that a group or society has for the behavior, beliefs, attitudes, and values of its members. Norms are enforced by **sanctions**, which are punishments or rewards for behaving in a way that is, respectively, against or in line with norms.

Norms can be classified by their formality or by their importance.

Formal norms are written down, specific, explicit, and typically are associated with penalties for violating them. A law is an example of a formal norm.

Informal norms are those that are generally understood but are not written down, not specifically defined, not explicitly stated, and typically do not have specific penalties associated with violating them. For example, when you enter an elevator, it is expected that you should turn around to face the doors. Though you would not be punished for facing the other direction, others would think your behavior is odd.

Mores (pronounced: more-ays) are informal norms that carry major importance for society and, if broken, can result in severe social sanctions. For example, imagine a woman in her mid 20's who is not married but decides to live with her boyfriend. Her parents are very religious and belong to a community in which only married couples can live together. In the parents' eyes, the daughter has broken a more, and the parents will levy sanctions accordingly.

> **MCAT STRATEGY > > >**
>
> Mores distinguish between right and wrong while folkways distinguish between right and rude.

On the flip side, **folkways** are informal norms that have less significance attached to them, yet they still shape and influence every day behavior. Breaking a folkway typically has less severe consequences than breaking a more. For example, if someone is at a fancy steak dinner and begins eating with their hands, they are breaking a folkway.

II. Deviance

Deviance refers to any violation of a societal norm, ranging from something as inoffensive as wearing shorts in a formal dress office to something as heinous as homicide. Deviance can also refer to a positive act, such as the sit-ins in the 1950's and 60's in which African Americans refused to leave restaurants and businesses that were labeled white-only.

Differential association theory posits that deviance and patterns of deviance can be learned through our interactions with others. The theory is based upon the notion that people commit crimes, at least in part, because of their associations with other people.

Stigma is the extreme disapproval of a certain person or group based upon their perceived deviations from social norms. For example, at the onset of the HIV epidemic of the 1980s, the general public stigmatized people who had contracted the disease.

III. Conformity, Compliance, and Obedience

In opposition to deviance, conformity, compliance, and obedience are ways that people adhere to norms.

Conformity refers to the matching of one's attitudes, behaviors, and beliefs to social norms. Conformity can be divided into **internalization**, which is the process of changing one's attitudes or behavior to fit in with a group, and **identification**, which is the acceptance of other people's ideas without thinking critically about them.

MCAT STRATEGY > > >

Remember, anyone can get compliance, but obedience is in response to authorities.

Compliance refers to a change in behavior in response to a direct request, typically from a person or group that does not actually have authority to enforce that change. Compliance is commonly used in marketing to sell products. Methods such as the **foot-in-door technique** take advantage of compliance: using the technique, a salesman uses a small request ("Can I have a minute of your time?" to gain compliance (you stop on the street) and then proceeds to made a larger request ("Will you donate to this cause?").

Obedience refers to a change in behavior in response to a direct request, but from a figure that actually has authority to enforce it. We are far more likely to obey than comply, simply because of the power the authority figure holds over us.

IV. Labeling Theory

Also related to deviance, stigma, and conformity is the **labeling theory**, which holds that labels that people are given socially affect how others see them, but also, how they see themselves. These labels can then motivate further deviance or conformity. For example, if someone is labeled an alcoholic by their friends or family, they could either be motivated to drink even more, deviating further, or else take actions to conform more to standard notions of how much is too much to drink.

7. Socialization

Socialization is the lifelong process through which people inherit, develop, and disseminate social norms, customs, and belief systems. It is through socialization that we develop the habits and skills necessary for successfully living in society.

I. Types of Socialization

Primary socialization refers to the learning of acceptable actions and attitudes during childhood, mostly from observation of our parents, siblings, friends, teachers, and other authority figures.

Secondary socialization refers to the process of learning what is acceptable and appropriate in a smaller, more focused section of society. Learning how to behave at school or in the workplace are examples of secondary socialization.

Anticipatory socialization refers to the process by which we prepare for future changes that we anticipate. For example, say a security officer will be switching to the night shift in a few weeks. In preparation, he will begin to shift his sleep cycle, so as to anticipate the demands of the shift change.

Resocialization is the process through which we get rid of old behaviors in order to take on new ones. The training of soldiers to obey orders and behave within the rigorous confines of military life is an example of resocialization.

II. Agents of Socialization

The factors that drive and have the most influence over our socialization change throughout our lives. When we are children, the primary drivers of socialization are our parents and family life. When we are teenagers, our social circles have a strong influence on our socialization. By the time we are adults, the workplace, as well as media, can have a strong effect on how we develop our habits. The following chart depicts some of the major agents of socialization.

Figure 3. Major Agents of Socialization.

8. Attribution

I. Attribution Theory

Attribution theory holds that people attempt to understand the behaviors of other people by attributing feelings, beliefs, and intentions to them. Behaviors can be attributed to internal causes, called **dispositional attribution**, or external causes, called **situational attribution**. Consider the following example: you are getting of the subway and someone, in a rush to get off the train, bumps into you with a lot of force and then runs off. A dispositional attribution would be to say, "That guy is such a jerk," while a situational attribution might be, "That guy must be late for work." So, dispositional attribution considers qualities of the person who is being observed and situational attribution considers situations that are affecting that person's behavior.

There are three factors that can influence whether attribution is dispositional or situational: consensus, consistency, and distinctiveness. **Consensus cues** are related to how common a person's behavior is, or how much it differs from standardly accepted behavior. The more abnormal it is, the more likely we are to form a dispositional attribution. **Consistency cues** are related to how consistent a person's behavior has been over time: the more consistent with past behavior, we more likely we are to form a dispositional attribution. **Distinctiveness cues** are related to how comparably a person behaves in different scenarios: the more the person's behavior varies, the more likely we are to form a situational attribution.

Another way of understanding attribution, **correspondent inference theory**, focuses more on the intentionality of a person's behavior. When someone does something that either helps or hurts us, and especially when it is unexpected, we are most likely to form a dispositional attribution.

Observation **Interpretation** **Attribution**

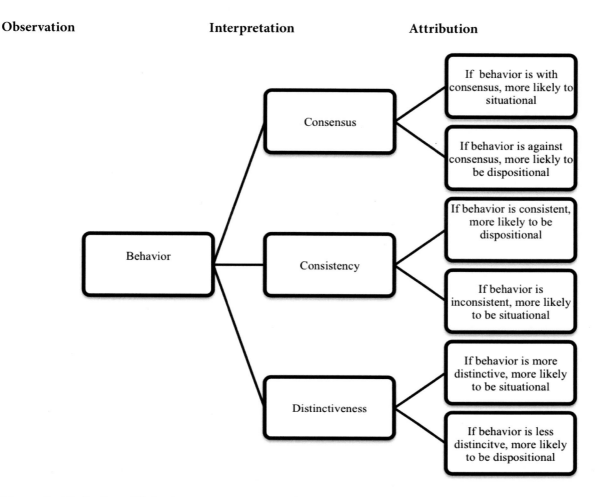

Figure 4. Attribution of Behavior.

II. Attribution Biases

Perhaps the most common way that our attributions are inaccurate is **fundamental attribution error**, the tendency to place less importance on the import of a situation or context on behavior, and instead place undue emphasis on dispositional or internal qualities in order to explain behavior. We have a tendency to think that people are how they act.

Moreover, we can often blame our own actions on situations but the actions of others on personality. This is called the **actor-observer bias**.

Similarly, **self-serving bias** is the tendency people have to credit their successes to themselves and their failures either to the actions of others or to situations.

Optimism bias is the tendency that people have to believe bad things only happen to other people and not them. Closely related to this bias is the just world phenomenon, the tendency to believe that the world is intrinsically fair and that all people get what they deserve.

The **halo effect** is the tendency many people have to see other people in black or white terms, as either good or bad. According to the halo effect, if you believe that someone is a bad person, your assumptions about them will be negative, even if those assumptions are inaccurate. For example, imagine you do not get along with an obnoxious coworker. You think she is a "bad" person. Somehow her family comes up in conversation, and you say that she is most likely a bad parent. The **physical attractiveness stereotype**, a specific variety of the halo effect, is the tendency to esteem someone more favorably for their personality traits based upon their attractiveness.

Attribute substitution refers to when a person must make a judgment or answer a question that is complex and substitutes a simple solution or heuristic for the actual solution. In this way, when someone tries to answer a difficult question, they may actually be answering a related but simpler question without knowing it.

III. Culture's Effect on Attribution

Different cultures encourage different ways of attributing behavior. For example, in Western cultures that have a more individualistic take on life and society, our successes and failures are more likely to be attributed to internal factors. Inversely, in Eastern cultures that have a more communal take on living in society, attributions tend to be more based on external factors.

9. Prejudice

The term **prejudice** refers to preconceived notion about a person, group, or thing that are either irrationally positive or negative and are made before having any kind of actual experience with that person, group, or thing. Prejudices are often made when it comes to race and ethnicity, but they can be made about most anything, from regions of the country to food to the best and worst toothpastes.

The three most significant social factors that influence prejudices are **class**, one's socioeconomic status, **power**, one's ability to achieve goals and control resources despite obstacles and **prestige**, the level of respect given to a person by others.

Discrimination is the active form of prejudice: it is acting in a particular, irrational way towards a particular group of people. For example, the segregation of American schools based on the skin color of students, with black students often placed in lower quality facilities with less resources, was discrimination against African Americans. Prejudice and discrimination based on race, and notions that one race is better than another, are known as **racism**.

Of course, schools were desegregated in the 1950's after the Supreme Court's landmark decision in *Brown vs. Board of Education of Topeka, Kansas*, but discrimination remained a problem in schools and the work force. As such, policy makers began to employ **affirmative action**, which were policies that took race and sex into consideration when considering employment or college enrollment, in order to better represent people belonging to minorities. Some have criticized affirmative action as being **reverse discrimination**.

Institutional discrimination refers to discriminatory actions, behaviors, and rules that are not only used by large institutions, but are part of those institutions' core operations and objectives. An example would be **apartheid** in South Africa, the race-based system of segregation system that the National Party governments of South Africa used to rule the country from 1948 to 1994.

Figure 5. The Entrance to the Apartheid Museum in Johannesburg, South Africa, Depicting How Facilities Were Segregated During Apartheid.

Prejudice can also be influenced by emotions and cognition. Oftentimes, prejudices come from a place of frustration or fear: when we have something or someone unknown seemingly blocking our path to some goal, hostility can be a natural reaction. This hostility can often be targeted at people, known as **scapegoats**, who actually have little to do with the problem or frustration, and are often underrepresented and marginalized. Jews became scapegoats in Germany for the poor economy between World War I and World War II.

As far as cognition, our brains seek to organize data into categories, using shortcuts to classify things in ways that often are simpler than they are reality (i.e. this person is black, this person is white, this person is wealthy, this person is poor, and etc.). This can obviously lead to prejudice, and in turn to stereotypes, which will be described further below.

Inversely, our brains also pick up on differences when it comes to categorizing. Distinctive people stick out in our minds and can often become representative of whole groups of people. For example, Asian students may be considered, in general, to be good at math because of a Chinese character who was good at math on a popular TV show. This is known as an **illusory correlation**.

10. Stereotypes and Stigma

A **stereotype** is a widely held but oversimplified image or understanding of a particular group of people or things based on outwardly obvious characteristics (gender, race, sexual orientation, and etc.). Stereotypes are, for the most part, attitudes that are based on little to no real information about a person, group, or thing.

I. Stereotype Content Model

The **stereotype content model** is a psychological theory that posits that stereotypes possess two primary dimensions, competence and warmth. The model centers around a hypothetical in-group that makes judgments about people. Competent groups are those held in high esteem by society and the in-group, and vice versa for incompetent groups. Warm groups are those that are not in direct competition with the in-group, and vice versa for low warmth groups. The model is illustrated below:

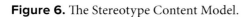

		Competence	
		Low	**High**
Warmth	**High**	**Paternalistic stereotype** low status, not competitive (e.g., housewives, elderly people, disabled people)	**Admiration** high status, not competitive (e.g., ingroup, close allies)
	Low	**Contemptuous stereotype** low status, competitive (e.g., welfare recipients, poor people)	**Envious stereotype** high status, competitive (e.g., rich people, feminists)

Figure 6. The Stereotype Content Model.

Paternalistic stereotype (or pity) is marked by low competence and high warmth, meaning the target group has a low social status and is not competitive with the in-group. The target group is looked down upon.

Admiration stereotype (or pride) is marked by high competence and high warmth, meaning the group has high social status and is not competitive with the in-group. This target group is respected and admired.

Contemptuous stereotype (or disgust) is marked by low competence and low warmth, meaning the group has low social status and is competitive with the in-group. This target group is viewed with disdain, contempt, and is considered annoying.

Envious stereotype (or envy) is marked by high competence and low warmth, meaning the group has high social status and is competitive with the in-group. The target group is viewed with jealousy, distrust, and bitterness.

Previously mentioned in Chapter 11, stigma is the extreme disapproval of a certain person or group based upon their perceived deviations from social norms. These deviations can often be unfair stereotypes. For example, at the onset of the HIV epidemic of the 1980s, the general public stigmatized people who had contracted the disease.

11. Self-Fulfilling Prophecy and Stereotype Threat

A **self-fulfilling prophecy** is a process through which stereotypes and perceptions of them can lead to behaviors that reinforce those stereotypes. Let us turn to Greek mythology for an example:

King Laius of Thebes was told by an oracle that his son would one day kill him. Therefore, his newborn son Oedipus, was left out in the wilderness to die. However, the infant was found and raised by others, and so was entirely ignorant of his origins. Like Laius before him, Oedipus was warned that someday he would kill his father and marry his mother, and so, believing his foster parents were his real parents, he left home forever. In his travels, he got into a fight with a stranger at a cross roads and ended up killing the stranger, who actually was Laius. Oedipus then married the widow of the slain man, Jocasta, who he did not know was his own mother.

In this mythological example, the stereotypes are the visions relayed by the oracles, and with incomplete knowledge, these stereotypes brought about the behavior that led those visions to fulfillment. So, both prophecies fulfilled themselves.

As another more contemporary example, say there are two fourth grade students, one who struggles at math, and one who excels. The one struggles is told he is bad at math and internalizes that belief, studying and working less. The one who excels is told he is excellent at math and internalizes that belief, studying and working harder. Both stereotypes end up reinforcing behavior, even though fourth grade is probably too young to make true judgments about a person's true propensity for mathematics.

Stereotype threat describes the feeling that people can have of being at risk of confirming or exemplifying negative stereotypes about a group that they belong to. This is typically a self-fulfilling fear.

The researcher Steven Spencer conducted a study in which men and women took a math test. He found that women performed worse on the test. However, if women were led to believe before the test that women, in general, perform as well as men on this test, their scores were comparable to those of men. Spencer posited that the negative stereotype of the mathematical abilities of women actually caused women to underperform on the test. So, fear of conforming to that stereotype actually caused them to do worse on the test and confirm that stereotype.

12. Ethnocentrism

Ethnocentrism is the evaluation of other cultures based upon preconceptions and ideas that come from the standards and customs of one's own culture. For an example, we can look to Imperialism, the practice of taking control of the lands of others. European imperialism began in the sixteenth century, with European nations colonizing territories in the Americas, Africa, and Asia. Europeans tended to believe the people and societies in these places were primitive, and that they ought to bring them up to speed, culturally and technologically. The judgments of the Europeans about these places in the "New World" were based on elements of their own cultures.

When talking about ethnocentrism, an **in-group** is a social group with which a person experiences a sense of belonging while an **out-group** is a social with which a person does not feel a sense of belonging. In the example above, a European explorer's in-group would be his nation, say Portugal, and his out-group would be the indigenous people of what is now known as Brazil.

Negative feelings about an out-group are not so much based on a dislike of the group or its characteristics and customs, but rather, those negative feelings tend to be rooted in favoritism for the in-group by comparison.

In order to combat the tendency towards ethnocentrism, cultural relativism can be employed. **Cultural relativism** is the idea that a person's beliefs and activities should be viewed and understood through the context of their own culture. In this way, differences in the behavior of people from different cultures are not measured as either superior or inferior: they are simply different.

This page left intentionally blank.

Practice Passage

Many adolescents make difficult choices in their pursuit of social needs. They seek out peer groups, feelings of safety, establishing identity, and decision-making. However, the choice to join a gang involves higher stakes with more potential for danger and other negative personal and social repercussions.

A peer group provides companionship and support. Henry Sullivan contended that all people have basic social needs that a peer group serves to fulfill. For adolescents living in certain low-income neighborhoods, peer group options may be limited, thus necessitating joining a gang to meet social needs.

In order to assess the presence of self-monitoring among gang members, a study was conducted in which adolescent gang members and non-members were rated on self-monitoring. Table 1 reports the percent of those groups who were considered to be high self-monitors. Self-monitoring is a strategy individuals use to manage their impressions they give others, by considering how their behavior corresponds to the behavior of their group. Individuals high in self-monitoring will adopt the behavior of their primary group, even if it is incongruent with their internal beliefs or social mores.

Table 1. Self-monitoring in Gang Members

Group	% Considered High Self-Monitors
Gang Members	58%
Non-members	32%

Adolescents feel a need to be safe like anyone else. However, with their increasing autonomy from their parents and their increasing involvement in their neighborhood and with peers, adolescents may feel more of a need to take it upon themselves to provide that safety themselves versus relying on their parents. In a dangerous neighborhood, individual protection may be insufficient; therefore a gang may provide protection for the adolescent.

Gangs provide a strong source of identity, with their distinct dress, signals, initiation, and customs. In an individual with no strong sense of identity from home, gang identity is a strong draw. Membership, even in a negatively perceived in-group, is better than no identity at all. To fulfill their expected role, the adolescent must adapt the customs and norms that the gang has established. This adaptation may be especially pronounced among adolescents who are high in self-monitoring.

1. According to Kohlberg, in what stage of moral development might an adolescent be in if the only deterrent to committing crimes in his gang that he considers is a legal sentence that he might receive?
   A. Obedience and punishment
   B. Interpersonal relationships
   C. Maintaining social order
   D. Social contract and individual rights

2. The passage suggests that all of the following play a role when an individual joins a gang EXCEPT:
   A. social isolation.
   B. social segregation.
   C. role strain.
   D. false consciousness.

3. In the dramaturgical perspective, an adolescent behaving in a more aggressive manner when he is with his gang and more non-aggressively when he is at home is demonstrating what type of contrast?
   A. In-group vs. out-group
   B. Ethnocentrism vs. relativism
   C. Front-stage self vs. back-stage self
   D. Central processing vs. peripheral route processing

4. In the study in the passage, the chi-square test was used to compare the percent of high self-monitors among adolescents in gangs versus those not in gangs. There was found to be a significant difference. What conclusions can be drawn from this finding?
   A. There is no difference in the percent of self-monitors between adolescents in gangs versus those not in gangs.
   B. There is a higher percent of self-monitoring gang members than non-gang members.
   C. There is a higher percent of self-monitoring non-gang members than gang members.
   D. It is not possible to determine the relationship between self-monitoring and gang status.

5. According to the passage information, if it was found that trauma correlates with self-monitoring, what must be true about the relationship between gang membership and trauma?
   A. There is no relationship between occurrence of trauma and gang membership status
   B. There is a higher incidence of trauma among gang members
   C. There is a higher incidence of trauma among non-gang members
   D. No conclusions can be made without further analysis

6. Many gang members hide their membership from their families and schoolmates, acting very differently when around these perceived out-groups. This deceit is most closely a form of:
   A. impression management.
   B. role strain.
   C. role exit.
   D. altruism.

7. How might an adolescent view his own deviant behavior if he comes to view his gang as his reference group versus society in general?
   A. He would likely not change his view of his behavior.
   B. He would likely view his behavior as more socially appropriate.
   C. He would likely view his behavior as less socially appropriate.
   D. He would likely not be able to judge his behavior.

Practice Passage Explanations

Many adolescents make difficult choices in their pursuit of social needs. They seek out peer groups, feelings of safety, establishing identity, and decision-making. However, the choice to join a gang involves higher stakes with more potential for danger and other negative personal and social repercussions.

Key terms: adolescent choices, gangs, social repercussions

Contrast: normal peer groups vs. joining a gang, the gang is a search for safety and identity and is much riskier with higher stakes

A peer group provides companionship and support. Henry Sullivan contended that all people have basic social needs that a peer group serves to fulfill. For adolescents living in certain low-income neighborhoods, peer group options may be limited, thus necessitating joining a gang to meet social needs.

Key terms: Henry Sullivan, peer group

Opinion: Sullivan = all have social needs peer groups can satisfy

In order to assess the presence of self-monitoring among gang members, a study was conducted in which adolescent gang members and non-members were rated on self-monitoring. Table 1 reports the percent of those groups who were considered to be high self-monitors. Self-monitoring is a strategy individuals use to manage their impressions they give others, by considering how their behavior corresponds to the behavior of their group. Individuals high in self-monitoring will adopt the behavior of their primary group, even if it is incongruent with their internal beliefs or social mores.

Key terms: self-monitoring, gang vs. non-gang, social mores

Cause and effect: ↑self-monitoring → ↑likelihood to adopt group behavior/customs/beliefs

Table 1. Self-monitoring in Gang Members

Group	% Considered High Self-Monitors
Gang Members	58%
Non-members	32%

Adolescents feel a need to be safe like anyone else. However, with their increasing autonomy from their parents and their increasing involvement in their neighborhood and with peers, adolescents may feel more of a need to take it upon themselves to provide that safety themselves versus relying on their parents. In a dangerous neighborhood, individual protection may be insufficient; therefore a gang may provide protection for the adolescent.

Key terms: safety, gang protection

Cause and effect: ↑autonomy as teenager → take control of their own safety → ↑attraction to gang

Gangs provide a strong source of identity, with their distinct dress, signals, initiation, and customs. In an individual with no strong sense of identity from home, gang identity is a strong draw. Membership, even in a negatively perceived in-group, is better than no identity at all. To fulfill their expected role, the adolescent must adapt the customs and norms that the gang has established. This adaptation may be especially pronounced among adolescents who are high in self-monitoring.

Key terms: self-monitoring is presenting an identity that corresponds to the group

Cause and effect: the search for identity leads adolescents to take on the gang identity

1. A is correct. In the obedience and punishment stage of moral development an individual is motivated to comply with social order solely by a punishment that he might expect for non-compliance.

2. D is correct. According to paragraph 2, financial and social factors result in many adolescents with few options for peer groups, which leads to them choosing a gang by default. This would suggest these people are isolated, or cut off from society (A, B). False Consciousness is an idea from Marxism that refers to ideology dominating the consciousness of exploited groups and classes which, at the same time, justifies and perpetuates their exploitation. For example, workers in an electronics factory in China being told by their managers if they work harder and harder for low wages, they may be rewarded with the opportunity to be promoted. As a result, the workers see the factory managers as potential allies, not the opposition that exploits them.
    C. Role strain occurs when a person has difficulty meeting the responsibilities of a particular role in his or her life. Paragraph 4 describes how many teenagers, when dealing with their increased autonomy, seek to ensure their own protection and safety rather than to rely on their parents. This leads them to seek out gangs for protection.

3. C is correct. An individual demonstrates his front-stage self when he is present in front of a group and acts in a certain way. He demonstrates his back-stage self when he is not in front of a group and feels freer to act more naturally.

4. B is correct. As indicated in the question, a significant difference was found in the chi-square test, indicating a difference in the percentages of the two groups. Visual inspection reveals that the percent of self-monitoring gang members is higher than the non-gang members.

5. D is correct. While the passage suggests there may be a relationship between trauma and self-monitoring, to conclude that there is a relationship between trauma and gang membership would require further analysis.

6. A is correct. Impression management is the process by which individuals try to control the impressions others form of them (i.e. self-presentation). The goal is for the individual to present themselves the way in which they would like to be thought of by the individual or group (e.g. their gang, classmates) they are with.

7. B is correct. If an adolescent comes to view his gang as his reference group, he would likely view his behavior as less deviant from the norm and thus view his behavior as being more socially appropriate.

Independent Questions

1. A group of several thousand nonviolent protesters united by a shared stance on a major political issue would most accurately be described as a(n):
   A. mob.
   B. craze.
   C. crowd.
   D. institution.

2. Suppose a teaching assistant prefers to grade undergraduate quizzes in a coffee shop, surrounded by numerous other people. However, this same individual prefers to study his most challenging graduate courses in the privacy of his apartment. The teaching assistant probably experiences increased productivity when grading quizzes in a public place due to the effects of:
   A. informal norms.
   B. self-serving bias.
   C. social facilitation.
   D. social loafing.

3. During the famous Stanford prison experiment, subjects were assigned to play the roles of guards or inmates in a mock prison setting. As the experiment progressed, the "guards" became shockingly abusive toward the "inmates" despite there being no real incentive for this behavior. Which aspect of the experimental protocol most likely contributed to this behavior?
   A. The "guards" were given explicit instructions by the researchers not to physically harm the "inmates."
   B. The "guards" were instructed to refer to the "inmates" only by their assigned inmate number, never by name.
   C. The researchers intentionally selected subjects with no history of violent crime or mental illness.
   D. The "guards" were encouraged to beat the "inmates" by the experimenter.

4. Suppose a tourist answers his cell phone while riding in an elevator with several other people. He continues to talk on his phone until the elevator reaches his floor. Several days later, the tourist overhears two people discussing how rude it is to have a phone conversation in an elevator. The tourist most likely violated a:
   A. formal norm.
   B. more.
   C. informal norm.
   D. subculture.

5. Which of the following describes an ascribed status?
   A. A student routinely professes his political views, making others aware that he is a Republican.
   B. A mother spends time with her children and is considered by many to be a caring parent.
   C. An armed robber is convicted by a jury of his peers and branded a felon.
   D. A child is born into the lowest level of the Indian caste system.

6. According to some sociological perspectives, deviant behavior is the result of unbalanced distribution of resources. Those without adequate resources are driven to deviance in order to survive. This perspective is LEAST consistent with which of the following scenarios?
   A. A schizophrenic woman without access to healthcare controls her delusions with heavy alcohol consumption.
   B. A homeless person resorts to pickpocketing in order to purchase a winter coat.
   C. A motorist, who was street racing, is found to be at fault in a fatal motor vehicle accident.
   D. A teenager sells illicit drugs, hoping to contribute to his family's income.

7. A particular individual routinely visits an online message board and avidly reviews the posted content. However, he rarely posts content of his own or joins in the online discussion, even when he has knowledge that might be valuable to the community. The actions of this individual are best explained by the concept of:
   A. self-actualization.
   B. social facilitation.
   C. social loafing.
   D. deindividuation.

8. Suppose a supervisor is reviewing a series of applications for an open position in a software engineering company. The supervisor notices that one of the applicants was born in Japan and consequently makes a note to interview this applicant first. The supervisor's belief that this applicant is probably more technically competent than the other applicants is an example of:
   A. prejudice.
   B. discrimination.
   C. ethnocentrism.
   D. groupthink.

Independent Question Explanations

1. C is correct. A crowd is a group of people in a single location that is united by a shared purpose. In contrast, a mob is a form of crowd with violent intentions, which contradicts the "nonviolent" part of the question stem (eliminate choice A). An institution is an established effector of social order with significant influence on one or more aspects of human behavior. The question stem does not provide any information to suggest that the protestors are part of an established societal element, making choice C a better answer than choice D. Choice B (a craze) is more closely related to a fad, making it unrelated to the question stem.

2. C is correct. Social facilitation refers to the tendency of individuals to perform better on straightforward tasks when in the presence of others. However, the social facilitation effect does not apply to the performance of more challenging tasks, such as learning complicated and unfamiliar material.

3. B is correct. The results of the Stanford prison experiment illustrate the effects of deindividuation and depersonalization. Regardless of their character or values, the "guards" acted in accordance with their arbitrarily assigned roles. This is an example of deindividuation, a loss of inhibition and identity, which typically occurs in situations of heightened arousal or strong depersonalization. The experiment established circumstances that facilitated depersonalization, including the provision of uniforms and the assignment of arbitrary numbers in place of names. Choices A and C would not encourage the behavior of the "guards," and choice D simply did not happen during this famous experiment.

4. C is correct. Informal norms include unwritten behaviors that are generally considered acceptable and expected by members of a society. Not speaking on the phone in an elevator falls into this category. Formal norms are more explicit and generally written down, often in the form of laws or rules. Mores are norms that are considered extremely important to upholding societal values and allowing the society to function. Subculture refers to a unique group within a culture that is different than the parent culture.

5. D is correct. Ascribed statuses are conferred by society, often irrespective of the efforts or actions of the individual. Castes are an extreme example of ascribed statuses. They are assigned at birth and there is generally very little mobility among them. In contrast, achieved statuses are earned by individuals based on merit and actions.

6. C is correct. If deviant behavior is purely motivated by utilitarian factors, this would not explain why some individuals might choose to drive recklessly and put other motorists at risk. All the other choices describe deviant behavior that results in some way from inadequate access to resources.

7. C is correct. Social loafing refers to the decreased contribution of individuals to a group effort when circumstances do not effectively assign individual responsibility. In this case, the individual in question is able to benefit from the content posted by other members of the online community without contributing anything of his own.

8. A is correct. The supervisor's prediction about the competence of this applicant is based on a belief about an entire group. Prejudice refers to the holding of a certain belief about an individual based on the group to which that individual belongs, rather than actual experience with the individual. In contrast, discrimination involves *actions* taken toward an individual that are motivated by beliefs about a certain group to which the individual belongs. The supervisor's act of giving this applicant priority over the others is certainly discrimination if he ends up doing so, but this question asks about the belief, not the action itself. Prejudice, which refers to the thinking that motivated such an action, is thus the best choice.

Social Interaction

0. Introduction

From an evolutionary perspective, society developed directly out of a need for human survival. With shared understanding, experiences, and methods of communication, we interact with society every day of our lives. These interactions take place within the framework of five general social structures: statuses, roles, groups, networks, and organizations. We learn to interact with society and others in society through the process socialization, which was discussed previously.

1. Status

A **status** is a socially defined position within society that is used to classify a person. The term is broad: a status can be anything from "mother" to "North Carolinian" to "musician."

Individuals typically have a **master status**, that is, the one that overshadows all others and determines one's place in society. For Roger Federer, the male tennis player with the most Grand Slam tournaments ever won (17), his master status is "tennis player," though he is also a "father," a "husband," and a "Swiss national."

The other two kinds of status are ascribed and achieved.

An **ascribed status** is one that is either given at birth or involuntarily assumed later in life. It is not chosen or earned, but assigned by society. A person's gender, ethnicity, and race are ascribed statuses.

An **achieved status** is one that is gained or earned through one's own effort. "Self-made millionaire," "Oscar-winning actor," and "licensed doctor" are achieved statuses.

2. Role

A **role** is a collection of behaviors, values, norms, attitudes and beliefs that are expected of a person holding a particular status. For example, a doctor is expected to be intelligent, caring, and very knowledgeable about medicine and the human body.

Every status can have multiple, varied roles attached to it. This collection of roles is known as a **role set**. These different roles are often defined by one's **role partner**, the person with whom one interacts. For example, imagine a seventh grade teacher. The teacher behaves in different ways when she is interacting with different role partners, like students, the administration, other teachers, or parents.

The term **role performance** refers to how well a person carries out a particular role. Perhaps the teacher mentioned above has an excellent grasp for her students and for what inspires them to study and work hard, but she struggles to relate easily to the school's administration. She performs the former better than the latter.

As we are often juggling multiple roles at once, struggles can arise.

The term **role conflict** refers to a difficulty in fulfilling the expectations of two or more roles at once. For example, imagine a father who is also a youth league baseball coach. As a father, he wants his son to be pitching, but as a coach, he knows another kid more deserves to be on the mound.

MCAT STRATEGY > > >

You feel strain when a single role creates a strain in you. Roles can conflict when multiple different roles place conflicting expectations on you. Remember conflict happens between two or more things (people, roles, etc.)

The term **role strain** refers to a difficulty in fulfilling multiple expectations within the same role. For example, imagine a babysitter who is struggling to keep up with three young children, the youngest of whom is in diapers. Within one five minute span she is trying to change the diaper, make lunch, and keep the older two from hurting each other. The role performance of each role suffers as undergoes role strain.

And, when she has had enough, the babysitter drops her roles and takes up some other identity (status). This is called role exit.

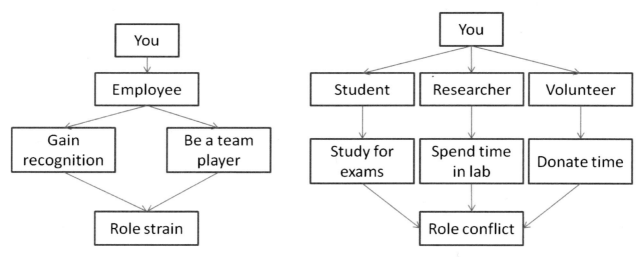

Figure 1. Illustrations of Role Strain and Role Conflict.

3. Groups, Networks, Organizations

I. Groups

Broadly speaking, a **group** consists of two or more people who identify and interact with one another. These people generally share values, interests, family, social placement, political ideals, or any other number of unifying factors. Human life tends to gravitate around groups: think about sports teams, schools, companies, governments, families, congregations, and etc. A lot of positive things come out of groups and the interactions between them, yet so do a lot of very negative things as well, including discrimination, war, and genocide.

There are several types of groups that are studied in sociology and group psychology.

A **family group** is generally determined either by birth, adoption, or marriage, joining people of different ages and sexes through strong emotional ties. A family group is typically united by blood (familial relationship) or law (marriage, adoption). Family groups can struggle to remain cohesive due to the differences in values that come with age gaps between members. This is especially true with teenagers in the family.

A **peer group** includes people of similar ages, statuses, and with similar interests, that have all chosen to join the group. Whereas a family group is not self-selected, a peer group is. A peer group can allow individuals feelings of belonging and friendship.

A **reference group** is a social group against which individuals can evaluate themselves. For example, if you are a medical school applicant, your reference group might be other people applying to medical school. How do you compare?

Mentioned in the previous chapter, an in-group is one to which a person belongs while an out-group is a group in which one does not feel a sense of belonging.

Groups can be classified as either primary or secondary.

A **primary group** features direct interaction between members with close and intimate relationships made that tend to last a long period of time. Families, close groups of friends, and teams can be examples of primary groups.

A **secondary group** features superficial interaction between members, with weak and not so intimate relationships made that tend to not last very long. A group of students working on a project and a group of coworkers at a temporary summer job can be example of secondary groups.

> **MCAT STRATEGY > > >**
>
> As is typical with lots of sociology on the MCAT, the terms can start to blur together, especially when they all seem to use ordinary conversational English. But the psych/soc section demands that you memorize the exact, technical definition, even for words as simple as "group."

The German sociologist Ferdinand Tönnies developed another theory for dividing groups into two, known as *Gemeinschaft and Gesellschaft*. *Gemeinschaft*, German for community, refers to groups, such as neighborhood and families, that are united by shared values, ancestry, and geographical location. *Gesellschaft*, German for society, refers to groups, such as nations and corporations, that are formed for the sake of mutual self-interest.

Smaller groups are easier to study than large groups, and a few notable methods have been developed to observe and analyze them. **Interaction process analysis** was a technique for observing and classifying the interactions between people in small groups. By the 1970s, it was revised into the **system for multiple level observation of groups**

(SYMLOG), which centers around three fundamental dimensions of interaction: instrumentally controlled vs. emotionally expressive, dominance vs. submission, and friendliness vs. unfriendliness.

The term **group conformity** refers to the power a group holds over its individual members. Often, the beliefs and values of individuals can be out of line with those of the group because individuals are willing to comply in order to fit in. This effect leads naturally to groupthink, mentioned in Chapter 12, which is when group members focus only on ideas and values shares within the group and ignore those outside of it, causing potential negative effects.

II. Networks

In terms of sociology, a **network** is an observable, chartable pattern of relationships between individuals and groups. A **social network** is a complicated, intricate web of social connections between people, with both direct and indirect links to different people and groups. Online social networks like Facebook and LinkedIn exemplify this: they allow you to connect not only with your friends, but also with their friends, the friends of those friends, and so on.

And **immediate network** is one that is dense, with close, direct ties between people. A **distant network** is looser and features weaker, less substantial ties between entities. Facebook and LinkedIn combine elements of both.

Figure 2. Visualization of Social Network Analysis (Larger Circles Represent Closer, More Immediate Relationships and Smaller Circles, Vice Versa).

III. Organizations

Within the context of sociology, an **organization** is a entity that comes together with a specific culture and structure, set on achieving specific goals. An organization is typically large, more impersonal than a group, and is generally organized as a hierarchy. Because of their deliberate organization, organizations can continue to function when individual members leave them (not so with some groups). Of course, this allows organizations to potentially last much longer than groups.

There are three general types of organizations: coercive organizations, normative organizations, and utilitarian organizations.

Coercive organizations are those for which members do not have a choice of joining. For example, a prison is a coercive organization.

Normative organizations are those which members join based on some shared, moral goal. For example, the American Red Cross volunteer division is a normative organization.

Utilitarian organizations are those in which members are paid for their efforts. These include businesses and corporations, from small town restaurants all the way up to McDonald's.

Another important term for understanding organizations and their structures is **bureaucracy**, a rational system of administration, control, and discipline. A typical bureaucracy has the following six defining characteristics, which were first noted by the German sociologist and political economist Max Weber:

> it has a formal hierarchical structure
> it is managed via a set of defined, specific rules and regulations
> it is organized by functional specialty, with different workers performing different, specialized tasks
> the organized has a unified mission that is either "up-focused," that is, to serve shareholders, a board, or some other entity that empowers it, or "in-focused", that is, to serve itself through maximizing profit or maximizing market share
> it is purposefully impersonal
> employment is based on technical qualifications, either advanced degrees or training

All of these characteristics mean that bureaucracies are not very adaptable and that they can be quite inefficient. The British naval historian C. Northcote Parkinson added a seventh characteristic to Weber's six, demonstrating that the management and professional staff of bureaucracies tend to grow at a steady, predictable rate, regardless of what the organization is actually doing. This is known as **Parkinson's law**.

The **iron law of oligarchy** posits that the majority of bureaucratic and democratic organizations eventually and naturally shift to being ruled by oligarchs, a group of elites.

4. Expressing Emotion

Expressing emotion is one of the important ways that we interact with other people, communicating internal states or feelings to others whether it is voluntary or involuntary. Inversely, detecting the emotions of others is also important.

First developed by Charles Darwin, the **basic model of emotional expression** posits that various forms of expression, including behaviors, postures, vocal changes, physiological changes, and facial expressions, are consistent with the theory of evolution. In other words, Darwin believed that these expressions of emotion should be similar across cultures, no matter how different those cultures nominally are. Since Darwin's time, scientists such as Paul Ekman, the man who developed the seven universal emotions, have found proof that Darwin was, for the most part, right: a significant number of human emotions are universally experiences are expressed in recognizable ways across different cultures.

Pl. 2

Figure 3. Photographs Illustrating Grief, from Darwin's 1872 Book, *The Expression of the Emotions in Man and Animals*.

On the other hand, the **social construction model** posits that there is no biological basis for emotions or their expression. Rather, this model holds that emotions are based entirely on experiences and social context. Therefore, emotions are expressed differently in different cultures, depending on the particular social norms of a particular culture.

Cultural expectations about emotions and how they ought to be expressed are known as **display rules**. Imagine an office situation in which the boss is a very clumsy guy. Almost every day, he trips and falls or drops his coffee mug, or something like that. The employees find this hilarious and want to laugh about it, but they cannot: the boss does not take well to people laughing at him, and has fired people before for this reason. As such, although they may want to, the employees do not laugh at the unintended physical comedy of their boss.

A **cultural syndrome** is a set of attitudes, behaviors, beliefs, norms, and values that are organized around some central theme and is shared near-unanimously among members of the same culture. A cultural syndrome helps to determine a society's rules for expression of a particular emotion. Take for example happiness: although it is almost universally considered a positive emotion, it is expressed differently in different cultures. In more individualistic Western cultures, happiness is individually attained and experienced. By contrast, in more communal Eastern cultures, happiness is more often an effect of collective, shared experiences. So, cultural syndromes are not only important in determining how emotions are expressed, but also in how they are actually experienced.

Gender can also affect how emotion is expressed. Though both men and women have about an equal capacity for **empathy**, the ability to personally identify with another person's emotions, research has shown that women are more likely to actually display empathy (i.e. crying or admitting genuine sadness or happiness in relation to another person's own emotion). This has to do with the fact that studies have shown that women are often better at reading emotional cues than men are, as well as societal expectations (generally, it is more acceptable for a woman to express sadness in public than it is for a man).

5. Self-Presentation

Self-presentation refers to the act of displaying oneself to others and to society at large through the means of culturally acceptable behaviors. In order to shape our self-presentation, we use **impression management**, the process through which we attempt to shape and influence how other people perceive us.

In terms of impression management, there are three "selves": the **authentic self**, who we really are, the **ideal self,** who we'd like to be, and the **tactical self**, who we pretend to be in order to meet the expectations other people have about us. This obviously mirrors the discussion of self-concept earlier in the book, which featured the actual self, the ideal self, and the ought self.

> ### MCAT STRATEGY > > >
>
> Get personal! It can help you memorize the various terms related to social interaction if you put those terms in the context of your own life. Think about how these terms relate to your own life, and how you interact with friends, family, and coworkers.

There are many kinds of strategies for impression management, two of them being assertive and defensive. Assertive strategies include bragging, talking oneself up, and wearing flashy clothes or accessories to alter how others perceive you. On the other hand, defensive strategies are meant to protect one's impression in the case of failure. One example of this is self-handicapping, the strategy of creating obstacles and excuses in order to divert blame when a person fails or doesn't reach his or her potential. For example, a student loudly proclaiming that he hasn't studied before test. He is defensively preparing for a bad grade so that if he does do poorly, it doesn't have to do with his innate intelligence, but rather, the fact that he didn't study.

The Canadian-American sociologist Erving Goffman used the **dramaturgical perspective** to understand impression management. According to Goffman, people imagine themselves playing certain roles, like actors in the theatre, while interacting in society. This means that our identities are not set, but rather, dependent upon the situations we are in and the people we are with. In keeping with the overall metaphor of life as theatre, social interactions are divided between front stage and back stage. In the **front stage**, the actor (the person) is in front of the audience (other people) and performs and dresses in accordance with the audience, the stage (the environment), and the script (social cues). In the **back stage**, when the actor is not "performing," she can be herself, not having to worry about anything other than comfort and personal taste.

6. Nonverbal Communication

Whereas **verbal communication** relies upon the use of words, either written, spoken, or signed, to transfer information, **nonverbal communication** refers to how we transfer information without words. Methods of nonverbal communication include eye contact, facial expression, gestures, tone of voice, body language, and the amount of space between two people. As far as the written word is concerned, punctuation, capitalization, and spacing are important means of nonverbal communication. Think of about texting, and how you use different symbols, capitalized letters, or punctuation to relay a verbal message with the feeling you can express in person. For example, consider the difference between these three texts: "I am so hungry," "I am so HUNGRY!", and "I AM SOOOOO HUNGRRRY!!!!!!"

7. Social Behaviors

Social behavior refers to interactions between members of the same species within a particular society. Attraction, aggression, attachment, and social support are all types of social behaviors.

I. Attraction

Interpersonal attraction refers to having positive feelings about another member of the species, and is the basic element of love, friendship, admiration, lust, and other kinds of close, social relationships. Several characteristics serve to heighten attraction, including proximity, similarity, appearance, self-disclosure, and reciprocity.

One's **proximity**, or geographical nearness to someone else, plays a big role in attraction. This is because the closer someone is, the more time we get to spend with them. A person who is closer is more accessible and that is attractive. In fact, proximity is one of the strongest predictors of friendship. In line with this concept is the **mere exposure effect**, which posits that people prefer repeated exposure to the same stimuli instead of to new stimuli.

Similarity between people is another influence on attraction: friends and people in serious romantic relationships are likely hold similar attitudes, backgrounds, beliefs, interests, and values.

Appearance has a strong influence on attraction, because physical attractiveness can significantly heighten the kind of draw another person has on you. Physical attractiveness can be such a persuasive force that research has shown that physically attractive people tend to be ranked higher for several personality characteristics and traits that have nothing to do with physical attractiveness.

Self-disclosure refers to the ability one has in a relationship to disclose one's closest fears, dreams, thoughts, and goals to one's partner. Self-disclosure can strengthen a relationship or friendship, but it must be reciprocal: if you are to share your intimate secrets with a person, they ought to share them back, or else they are taking advantage of your vulnerability, which would weaken the relationship. **Reciprocal liking** is the term used for when a person likes another more because they know that other person likes them back. In general, reciprocity is an important element of a healthy relationship.

II. Aggression

Aggression is essentially the opposite of attraction: it refers to behavior or attitudes that are hostile, assertive, and attacking. Aggression is typically used to cause harm, bodily or otherwise, to another person, or to assert one's social dominance over others. Aggression can be physical (physical intimidation, actual fighting), or can be communicated either verbally (taunts) or non-verbally (offensive gestures).

Figure 4. A Tiger Modeling Aggressive Behavior.

From an evolutionary standpoint, aggression was used as a means of protecting precious resources like food and water, or else demonstrating social dominance, and therefore, sexual fitness (this can still be observed in many animals). Today, humans use aggression to get ahead in the world, to wage war, to play sports, and in many settings, still demonstrate dominance over others (think of bullies, gangs, and even politics).

The amygdala is in part responsible for aggression, as its function is to associate incoming stimuli with correspondent punishments and rewards. An activated amygdala can increase feelings of aggression, though the prefrontal cortex typically exerts control over the amygdala, diminishing impulsive feelings. This is why damage to the prefrontal cortex has been linked to a increased likelihood of aggressive behavior.

Another physiological element of aggression, hormones, and particularly testosterone, play a role in causing aggressive behavior. This may be why men are more likely to exhibit aggression than women are.

The three main predictors for aggressive behavior are genetic, neural, and biochemical. Studies of identical twins, in which separated twins both exhibit tendencies towards aggression, have proven the role of heredity in passing on a penchant for aggression. Neurally, as mentioned before, the amygdala can play a role in aggression while the prefrontal cortex plays a role in inhibiting this. Any damage or disorder of these areas can affect aggression. Biochemically, hormones like testosterone can heighten feelings and acts of aggression, but so too can chemicals that are consumed, like alcohol, which limits inhibition, making aggressive behavior more likely.

Certain situations can also heighten the likelihood of aggression. The **cognitive association model** posits that we are more likely to respond to stimuli in an aggressive manner when we are experiencing negative emotions or physiological feelings. For example, we are more likely to snap at our friends when we are hungry, tired, frustrated, or in pain. This model works on a large-scale level as well: for example, riots are more likely to happen on very hot days.

Similarly, the **frustration aggression principle** finds that we are more likely to behave aggressively when we are blocked from reaching a goal.

Aggressive behaviors are more likely to be repeated if they are reinforced. For example, think back to the prototypical school bully. If every time the bully aggressively asks smaller kids for their lunch money, they give it, then he is more likely to keep asking, and to use aggression as a tactic.

Aggression can also be stimulated by ostracism: the loner on the outside of social groups is more likely to behave aggressively than those who are in strong, positive relationships. This can, at least in small part, account for many mass shootings in schools and public places.

III. Attachment

Attachment refers to the emotional connection between a child and a caregiver that is established from birth. The study of attachment began in earnest after World War II when the British psychologist John Bowlby began noticing the negative effects that isolation had on children who had been orphaned during the war. Later, the American-Canadian developmental psychologist Mary Ainsworth took Bowlby's theories and developed them further, claiming that, in order to develop appropriately, infants need the security of a conscientious caregiver from the first six months to two years of life.

There are four main types of attachment that are studied: secure, ambivalent, avoidant, and disorganized, the latter three of which lead to the deficits in social skills as a child grows.

Secure attachment refers to when a child has a constant caregiver and is therefore able to explore and learn about the world, knowing he or she has a secure, constant base to return to. Secure attachment is considered crucial to healthy social development.

Figure 5. A Mother and Child Modeling Secure Attachment.

Ambivalent attachment refers to when the child's caregiver is inconsistent, sometimes response to the child's needs, and sometimes not. Because of this on-off effect, a child will be distressed when separated from the caregiver, but more ambivalent upon his or her return.

Avoidant attachment refers to when a child's caregiver provides little to no response to the child's needs, effectively providing no safe base. Children in this situation are likely to show no preference between the caregiver and a total stranger. As such, the show will show little to no distress when separated from a caregiver, and little to no elation upon his or her return.

Disorganized attachment refers to when a child's caregiver behaves erratically and is typified by a disorganized pattern of behavior in response to the caregiver's absence and presence.

IV. Social Support

Social support refers to the perception, whether it is true or not, that one is cared for and supported by a social network. Social support can come from friends, family, loved ones, and even a wider group of acquaintances (for example, your "friends" on Facebook). Social support can be emotional (ex: empathy and condolences), esteem-based (ex: "hey you can do it!"), material (ex: money or other material goods), informational (ex: mentorship from someone further along in your professional feed), and network-based (ex: a group hug, or lots of people liking your status update on Facebook).

Social support can help to lessen the occurrences of depression and anxiety, and can also lessen one's inclination towards other mental health issues and substance abuse. Additionally, people with low social support have been shown to have higher mortality rates from many diseases, proving how important social support is for quality of life.

V. Biological Explanations for Social Behavior

Foraging behavior refers to an animal's search for and use of food resources. For many animals, acquiring an adequate food source can take a lot of energy, and so, they have adapted to do it as efficiently as possible. Moreover, because environments are constantly changing, it is important that animals are adaptable in their foraging behavior: those that are not will be less likely to reproduce. Young animals (including humans) learn how to acquire food and eat most efficiently from observing others.

Mating behavior is another social behavior rooted in biology, in the very need for reproduction and continuation of the species. The three primary types of mating are **monogamy** (one, exclusive mating relationship), **polygamy** (a male has relationships with many females, known as **polygyny**, or a female has relationships with many males, known as **polyandry**), and **promiscuity** (members of opposite sexes mate randomly and without exclusivity). Though most animals are essentially bound to one type of mating, humans can, depending on their circumstances and society, use any of the three types.

Mate choice refers to the deliberate selection of a mate based on attraction, and the selectiveness with which this choice is made is known as **mate bias**. Mate choice can provide **direct benefits** (protection, emotional support, material gain), or **indirect benefits** (stronger, more capable offspring).

There are five more specific benefits that can come with mate choice: phenotypic benefits, indicator traits, genetic capability, sensory bias, and Fisherian selection.

Direct phenotypic benefits are traits that can be outwardly observed and make a potential mate more attractive by indicating the potential mate will have more viable offspring than another. Take for example, the great reed warbler, a songbird that breeds throughout Europe and Asia. Female warblers are more attracted to the males with a larger song repertoire because they tend to produce more viable offspring.

Indicator traits are those that signal the overall good quality (health, strength, well-being) of a potential mate. For example, female cats tend to be more attracted to male cats that are well groomed, with clean coats. A dirty coat can signify either some kind of genetic weakness or disease, or else malnutrition. Any of these qualities make a dirtier cat less attractive than a clean cat. In most cases, it is fair to say the same idea applies to humans (we typically look for well-groomed mates).

Genetic capability refers to how well the genes of two mating animals work together to create viable offspring. In this way, an animal might be better served with another whose genetic make up is comparable to its own.

Sensory bias refers to the preference for a trait that develops in a non-mating context and is then adapted or exploited by an animal to attract a mate. For example, freshwater fish in Trinidad and Tobago prefer to mate with males that have some orange coloration on them. Outside of mating, these fish show a marked preference and interest in objects that are orange, giving some proof that the mating preference arose from this every day preference. The reason may be that orange fruits from trees occasionally fall into streams and provide an easy, accessible meal. The fish able to get to these fruits first are most likely to take sustenance from them, and may be more sexually fit.

Fisherian selection refers to a trait that has no effect on survival or viability but becomes more and more pronounced or bold over time, making it a trait that members of the opposite sex find attractive. If this effect is strong enough, it can overpower natural selection. The classic example is the male peacock, with its large, bright, conspicuous plumage. The bigger your plumage, the more mates you attract, though this doesn't guarantee increased viability of offspring. Rather, it guarantees more offspring for the male.

Figure 6. Male Peacock with Full Plumage.

Inclusive fitness refers to the number of offspring an animal has, how well it supports those offspring, and how well its offspring support other organisms in a group. An animal can bolster its inclusive fitness, and thereby, its genetic success, by performing **altruistic behaviors**, those that help other members of the group survive and thrive. Occasionally, this comes at the expensive of the survival or success of the animal performing the behavior. For an example, dolphins have been observed helping other sick or injured dolphins by swimming under them for hours on end, even taking them up to the surface so they can breathe.

Game theory, originally used to study decision-making in terms of economics, policy, and mathematics, can also be used by scientists to study social behavior in animals. Evolutionary game theory can be used to study how something seemingly selfless like altruism can fit into the larger notion of natural selection.

Game theory centers on players, the actions and information available to these players at any given point, and the rewards associated with decisions or actions. When studying evolutionary or biological game theory, the pay off is typically sexual fitness.

8. Discrimination

Discrimination is the active form of prejudice: it is acting in a particular, irrational way towards a particular group of people. For example, the segregation of American schools based on the skin color of students, with black students often placed in lower quality facilities with less resources, was discrimination against African Americans. Prejudice and discrimination based on race, and notions that one race is better than another, are known as racism.

Institutional discrimination refers to discriminatory actions, behaviors, and rules that are not only used by large institutions, but are part of those institutions' core operations and objectives. An example would be apartheid in South Africa, the race-based system of segregation system that the National Party governments of South Africa used to rule the country from 1948 to 1994.

Practice Passage

Being in the presence of others, particularly strangers, typically causes physiological arousal. Research shows that, in the presence of groups, individuals tend to demonstrate proficiency in dominant responses. Dominant responses are those which are well-rehearsed and familiar to the performer. However, if the task is complicated or novel, observed performance quality decreases.

Social facilitation can be observed when researchers introduce confederates who are meant to observe the subjects performing. The percentage of success of those individuals is recorded before the confederates are introduced and after they are introduced. The participants are classified according to their proficiency in the task as being either high-performers or low-performers. A study in which researchers observed basketball players and recorded their percentage of shots made before and after introducing confederates was conducted with the results presented in Table 1.

Table 1. Task Performance

Performance Level	Before Confederates	After Confederates
High	68%	74%
Low	42%	36%

Groups also impact individual behavior through deindividuation. This refers to people feeling that they are less personally responsible for their behavior in a group and as a result behaving in ways they normally wouldn't while alone. Deindividuation changes individual behavior through anonymity and diverting the individual's attention away from his own values. An example of the deindividuation that can occur in a group was provided by researchers who observed children trick-or-treating for Halloween. The researchers put out candy and instructed children to only take one piece. Conditions that fostered children only taking one piece included having the children asked their name, being alone, and having a mirror present in front of the candy.

Group opinions tend to become more strongly held after group discussion. A reason for this is that the group is likely to hear more arguments of the opinion the group is favoring. Group members will hear these arguments and become more persuaded and also continue to further the argument in extreme directions.

1. According to the data, what group might be most likely to perform well in front of a group?
    A. Good students performing novel calculations
    B. Poor singers performing a song
    C. Unskilled mechanics changing a tire
    D. An experienced factory worker performing a duty on an assembly line

2. Which of the following would be LEAST helpful as a way to avoid groupthink?
    A. Have group members with a variety of views on the topic
    B. Record individual views before topics are discussed
    C. Include individuals in positions of authority in the group
    D. Present all sides on the issue

3. What could be done to avoid inflammatory rhetoric in online commentary?
    A. Allow individuals to gravitate towards topics they feel passionate about
    B. Allow the online group to rebuke the commentators
    C. Require users to use their actual names
    D. Ask difficult questions, requiring non-dominant answers

4. A group member presenting a more extreme opinion than another group member who he views as high status in order to appear favorable to the group is known as what process?
   A. Upward social comparison
   B. Downward social comparison
   C. Lateral social comparison
   D. Inverse social comparison

5. According to the passage, all of the following factors would help the low-performing group perform better EXCEPT:
   I. the use of modeling to familiarize subjects with the task.
   II. to have subjects perform in front of observers.
   III. to place observers behind one-way mirrors during task completion.
   A. I only
   B. II only
   C. III only
   D. I and III only

6. The researchers expected the observing confederates to have on a subject performance if they were discovered, this is mostly likely due to:
   A. the Hawthorne effect.
   B. inclusive fitness.
   C. ascribed status.
   D. role conflict.

7. The shift in opinion discussed in the fourth paragraph is most closely identifiable as:
   A. conformity.
   B. groupthink.
   C. group polarization.
   D. obedience.

Practice Passage Explanations

Being in the presence of others, particularly strangers, typically causes physiological arousal. Research shows that, in the presence of groups, individuals tend to demonstrate proficiency in dominant responses. Dominant responses are those which are well-rehearsed and familiar to the performer. However, if the task is complicated or novel, observed performance quality decreases.

Key terms: physiological arousal, dominant responses

Cause and effect: presence of others → arousal, ↑ performance on familiar/dominant behaviors, ↓performance on complicated tasks

Social facilitation can be observed when researchers introduce confederates who are meant to observe the subjects performing. The percentage of success of those individuals is recorded before the confederates are introduced and after they are introduced. The participants are classified according to their proficiency in the task as being either high-performers or low-performers. A study in which researchers observed basketball players and recorded their percentage of shots made before and after introducing confederates was conducted with the results presented in Table 1.

Key terms: social facilitation, high/low-performers, confederates

Cause and effect: the effect of observers on basketball performers was observed

Table 1. Task Performance

Performance Level	Before Confederates	After Confederates
High	68%	74%
Low	42%	36%

Table 1 shows us that high performers do better when being watched and low performers do worse

Groups also impact individual behavior through deindividuation. This refers to people feeling that they are less personally responsible for their behavior in a group and as a result behaving in ways they normally wouldn't while alone. Deindividuation changes individual behavior through anonymity and diverting the individual's attention away from his own values. An example of the deindividuation that can occur in a group was provided by researchers who observed children trick-or-treating for Halloween. The researchers put out candy and instructed children to only take one piece. Conditions that fostered children only taking one piece included having the children asked their name, being alone, and having a mirror present in front of the candy.

Key terms: deindividuation

Cause and effect: deindividuation → anonymity and reduces focus on personal values → abnormal (for self) behavior

Group opinions tend to become more strongly held after group discussion. A reason for this is that the group is likely to hear more arguments of the opinion the group is favoring. Group members will hear these arguments and become more persuaded and also continue to further the argument in extreme directions.

Key terms: polarization, norm, social comparison

Cause and effect: group discussion → polarize group opinions/attitudes since arguments that favor the group opinion are heard more than contrary opinions

1. D is correct. According to the data individuals who perform best in front of groups are those who are good at their task and for whom the task is routine.

2. C is correct. If individuals in positions of authority are in the group then the group members may be more inclined to try to curry favor with these individuals, which could lead to groupthink.

3. C is correct. According to the passage, individuals often behave in ways they would not normally behave if they feel they are anonymous and have been deindividuated.

4. A is correct. In an upward social comparison, individuals compare themselves with group members who are seen as having high status.

5. B is correct. I: If the subjects were familiarized with the task (e.g. practice) this would likely improve performance. III: If the observer's effect were mitigated by placing them in an unseen location, this is also likely to improve performance of the low-performing group. II: This is contrary to what the passage described regarding the observer effect.

6. A is correct. The researchers expected known observation to impact subject performance. The alteration of behavior by the subjects of a study due to their awareness of being observed is known as the Hawthorne effect.
    B. Inclusive fitness is also known as kin selection. This is most often used to help explain altruism. Genes are selfish, and will encourage behavior which allows them to continue.
    C. Ascribed status is the social status a person is assigned at birth or assumed involuntarily later in life.
    D. Role conflict occurs in any situation in which a person is expected to play two incompatible roles. For example, a physician will suffer role conflict if forced to make difficult medical decisions for a family member.

7. C is correct. People placed into a group will typically have some overriding attitude toward the situation they are presented with. Over time and with discussion, the group's attitude toward that situation may change in such a way that the group attitude is enhanced and strengthened. This is group polarization.

Independent Questions

1. Derek, a college junior, is seven feet tall. "Tall person" is thus most likely one of Derek's:
   A. achieved statuses.
   B. ascribed statuses.
   C. master statuses.
   D. role sets.

2. A doctor is treating a pediatric patient whose parents are refusing vaccinations for the patient. The doctor feels emotionally distraught because she wants to protect the child from preventable illnesses while also respecting the parents' autonomy. Which of the following describes this social interaction?
   A. Role status
   B. Role conflict
   C. Role exit
   D. Role strain

3. Which of the following is not considered a characteristic of an ideal bureaucracy?
   A. A hierarchy of authority
   B. Informal or unwritten codes of conduct
   C. Impersonality
   D. Efficiency

4. Philip works as a teller at a local branch of an international bank. Philip and the other employees of the branch are part of the same:
   A. normative organization.
   B. utilitarian organization.
   C. coercive organization.
   D. primary group.

5. A student holds a part-time position at a pizza kitchen in order to finance her education. She speaks and acts differently around her coworkers at the pizza kitchen compared to when she is comfortable with her small group of friends. This difference in behavior is best explained by the:
   A. structural functionalism theory.
   B. dramaturgical approach.
   C. rational choice theory.
   D. Sapir-Whorf hypothesis.

6. Peter, a two-year-old child, is dropped off at daycare by his mother. He cries when his mother leaves, but he is comforted by a daycare provider shortly after and plays happily until his mother returns. At that point, he smiles and runs into her arms. With regard to his connection with his mother, Peter displays:
   A. secure attachment.
   B. ambivalent attachment.
   C. disorganized attachment.
   D. avoidant attachment.

7. Patricia and Sarah have been best friends since they were in grade school, and they are both currently accountants at the same company. Recently, Sarah was the maid of honor at Patricia's wedding. Which of the following best describes Patricia and Sarah as a social group?
   A. A secondary group and a dyad
   B. A secondary group and a triad
   C. A primary group and a dyad
   D. A primary group and a triad

8. Which of the statements below is NOT accurate with regard to organizations?
   A. Organizations are typically larger than groups.
   B. Organizations always have hierarchical structures.
   C. Organizations have their own goals and cultures.
   D. Organizations typically continue to function even after some members leave or quit.

Independent Question Explanations

1. B is correct. "Tall person" is a position that Derek holds within society, making it a status. Specifically, since Derek did not voluntarily assume or work for his height, it is an ascribed status, just like race or ethnicity. Individuals generally have multiple ascribed and achieved statuses, but they only have one master status, a term which refers to the status that most defines one's place in society. We have no way of knowing whether "tall person" is Derek's master status, so choice C can be eliminated. Finally, a role set is the collection of behaviors, values, and norms associated with a status, not the status itself.

2. D is correct. Role strain occurs when an individual feels conflict between different requirements of one role. In this case, the doctor is feeling pulled by patient care versus patient autonomy, both of which are requirements of her role as a doctor. In contrast, role conflict refers to a clash between two separate roles.

3. B is correct. Characteristics of an ideal bureaucracy include a hierarchy of authority, promotion based on achievement, specialized division of labor, impersonality, written rules of conduct, and efficiency. Informal, unwritten codes of conduct are not characteristic of an ideal bureaucracy.

4. B is correct. A utilitarian organization is one that pays its members, typically a business or corporation. Here, Philip and his co-workers are employees of the bank, making them part of the same utilitarian organization. A normative organization is composed of volunteers who share a moral purpose or goal, and a coercive organization is formed of members who are forced to join, such as prisoners. There is no indication that Philip and his co-workers are very close or have known each other for a long time, so we cannot conclude that they form a primary group.

5. B is correct. The dramaturgical approach is a subset of symbolic interactionism that proposes that each individual plays a certain role according to the circumstances and people surrounding them—in other words, their audience. The individual might perform a certain way (termed her "front-stage self") in front of individuals around whom she is not comfortable, while performing entirely differently when alone or when comfortable around close friends (her "back-stage self"). The structural functionalism theory can be eliminated here because this theory describes the ways that different parts of society work together, which does not apply to this question. Additionally, the Sapir-Whorf hypothesis is a language theory, and does not describe the student acting differently at work than with friends.

6. A is correct. Attachment develops between a parent and child during the first few years of life. Various styles of attachment exist. Here, the child prefers his mother to a stranger and is upset when she leaves, but he is able to quickly recover and enjoy playing and learning about the world. This is an indication of secure attachment. A child who displays ambivalent attachment would not be able to quickly recover from his distress and would likely show more ambivalence (mixed feelings) when his mother returned. Disorganized or disoriented attachment is marked by confusion or contradictory behavior, which Peter is not said to show. Finally, a child who has an avoidant attachment with his mother would not be distressed when she left him at the daycare.

7. C is correct. A dyad is the smallest possible social group and consists of only two individuals. Since Patricia and Sarah comprise two people, a group that contains them alone is a dyad. (Note that a triad is a social group composed of three individuals.) Additionally, since the two women have had a close, long-lasting friendship and regularly interact, they represent a primary group.

8. B is correct. Not all organizations have hierarchical structures, although many do. Organizations are entities that are generally larger than groups, that have their own goals and cultures, and that usually continue functioning even after one or more members exit the organization (a fact that is not true of many groups).

This page left intentionally blank.

Social Structures

CHAPTER 11

0. Introduction

A **society** is a group of people who live in a delineated area and who, for the most part, have a shared culture. **Sociology** is the study of society: sociologists are concerned with how society is created, how we all behave and interact within it, how we define what is normal and abnormal within that society, and how these preferences are institutionalized.

Social structures are organizational systems within society that center around characteristic, definable patterns of relationship between people and institutions.

1. Theoretical Approaches

Because a society as a whole is a very large entity, and therefore difficult to measure and observe on a detailed level, sociologists use several theoretical approaches to understand how society works.

I. Functionalism

Functionalism, the oldest of the many theoretical approaches to sociology, is the study of every part of a society and how they all function. Early sociologists, including Émile Durkheim, often considered the father of sociology, viewed whole societies as living organisms, with each part of them comparable to organs in organisms, each performing its own function. Durkheim theorized that the parts of society work together to maintain a **dynamic equilibrium**, and that only healthy societies can actually maintain such equilibrium.

In the context of functionalism, the term **function** refers to the benefits created by a person or entity's actions. Inversely, the term **dysfunction** refers to the negative or harmful effects brought about by a person or entity's actions. Furthermore, functions are classified as either manifest or latent. **Manifest functions** are those with intended consequences while **latent functions** are those with unintended consequences. The manifest consequence of a big public school is to educate the populace while its latent function is to provide jobs to the community.

II. Conflict Theory

Unlike functionalism, which views society as harmonious and its many parts working mostly cooperatively, **conflict theory** stresses the competition for resources between different groups of people. Based on the works of Karl Marx, conflict theory acknowledges that scarcity of resources creates competition for all forms of resources (material, social, and political). Because certain groups are able to amass more resources than others, they maintain their resources by creating social structures and institutions that keep others from advancing towards positions of power. These structures and institutions in turn maintain a certain social order. In this way, one group can come to dominate others because of its success in acquiring and maintaining resources.

III. Symbolic Interactionism

Symbolic interactionism is the study of the many ways people interact through the shared understanding of **symbols**, which are simply anything to which we attach meaning. Therefore, words, gestures, body language, and sounds are symbols. In this approach to sociology, symbols are crucial to our understanding of society, also to our communication with other members of society. Often times these symbols do not match between different cultures, and so, part of joining another culture is the process of learning is system of symbols. For example, a thumbs up in America signifies a sign of approval whereas in Australia (and with a little thrust upwards), it means "up yours," obviously an insult.

Figure 1. The Thumbs Up, a Common American Symbol.

Unlike functionalism and conflict theory, which work from a macro perspective, symbolic interactionism take a micro approach to sociology.

IV. Social Constructionism

Social constructionism examines how people in a society develop jointly constructed understandings of the world, called **social constructs**. These social constructs arise from people coming together, communicating with one another, and deciding upon the significance of something. Intangible things like justice and honor can be social constructs, and so can tangible things, like money. Think about money: it is inanimate, made of paper or metal, and only has value because society has come together and agreed that has value. No pun intended, we all buy into the idea of money, and therefore, money has financial value.

> **MCAT STRATEGY > > >**
>
> The common theories of sociology are a popular source of MCAT questions. Make sure you commit these definitions to memory!

2. Education

Education is the process of receiving or giving formal instruction, often in a school setting. Sociologically speaking, the manifest function of schools and other educational institutions is to pass down knowledge in the form of information, facts, figures, and mental and academic processes. Another manifest function is to give fitting status to those who have completed particular levels of education. The latent functions of schools include socialization, the creation of statuses based upon achievements or level of degree, the stimulation of students to continue learning outside of school, and reinforcement of the role of education in society.

Though a good education is often considered to be an important factor in having a successful life in society, not everyone has access to a good education, and therefore, to the success that can come with it. Many public schools in poor areas have inadequate facilities and are lacking in teachers, but the private schools in these areas are too expensive. Therefore, students from poor families are not given the same opportunities as students with wealthy parents, or else students who live in areas with strong public schools. This problem, along with many others, is an important one to which sociologists devote their research.

3. Family

A **family** is a group of people related in some significant way, either by blood, marriage, adoption, or law, that have some have some degree of responsibility in relation to each other. In some ways, a family functions like a small unit of society, providing for socialization, companionship, education, protection, resource gathering, reproduction, and social status.

A family has leaders, typically the parents, who have the most authority to make decisions and enforce rules. In an **egalitarian family**, both parents have equal power. In a **patriarchy**, men have the most authority, and in a **matriarchy**, women have the most authority.

> **MCAT STRATEGY > > >**
>
> When it comes to culture, nothing trumps family. The family serves as the primary agent of socialization and the primary agent of enculturation.

Extending out from family, **kinship** refers less to our blood relations and more to who we consider belonging to our family (who do you spend holidays with, who keep in touch with, and etc.). For example, family friends who have been around so long that they are called "aunt" and "uncle": they are not blood related, but they are kin. Of course, brothers and sisters and grandparents and uncles and cousins can also kin. When kin groups derive equally from both your parents, that is referred to as **bilateral descent**. When kin groups are derived more from either the paternal or maternal side, they are known as patrilineal or matrilineal, respectively.

There are many different kinds of families, not just the nuclear family with a mother and a father and children. Some families include kin, particularly in societies where the extended family is more valued. Many families are altered by divorce, with parents splitting and taking turns having custody of the children. In some families, the parents are not married, but live together and engage in the family-rearing activities a married couple would. Some families have homosexual parents, with two fathers or two mothers. Though still somewhat taboo, legal and cultural strides are being made in America for gay marriage and family-rearing to continue becoming more acceptable.

4. Religion

Within the context of sociology, the term **religion** refers to patterns of beliefs, practices, and organizational forms that seek to address the meaning of life while creating a sense of community.

There are four major types of religious organizations: churches, sects, state religion, and cults.

Churches are religious organizations that are thoroughly integrated into society and that are interested not only in the sacred and holy, but in the daily and mundane as well. They are typically organized by a codified set of rules, and though many people are born into particular churches, they generally allow people to join later in life. The Presbyterian and Catholic churches are examples.

Sects are religious organizations that are notably not integrated into society, often formed after a split from a larger, more defined religious organization. Members are typically born into a sect, or else must convert. In more extreme cases, sects may withdraw from society at large to practice their beliefs in a more controlled setting. An example is the Church of Jesus Christ of Latter-Day Saints (Mormonism), which split from Christianity.

A **state religion** is a religious organization that includes most members of a society, is officially recognized, and sometimes does not tolerate other religions. A state religion is not necessarily a **theocracy**, that is, a government based on religious principles, run by religious figures. For example, the state religion of Sweden is Lutheranism: it is legally regarded as such, though the government is secular. Iran, on the other hand, has a theocratic government: its state religion is Islam and its government is informed by principles of Islam.

A **cult** is a relatively small religious organization that has beliefs and practices that are typically far outside of what a society regards as normal or even acceptable. A cult that survives and grows can become a major religion, as Christianity did.

The five major world religions are considered to be Christianity, Islam, Judaism, Hinduism, and Buddhism.

From a functional sociological perspective, religion can give people meaning and purpose for their lives, as well as it can bring people together (or inversely pull them apart) and create a means for social change (or inversely social control). In this way, religion is a powerful social institution that can have a lot of influence over people and society, and can bring about both positive and negative effects.

5. Government and Economy

Government refers to the system by which a state or community is run. **Economy** refers to the wealth and resources of a state or community, with particular attention paid to the finite amount of goods and services that are produced, distributed, traded, and consumed.

The government of the United States is based on **rational-legal authority**, meaning it is based on legal rationality, legitimacy, and bureaucracy. The US economy is based on **capitalism**, meaning resources and methods of production or trade are privately owned and are used to generate profit. It should be noted that the US economy is not purely capitalist, as the government does have interventionist programs that regulate capitalism. The US more accurately exemplifies **state capitalism**, in which companies are, for the most part, privately run, but the government runs some major institutions, like schools and the military. The US also has elements of **welfare capitalism**, a system in which companies are privately run but the government has a network of social welfare programs. Many of the countries of Western Europe actually typify this kind of economy more than America does.

Other governments around the world may derive their power from **traditional authority**, that is, power that is passed down through tradition and custom.

And on the flip side of capitalism, **socialism** is an economic system in which resources and the methods of production are collectively owned by all people of a state or community. Whereas capitalism encourages individual goals, socialism encourages collective goals.

6. Health and Medicine

The institution of **healthcare** and the practice of **medicine** aim to maintain and improve the health of individuals, as well as society as a whole. Ideally, healthcare addresses not only individual issues, ailments, sicknesses, and diseases, but also strives to make people healthier in general. So, healthcare as a field is occupied with helping people who are sick, but also researching and educating on ways that people can avoid being sick in the first place. This is the ostensible goal of such organizations as the Food and Drug Administration, which seeks to promote public health by regulating foods and substances that can be unhealthful.

Sociologists study how healthcare affects people, how it improves over time, how it sometimes does not, and reasons why that may be. Moreover, sociologists are interested in **medical ethics**, the system of moral judgments and values that apply to the practice of medicine. According to *Principles of Biomedical Ethics* by Tom Beauchamp and James Childress, the four primary tenets of medical ethics are **beneficence** (a doctor has responsibility to act in the best interests of the patient), **justice** (a doctor has a responsibility to give healthcare service fairly and justly, as in, to not give one patient worse care than another), **non-maleficence** (a doctor has a responsibility to not harm a patient), and **respect for autonomy** (a doctor has a responsibility to respect the wishes of a patient, though there are some exceptions, like when a patient has a psychiatric illness or disorder that obscures rational thinking).

Another phenomena related to health that sociologists study is how social rank or class can affect health. For example, obesity is a notably larger problem in low-income communities that in those with middle to high-income. One of the many reasons for this is the occurrence of **food deserts**, areas in which fresh food is difficult or impossible to find. These are most often found in densely populated, low-income environments, like the so-called "bad neighborhoods" or major cities.

7. Elements of Culture

Culture is the amalgamation of beliefs, norms, and values that a certain group of people share. The term refers, essentially, to the collective lifestyle of a group of people, whether it be a community or a state.

I. Material Culture

The term **material culture** refers to the physical objects that have been made or are used by a particular culture. These includes jewelry, architecture, artwork, tools, clothing, money, and even food. Some cultures, such as American culture, place higher value on material objects (for example, cars and houses) than others.

II. Symbolic Culture

Symbolic culture refers to the symbols and ideas that are used by a particular culture. These include words ("Hello"), gestures (thumbs up), signs (a stop sign), and rituals (funerals and weddings). These symbols can differ widely from culture to culture. Often times, material objects are the physical manifestations of culturally important symbols. For example, possessing an expensive car and house is a way of engaging with the so-called "American Dream," the idea that people in America, if they work hard, can make themselves successful and wealthy. Another, perhaps more idealistic symbol, is the Statue of Liberty, which represents individual liberty, equal opportunity, and inclusiveness (as the inscription reads, "Give me your tired, your poor, / Your huddled masses yearning to breathe free, / The wretched refuse of your teeming shore. / Send these, the homeless, tempest-tost to me, / I lift my lamp beside the golden door").

Figure 2. The Statue of Liberty.

III. Language

Described fully earlier, language is the complex system of symbols that allows people to communicate with one another, and to share what is going on in their heads. Furthermore, language allows for the transmission and maintenance of culture. Also mentioned earlier, the linguistic relativity hypothesis, also known as the Whorfian hypothesis (named after linguist Benjamin Whorf), holds that our perception of reality is shaped by the structure and content of our language. He believed that language affects cognition more than cognition affects language.

IV. Beliefs, Norms, Rituals, and Values

A **belief** is something that people accept and hold to be true. A **value** is something that is held to be important in life, enough so that it influences the way people make decisions and behave. The beliefs and values of a society may not always be fully put into practice: equality and equal opportunity are values that are held to be important in America, and yet, history and current event show that not everyone in our country has an equal opportunity to succeed.

Discussed earlier, norms are the rules, spoken or unspoken, that define what is and isn't acceptable as far as the behavior, beliefs, attitudes, and values of a society.

A **ritual** is a ceremony consisting of a series of actions that are performed in a particular order and that reflect the values of a culture. Moreover, particular materials objects and symbols are often involved. An wedding is an example of a ritual, with a prescribed order of actions and certain material objects (wedding dress, bouquet, etc.) and symbols (the sharing of vows, the altar, the veil, etc.). Of course, rituals can vary based upon cultural backgrounds and personal preferences.

Figure 3. A Catholic Wedding.

V. Evolution's Effect on Culture

Culture allows for people to pass ideas and information from generation to generation. This allows for social, cultural, and perhaps even evolutionary progress to be made: every generation can take what all those before it have learned and work from there to continue solving problems.

Think about the very first humans that had language to communicate with. They developed rudimentary norms and social rules. Over thousands of years, those norms and social rules evolve and become more refined as certain cultural groups are selected for and become more dominant in human society. Perhaps, over those thousands of years, through natural selection, human beings evolved, cognitively speaking, to better understand, communicate, and internalize norms and values. Essentially, particular genetic traits in early humans were evolutionarily favored over others because of cultural values, beliefs, and practices that were pervasive in early human society.

For example, consider the practice of cooking. An early human discovered that fire could be used to make food more easily digestible. Cooking caught on and was spread by social learning: early humans taught each other how to cook. Once it was spread, cooking became a driver of natural selection, and those with smaller digestive tracks, teeth, and stomachs passed on their genetic material. Through evolution, as these organs got smaller, perhaps more resources were available for brain development. Thus cooking, an accidental discovery passed through early humans by rudimentary culture, may have had some part in shaping the evolution of man.

8. Interactions Between Cultures

When multiple cultures exist within a society, and this most often the case, they will inevitably interact, whether that be positively or negatively.

I. Ethnocentrism and Cultural Relativism

Discussed more fully in Chapter 12, ethnocentrism is the evaluation of other cultures based upon preconceptions and ideas that come from the standards and customs of one's own culture. This can exacerbate differences between different people of different cultures. Inversely, cultural relativism is the idea that a person's beliefs and activities should be viewed and understood through the context of their own culture. In this way, differences in the behavior of people from different cultures are not measured as either superior or inferior: they are simply different.

II. Culture Shock

Culture shock refers to the feeling of disorientation that can be felt by someone who is suddenly subjected to or immersed into an unfamiliar, new culture. Students that study abroad, particularly in countries with notably different cultures from their own, often experience this.

III. Culture Lag

Culture lag is the tendency of material culture to evolve and change faster than symbolic culture. So, culture lag represents a conflict of culture that can happen within one single culture. For example, consider technology. The material culture of consumer technology evolves and develops much faster than our ability to understand it symbolically. Conflicts, like the current debates about online privacy that are prevalent, can arise out of this tension.

IV. Cultural Diffusion

Cultural diffusion is the process by which a cultural phenomenon spreads through a culture and outward into other cultures. Take for example, a restaurant chain like McDonald's, which started with one single location. McDonald's succeeded and proliferated throughout the United States. Today, you can find a McDonald's in most countries around the world. Coca-Cola is the same way. Another example is the spread of the cell phone: at one point in time, only business people and doctors carried cell phones, people who needed to communicate on the go and who could afford them. Today, most Americans have one.

V. Cultural Assimilation and Multiculturalism

Cultural assimilation is the process by which a particular group's culture begins to resemble that of another. Take for example Italian immigrants to New York City: having left Italy and taken up residence in the bustling city, immigrants began to take on qualities of New York culture. Inversely, people already in New York began to incorporate elements of Italian culture. Take pizza for an example.

Typically, the four factors that measure completeness of assimilation are geographic distribution, intermarriage, language acquisition, and socioeconomic status.

Assimilation can be slowed by the development of **cultural or ethnic enclaves**, that is, neighborhoods or areas with a high concentration of people from one distinct culture or ethnicity. New York's China town: walking through, you can easily pretend you are in China, as people speak Chinese and signs are written in Chinese.

Figure 4. New York City's Chinatown, Located in Southern Manhattan.

Practice Passage

Multiple biopsychosocial factors impact the effect of medicine on patients. Ethnicity and culture have been observed to impact the biological response to medication, especially considering genetic variance between ethnicities. One way culture may impact medication response is through diet. For example, researchers have found that when immigrants' diets change from that of their native country to that of their new country, their drug response also becomes more similar to that of the individuals in their new culture.

In a study in which the efficacy of a new drug for depression was examined, scientists evaluated improvement study participants had compared to those taking placebo. The researchers conducted the study on three different continents, with differing cultures. Researchers assessed the average improvement (%) of participants taking the drug compared to those taking placebo, separated by location. The difference in improvements between continents was also tested (p = 0.004).

Table 1. Drug Efficacy

	North America	Asia	Africa
Improvement compared to placebo group	25%	33%	38%

Cultural differences among doctors also influences medication efficacy. First of all, doctors may be influenced by their culture in how they prescribe medication. Insurance providers, health organizations, or the patient's own expectations can also impact prescription. Additionally, research has shown that Caucasian doctors are far more likely to over-pathologize African-American and Hispanic patients.

Asian cultures often employ alternative remedies, such as natural medication, physical healing techniques, and alternative health care providers. These practices are typically viewed as being more safe and non-invasive than taking pharmaceuticals. However, these practices can impact other treatment regimens. As a result, Asian patients may be assessed for engagement in alternative treatments, to evaluate their willingness to use prescribed medication.

The form, color, and amount of the medication can affect the way it is viewed as well. Western Caucasians were found to regard white capsules as analgesics while many Muslims are averse to taking medications containing alcohol derivatives due to religious beliefs. Patients may not disclose their aversion to taking a certain medicine and may assume that there are no alternatives.

1. Which of the following would least likely account for the difference in drug efficacy seen in the study?
   A. Different cultural expectations of the efficacy of the drug
   B. Cultural differences affecting drug pharmacokinetics
   C. Cultural differences in the relationship between study researcher and participant
   D. Immigrant participants' diets may have changed

2. A survey of doctors at a hospital reveal that 84% are diagnosing Hispanic patients with more severe disorders compared with Asian patients, despite similar clinical and laboratory findings. This likely due to:
   A. individual discrimination.
   B. Institutional discrimination.
   C. both individual and institutional discrimination.
   D. neither individual nor institutional discrimination.

3. Which of the following is NOT a question that would helpful for gauging the conscious bias a patient may have towards their prescribed medication?
   A. How do you feel about this prescription?
   B. Are you using any other treatments for your condition?
   C. What do you think of the shape of this medicine?
   D. What might prevent you from taking the medicine as directed?

4. According to the passage, what would be the LEAST effective public health strategy to consider cultural factors in medicine?
   A. Encouraging immigrant patients to retain the diets of their native country
   B. Informing doctors about cultural factors for which to assess
   C. Providing patients with information about drugs and natural healing
   D. Requiring pharmaceutical companies to disclose with what cultures drugs have been evaluated

5. Many doctors report that new immigrants often adapt to medical norms and expected behaviors more quickly if they are still school-aged. This is most likely due to:
   A. formal curriculum.
   B. hidden curriculum.
   C. educational segregation.
   D. educational stratification.

6. A follow-up study on patient-physician relationships revealed that patients will often choose their physician based on how much they feel their input is valued by the doctor during visits. This evaluation of give and take with their doctor best exemplifies which sociological approach?
   A. Rational choice theory
   B. Conflict theory
   C. Social constructionism
   D. Social exchange theory

7. All of the following are methods by which the researchers could remove some of the location effects from the study EXCEPT:
   A. Considering the expectations of the participants and the pill administration method
   B. Distinguishing the placebo pill from the trial medication
   C. Measuring the pharmacokinetic effects of the drug
   D. Including a cultural questionnaire during diagnosis and treatment plans.

Practice Passage Explanations

Multiple biopsychosocial factors impact the effect of medicine on patients. Ethnicity and culture have been observed to impact the biological response to medication, especially considering genetic variance between ethnicities. One way culture may impact medication response is through diet. For example, researchers have found that when immigrants' diets change from that of their native country to that of their new country, their drug response also becomes more similar to that of the individuals in their new culture.

Key terms: factors, impact of medicine, culture, ethnicity

Cause and effect: via genes/diet, ethnicity/culture can change how people respond to drugs

In a study in which the efficacy of a new drug for depression was examined, scientists evaluated improvement study participants had compared to those taking placebo. The researchers conducted the study on three different continents, with differing cultures. Researchers assessed the average improvement (%) of participants taking the drug compared to those taking placebo, separated by location. The difference in improvements between continents was also tested (p = 0.004).

Key terms: drug efficacy, placebo, % improvement

Cause and effect: the effects in Table 1 were significant (p < 0.05)

Table 1. Drug Efficacy

	North America	Asia	Africa
Improvement compared to placebo group	25%	33%	38%

Table 1 shows us that max effect = Africa, min = N. America

Cultural differences among doctors also influences medication efficacy. First of all, doctors may be influenced by their culture in how they prescribe medication. Insurance providers, health organizations, or the patient's own expectations can also impact prescription. Additionally, research has shown that Caucasian doctors are far more likely to over-pathologize African-American and Hispanic patients.

Key terms: cultural differences among doctors, over-pathologize

Cause and effect: physician culture also affects how drugs are used; white doctors overtreat black/ Hispanic patients

Asian cultures often employ alternative remedies, such as natural medication, physical healing techniques, and alternative health care providers. These practices are typically viewed as being more safe and non-invasive than taking pharmaceuticals. However, these practices can impact other treatment regimens. As a result, Asian patients may be assessed for engagement in alternative treatments, to evaluate their willingness to use prescribed medication.

Key terms: Asian culture, alternative treatments

Cause and effect: Asian patients more likely to engage in alternative remedies → alter drug compliance

The form, color, and amount of the medication can affect the way it is viewed as well. Western Caucasians were found to regard white capsules as analgesics while many Muslims are averse to taking medications containing alcohol derivatives due to religious beliefs. Patients may not disclose their aversion to taking a certain medicine and may assume that there are no alternatives.

Cause and effect: the medium the medicine comes in can affect patient reaction to it

Contrast: White patients view white pills as pain-killers

1. D is correct. While a change in diet due to immigration may affect the pharmacokinetics of the individual, the result is that the drug would then behave similarly to the place to which he migrated. This answer does not account for the cultural differences.

2. C is correct. Doctors likely have their own cultural biases and in addition are trained at institutions that may not promote multicultural competency.

3. C is correct. The appearance of the medicine, for example shape or color, and how it affects a patient's view of it is largely an unconscious process. Therefore asking a patient about it would likely not yield helpful information.

4. A is correct. According to the passage, the change in diet can affect the pharmacokinetics of a drug. However, this can be accounted for so patients do not necessarily need to change their diet.

5. B is correct. A hidden curriculum is a side effect of education. This refers to any lessons which are learned but not openly intended to be taught. This includes cultural norms, values, and beliefs teachers may convey in the classroom and the social environment.

6. D is correct. Social exchange theory posits that human relationships are formed by the use of a subjective cost-benefit analysis and the comparison of alternatives.
   A. Rational choice theory is the principle which states that individuals always make logical decisions. These decisions provide people with the greatest benefit or satisfaction, or are in their highest self-interest.
   B. Conflict theory posits that tensions and conflicts arise when resources, status, or power are unequally distributed between groups in society and that these conflicts become the engine for social change.
   C. In social constructionism, society is viewed as both as a subjective and an objective reality. Meaning is shared, thereby constituting an agreed-upon reality.

7. B is correct. Distinguishing the medication to the participants would eliminate the usefulness of having a placebo pill.
   A. This is helpful because if participants expect that the pill will work the placebo effect may mask actual effects.
   C. This will help because then researchers have a more unbiased measure of the effects of the drug.
   D. According to the passage, this method is helpful because culture can impact diagnosis, resulting in participants with different severities of pathologies across sites.

Independent Questions

1. Which of the following assertions about mass media is most consistent with the conflict theory of sociology?
   A. Mass media propagates the views and agenda of the wealthy elite, thus reflecting class tension.
   B. Mass media has limited inherent influence, but individuals apply their own subjective reality to it.
   C. Individuals weigh the value of different mass media outlets, using logic to choose which ones are best.
   D. Individuals are likely to carefully consider the content of mass media only if the subject interests them.

2. Which of the following is primarily a micro-sociological theory?
   A. Conflict theory
   B. Structural functionalism
   C. Symbolic interactionism
   D. Welfare capitalism

3. A construction worker injures his arm and requires a month off work to properly recover. According to the sick role concept, staying home for a month rather than going to work would most likely:
   A. be considered deviant behavior, because being employed is a societal norm.
   B. be considered deviant behavior, because individuals who are sick or injured are expected to continue working.
   C. not be considered deviant behavior, provided the worker makes a genuine attempt to recover.
   D. not be considered deviant behavior, because sick individuals are not expected to return to work.

4. The Russian government controls certain aspects of the Russian economy, including the defense industry and the extraction of certain strategic resources. However, many other economic sectors are controlled by privately owned entities. Which of the following most accurately describes the Russian economy?
   A. Mixed
   B. Planned
   C. Market
   D. Traditional

5. During the British Raj in India, considerable effort was made to impose British values on the native Indian population. This was accomplished through organized educational efforts and religious proselytizing. The cultural effects of the British presence in India are most closely associated with the concept of:
   A. culture shock.
   B. cultural diffusion.
   C. cultural lag.
   D. ethnocide.

6. The collection of systemic obstacles that hinders the progress of women in professional and societal settings is known as the:
   A. glass ceiling.
   B. stereotype threat.
   C. self-fulfilling prophecy.
   D. bamboo ceiling.

7. In a certain island culture, women are seen as subservient to men, and they are relegated to work such as cooking and cleaning while the men earn money for the family. A sociologist describes this culture by saying "The men and women each do their own work, and this keeps the parts of society working together smoothly." This statement best exemplifies:
   A. conflict theory.
   B. social constructionism.
   C. structural functionalism.
   D. symbolic interactionism.

8. In Saudi Arabia, it is illegal to publicly practice any religion other than the dominant state religion. In accordance with the Saudi legal system, some individuals have received criminal charges for converting to a religion other than the accepted state religion. The dominant religious organization in Saudi Arabia is most accurately described as a(n):
   A. ecclesia.
   B. church.
   C. cult.
   D. sect.

Independent Question Explanations

1. A is correct. Conflict theory is based on the premise that all members of society must compete for limited resources. Conflict theory suggests that institutions, including mass media, are put in place to perpetuate inequality between those who control the means of production and those who serve as laborers.

2. C is correct. Symbolic interactionism is an interpretation based on everyday interactions between individuals. For this reason, symbolic interactionism operates on the micro level of sociology. (This does not mean that it has nothing to do with the "big picture"—in contrast, these individual social interactions ultimately determine the nature of the society as a whole.) Structural functionalism and conflict theory are macro-level sociological theories, which examine society in terms of large-scale effectors, such as institutions and other social structures. Welfare capitalism is capitalism that includes a concern for public welfare, but it is not a micro-sociological theory.

3. C is correct. According to the sick role concept, society accepts the fact that sick people may not be able to contribute to society as much as they did when they were not sick. However, sick individuals are expected to adopt the sick role, which involves making a genuine effort to recover in order to ultimately resume their previous role in society.

4. A is correct. Mixed economies include both publicly and privately controlled means of production. Therefore, mixed economies include elements of both market and planned economies, making choice A a better answer than choices B or C. Note that this description does not correspond to a traditional economy, which is characterized by customs of the culture and can typically revolve around a barter-based system.

5. B is correct. Cultural diffusion is the transfer of cultural elements from one group to another. These elements can include religious practices, values, norms, and language. In contrast, culture shock (choice A) is a disoriented feeling experienced by an individual who is subjected to another culture. Choice C (cultural lag) is the idea that the symbolic culture of a society takes time to catch up with advancement in material culture, most notably technology. Finally, choice D, ethnocide, is the systematic destruction of the culture of a group of people; this option is incorrect here because we are given no evidence that elements of Indian culture were destroyed.

6. A is correct. The glass ceiling describes the barriers that impede the ascension of women to higher positions in society. It is often applied to the observation that women in professional settings do not have as many opportunities for promotion compared to their male counterparts. The bamboo ceiling is a derivative of this term that refers to the similar barriers that restrict the opportunities for Asian Americans. Stereotype threat refers to the fear people have to conform to the perceived stereotypes of their group, which is not a match for the information provided in the question stem. Finally, self-fulfilling prophecy also does not fit here because this describes the phenomenon where predictions of a event result in it happening.

7. C is correct. A main tenet of structural functionalism is that the different elements of society work together to keep the society functioning. Structural functionalism also generally has a relatively positive outlook on the "status quo," or the way society is now. (This contrasts with conflict theory, the proponents of which believe that social institutions act to keep certain groups oppressed.) Since the statement given in the question stem mentions different components of society working together, and since it does not seem overly concerned with the imbalance between men and women, structural functionalism is the best choice.

8. A is correct. An ecclesia is a religious organization that holds a great degree of influence over the state and does not tolerate other religions. This is consistent with the description of the dominant religion in Saudi Arabia, since religious laws are incorporated into the official state legal system and actively enforced by the government.

This page left intentionally blank.

Demographics and Inequality

0. Introduction

Demography is the study of certain statistics that illustrate how human populations change over time, making it, essentially, the mathematical branch of sociology. These statistics are known as **demographics** and can be gathered either informally (a small scale poll) or formally (a census).

Social inequality is rooted in **social stratification**, the system by which society ranks categories of people into a hierarchy, whether this is done officially and intentionally or unofficially and unintentionally. When it comes to access to resources, jobs, behaviors, attitudes, and lifestyles, there are notable gaps between these categories, or social classes. Often, those gaps can be very substantial, creating inequality between social classes.

Three of the primary systems of social stratification are the caste system, the class system, and the meritocracy system. A **caste system** features closed stratification, meaning people are not able to change the class they are born into. A **class system** divides society into less rigid classes which are comprised of people of similar wealth and education and are open to people from lower classes if they can acquire enough wealth and education through hard work and good luck. A **meritocracy** is based solely on personal effort to determine a person's social standing: this is an ideal system and has likely never been fully put to practice (though American society does have elements of meritocracy).

1. Demographic Structure of Society

Though there are actually hundreds of demographics that can be used by demographers to study population changes, the most common demographics are race and ethnicity, age, gender, sexual orientation, and immigration status.

I. Race and Ethnicity

Both race and ethnicity are actually social constructs. **Race** refers to the observable, physical differences between different groups of people. **Ethnicity** refers to differences of language, religion, nationality, and other cultural factors between different groups of people. Unlike race, one can choose whether or not to display one's ethnicity. **Symbolic ethnicity** refers to a very specific, often singular connection to ethnicity when one's ethnic identity is not displayed on a regular basis. For example, many people of Irish descent celebrate being Irish on one day of the year: St. Patrick's Day.

The U.S. census taken every year measures the following races: White, Black/African American, Asian American, American Indian / Alaskan Native, Native Hawaiian / Pacific Islander, some other race, and two or more races. Additionally, only two ethnicities are measured: "Hispanic or Latino", or "not Hispanic or Latino." Below is a chart reflecting the 2010 US Census numbers for race and ethnicity.

Race Category	Percentage of US Population in 2010
White	72.4%
Black / African American	12.6%
Asian American	4.8%
American Indian / Alaska Native	0.9%
Native Hawaiian / Pacific Islander	0.2%
Some other race	6.2%
Two or more races	2.9%

Table 1. U.S. Census Data for Race in the USA in 2010.

Furthermore, the 2010 US Census that 16.3% of Americans considered themselves to be ethnically Hispanic or Latino.

II. Age

As the science of medicine and healthcare improve, many people are living longer lives. Add in the fact that the baby-boomer generation that was born after World War II is entering old age and it's no surprise that the group of those 85 and older is the fastest growing age demographic. According to some estimates, by the year 2030, over 70 million Americans will be over the age of 65.

The chart below illustrates how the US population has shifted older over the past 50 years, with both "45 to 64" and "65 and over" demographics increasing over time while "Under 18" significantly decreased.

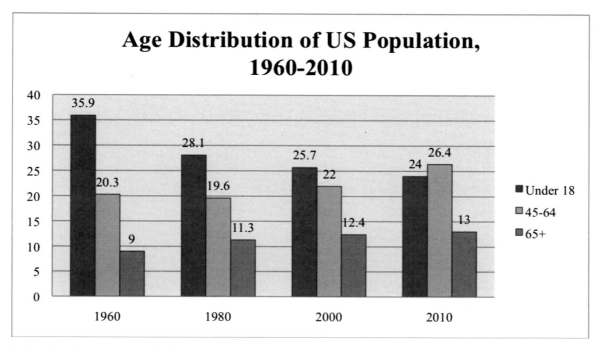

Figure 1. Age Distribution in the US by % from 1960 to 2010.

Ageism refers to prejudice or discrimination based on age, and it's a two way street: a young person may be considered inadequate for a job opening even if they have the skills necessary while older employees can sometimes be considered to be frail, weak, and less intelligent. Considering the growing age gap, ageism may become more common and prevalent.

III. Gender

Gender refers to the state of being a particular sex, either male or female, and corresponds not to physical differences (sex organs), but behavioral, cultural, and psychological traits. Importantly, sex and gender are not synonymous: **sex** refers to the biologically determined sex chromosomes of a person and the accompanying anatomy (the XX genotype corresponds to females and the XY genotype corresponds to males).

Gender inequality refers to the empowerment of one gender over another, either intentionally or not. It is typically accepted that there is still inequality between men and women, with men given more power in society, but this continues to shift as women become more empowered in modern society (at least in the USA).

As of the 2010 census, the American population is 50.8% female and 49.2% male.

IV. Sexual Orientation

Sexual orientation refers to a person's sexual identity insofar as who they are sexually attracted to. The three major categories of sexual orientation are heterosexual (attracted to members of the opposite sex), bisexual (attracted to members of both sexes), and homosexual (attracted to members of the same sex).

The American biologist and sexologist Alfred Kinsey developed a scale for measuring sexual orientation, ranging from a score of 0, representing exclusive heterosexuality, and a score of 6, representing exclusive homosexuality. Kinsey found that most people fell somewhere between the two extremes.

V. Immigration Status

Immigration status refers to whether or not a person was born in another country before moving to the US. According to the 2010 Census, 12.9% of people in America were born in another country, making them immigrants. For that census, 53.1% of immigrants came from Latin America and the Caribbean, with Mexico having the highest representation of a single nation at 29.3%.

2. Demographic Shifts

Simply put, **demographic shifts** are changes in the makeup of a population over time. One such demographic shift has been the near doubling of the United States population since 1950, owing to changes in fertility rate, mortality rate, and migration, the primary drivers of demographic shifts.

Fertility rate is the average numbers of children born to a woman during her lifetime in a certain population. It is measured as both **crude birth rate**, the annual number of births per 1,000 people, and **general fertility rate**, the annual number of births per 1,000 women of childbearing age. Since 1950, fertility rates have actually trended downward over time, though the rate is still above two per woman, signifying that fertility rate still contributes to the growth of the US population. In developing parts of the world, like many African countries, fertility rate is the primary driver of population growth, with some countries having a fertility rate as high as eight children born per woman.

Mortality rate is the number of deaths within a population during a certain amount of time. Typically, it is measured in deaths per 1,000 people per year. Since 1950, the US mortality rate has decreased significantly, contributing to the increased average age of the US population (the declining fertility rate also contributes). In other parts of the world, high mortality rates are a serious block to population growth.

MCAT STRATEGY > > >

Don't confuse demographic shifts with "demographic transition." The latter term refers specifically to a four-stage process which includes several demographic shifts.

Migration is broken down into immigration, the movement of people into a new geographic space, and emigration, the movement of people out of a geographic space. The United States has greater net immigration than emigration, which contributes to our country's population growth, as well as the growth of racial and ethnic diversity.

While the term demographic shift refers to the general change of the makeup of population over time, the term **demographic transition** is a specific iteration of demographic shift, accounting for changes in fertility and mortality rates as a country develops from a preindustrial to an industrial, modern economic system. It is broken down into the following four stages:

In **Stage 1**, a society is preindustrial and has high fertility and mortality rates.

In **Stage 2**, a society sees significant enough improvements in healthcare, sanitation, nutrition, and wages that the mortality rates drops.

In **Stage 3**, a society sees a decrease in fertility rate due to a move from an agricultural to an industrial economy, as well as improvements in contraception and women's rights. In Stage 3, in order for children to be productive in society, they must go to school for many years. Furthermore, they may need to be supported by their parents for longer than they formerly were, which encourages families to have fewer children.

In **Stage 4**, a society becomes fully industrialized and both fertility and mortality rates are low.

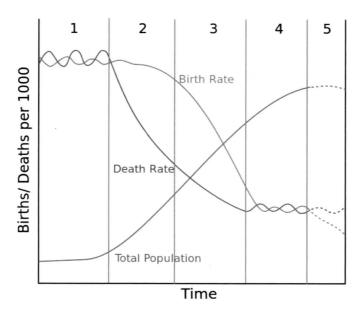

Figure 2. The Progression of Society from Stage 1 to Stage 4 (With an Additional Fifth Stage That Scientists are Beginning to Posit Could be a Less-Fertile Future).

3. Globalization

Globalization refers to the process by which the exchange of worldviews, products, services, ideas, and other cultural ideas leads to international integration. This lessens geographical constraints on businesses, ideas, and people. One of the benefits of globalization is that in-season produce can be shipped from countries across the world, where produce that is currently out of season in the US is in-season. Globalization also accounts for the spread of major international businesses, and increased manufacturing. As such, one of the negative effects of globalization is the pollution that this business growth brings with it.

Urbanization refers to the shift of populations from rural to urban areas. One of the drivers of urbanization has been the decline in the worldwide agricultural jobs: simply put, there are more job opportunities in major cities.

According to the United Nations, over half of the world's population lives in urban areas. Most all cities have quite diverse populations, and are also often divided along socioeconomic lines. As far as the poorer populations go, ghettoes and slums can develop. A **ghetto** is an area that typically has a high concentration of a specific racial or ethnic group and is formed as a function of socioeconomic inequality. A **slum** is more extreme: it is an extremely populated area that often has make-shift housing and poor to non-existent sanitation systems.

4. Social Class

The term **social class** most often refers to the divisions of a society based on **socioeconomic status**.

I. Aspects of Social Stratification by Class

One's socioeconomic status is determined primarily by how much or how little one has of the following: power (ability to make people do things), property (assets, income, wealth, etc.), and prestige (reputation or social standing).

Ascribed and achieved status, mentioned earlier, also play a role in determining one's socioeconomic status: in a caste system, one's socioeconomic status is ascribed while it is achieved (or at least more so) in a class system.

Another important determinant of one's social class is **social capital**, the collective or economic benefits derived from preferential treatment and cooperation between groups. Essentially, the more you invest in society and social groups, the greater the reward. The wealthier you are, the most social capital you are likely to have. One of the major ways social capital plays out is in social networks: people in higher socioeconomic classes typically have better connections. For example, someone with a higher socioeconomic status that is looking for a job is more likely to have a connection with someone that can help her than get a good job than someone with a lower socioeconomic status.

The former refers to a social network with **strong ties**, typically characteristic of a smaller, but tighter group of peers and extended family that is relatively powerful. The latter refers to a network with **weak ties**, characteristic of a bigger network that is relatively less powerful.

Another factor that can influence social stratification is **anomie**, which refers to the breakdown of social bonds, such as social norms, between individuals and communities. Sociologists use **strain theory** to study how the social breakdown characteristic of anomie can lead to social deviance and crime, which can in turn reinforce social stratification.

MCAT STRATEGY > > >

Keep the different kinds of capital clear in your memory. Capital = financial resources. Social capital = value from who you know. Cultural capital = value that comes from something other than money or social connections (e.g. dressing well, having a good vocabulary).

II. Models of Social Stratification

There are several academic models used by sociologists to account for social stratification. One of them, developed by the American sociologists William Thompson and Joseph Hickey in 2005, breaks society down into the following social classes:

> The upper class, which contains 1% of people, accounts for celebrities, business executives, heirs, and other extremely wealthy people, typically with an annual salary greater than $500,000.
> The upper middle class, which contains 15% of people, accounts for highly-educated professionals and managers, typically with an annual salary ranging from the high 5-figures to well over $100,000.
> The lower middle class, which contains 32% of people, accounts for semi-professionals and craftsmen with some college education, typically with an annual salary ranging from $35,000 to $75,000.
> The working class, which also contains 32% of people, accounts for clerical and blue-collar workers who often have low job security, little to no college education, and who make between $16,000 and $30,000 annually.
> The lower class, which contains 14 to 20% of people, accounts for poorly paid or impoverished people, many of whom rely on government welfare.

Remember, this is only one of the models sociologists use for studying social stratification, though in general, most models contain an upper class, a middle class (can be further subdivide into upper, middle, and lower), a working class, and a lower class.

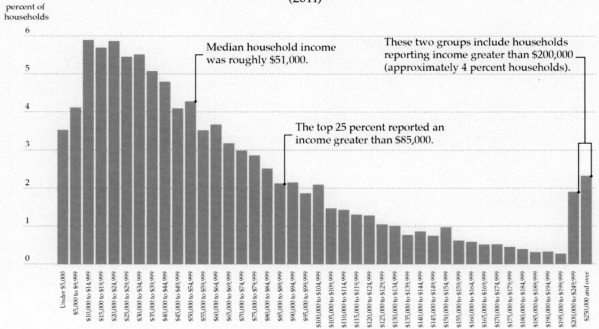

Figure 3. Distribution of Annual Household Income in the US in 2012 (The X-Axis is Income, from Low to High).

II. Poverty

Any discussion of social class would be remiss without the inclusion of **poverty**, which refers to the state of having low socioeconomic status and few resources, financial or otherwise.

Social reproduction refers to the idea that social inequality can be passed from one generation to the next: in other words, the qualities of poverty, including a lack of resources, feelings of apathy and isolation, and little knowledge about financial matters, can be spread from one generation to the next, from parents to children. Likewise, the qualities of being wealthy can be passed on.

Poverty exists in either absolute or relative terms. **Absolute poverty** refers to deprivation of basic needs like food, potable water, shelter, and healthcare. **Relative poverty** refers to the condition in which a person lacks the minimum income or resources needed to maintain the average standard of living for a community or society. So, the poorest people in America, for the most part, suffer from relative poverty: they are still better off than the poorest people in the poorest countries of the world. Those are the people who suffer from absolute poverty. For example, imagine a public school teacher and an actor who live together on the Upper West Side of Manhattan. These two struggle to get by and are poor, relative to the average standard of living in Manhattan. They do, however, have access to food, water, and shelter, making them much better off than those who suffer from absolute poverty in places like Haiti, for example, where 77% of the population lives in poverty.

People who live in poverty can often be subject to **social exclusion**, or relegation to the fringe of society. This can be due to the feelings of powerlessness and alienation that poverty can cause. In a vicious cycle, this kind of thinking can perpetuate patterns or poverty by creating obstacles to self-betterment and financial independence.

5. Social Mobility

Social mobility refers to the movement of individuals or families within or between social classes.

I. Upward and Downward Mobility

Typically, a chance in social class represents a move either up or down. **Upward mobility** refers to a movement up to a higher social class, a move up the ladder of society. Upward mobility is celebrated in the USA and is intrinsically bound with the notion of the "American dream." Imagine a young man from a poor, rural family who is a very talented baseball pitcher. Say that he receives a full ride scholarship to college and only two years later is drafted to a Major League time with a salary of $10,000,000 per year. This is upward mobility exemplified. Downward mobility refers to a movement down to a lower social class and is obviously not held in as high regard as upward mobility.

II. Intergenerational and Intragenerational Mobility

Intergenerational mobility refers to social mobility between generations, typically between parents and children. For example, the pitcher mentioned above attains a higher social class than his parents ever did. **Intragenerational mobility** refers to different degrees of social mobility of members of the same generation. Say the pitcher had a brother who was not so lucky: the pitcher attains a higher social class than his brother, though they both belong squarely to the same generation.

III. Meritocracy

In America, the idea is that one's merit, one's intelligence, one's diligence, one's drive will take that person to the next level of society. America has never completely been a full meritocracy, but rather, has incorporated the idea of meritocracy into its identity. However, some fear that the country continues to lean further away from meritocracy and closer to **plutocracy**, that is, rule by and mostly for the upper classes.

6. Spatial Inequality

Spatial inequality refers to the unequal distribution of resources and services between different areas and locations. This can explain how so-called "bad neighborhoods" develop in cities. Areas with less resources and less economic activity will almost always have less political and commercial influence, and as such, will not attract promising, attractive businesses, but rather, trash-smoldering plants, water refineries, and chemical manufacturers. Spatial inequality can be discussed on three major levels: residential, environmental, and global.

Residential segregation refers to the process by which groups are separated into different neighborhoods, often by class, race, or ethnicity. Furthermore, the existence of segregated neighborhoods in itself serves to strengthen this effect, enforcing residential segregation. Low-income areas tend to have a whole slew of negative qualities, including higher rates of poverty and homelessness, lower quality schools, higher rates of unemployment, and more crime. On the other hand, high-income areas tend to have greater wealth in general, higher quality schools, lower rates of unemployment, and less crime.

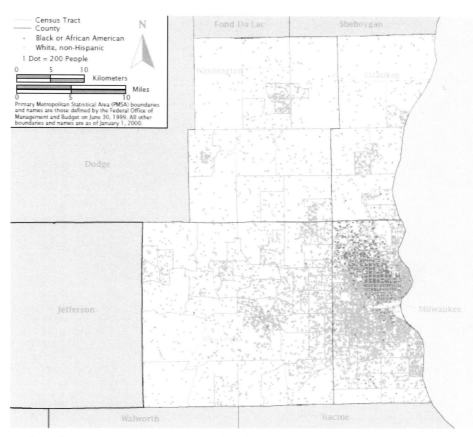

Figure 4. Residential Segregation in Action in Milwaukee, WI (Orange Dots Represent 200 White People, Blue Dots Represent 200 African-American People).

Additionally, the difference between living in a rural and urban setting is notable: an urban area lends a person far more anonymity and opportunities, giving people with an urban background perhaps more of a chance to deny their familial history and move upwards socially. It is easier for someone with a rural background to fall into an occupation traditional to one's family.

Essentially, the place you come from has a major influence on how you interact with other people and how able you are to advance higher in society.

Environmentally speaking, low-income neighborhoods are more likely to be exposed to environmental hazards like the trash-smoldering plants, water refineries, and chemical manufacturers mentioned above. The cheaper the housing market of an area, the more likely these kind of businesses will open up shop. Pairing agents of pollution like these with low quality housing stock, high population density, and less quality nutrition (i.e. food deserts), low income areas can see higher numbers of serious medical problems than high income areas.

Finally, **global inequality** refers to the stratification of resources. opportunities, and power between different countries. Basically, some countries have more access to resources than others, and having resources is pivotal in bringing about opportunity and power.

In a country like Haiti, where 77% of the population lives in poverty, people must focus more on attaining basic needs like food and water, and simply cannot put as much energy into the work, education, and self-betterment that are required for upward social mobility.

Add in the fact that the Earth's population has easily crossed the 7 billion mark, and that it may possibly hit the 10 billion mark by 2050: the growing scarcity of resources, and the further stratification of them (more people splitting less resources), will become even greater problems.

7. Health Disparities

Social epidemiology is the study of how health and illnesses are distributed across populations and how societal factors influence this distribution. Disparities exist between certain people and areas within countries, and between countries themselves. Figure 16. below demonstrates how the global disparity between life expectancy in different countries (note how Africa has by far the highest concentration of low life expectancy).

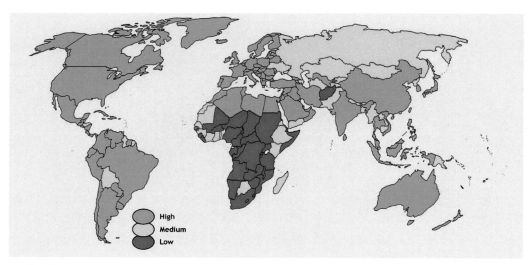

Figure 5. General Life Expectancy at Birth (Medium Grey = High, Light Grey = Medium, Dark Grey = Low).

I. Gender-Related Health Disparities

In most countries around the world, women have high life expectancies than men. On the whole, this is due to the fact that men have higher mortality rates for major diseases like cancer, diabetes, and heart disease, as well as the fact that men are far more likely to die from accident, homicides, or suicides than women are. Moreover, from a sociological perspective, men are likely to be risk-takers and to engage in dangerous activities (alcohol and drug use, speeding, fighting) or work (mining, military, police.)

Though men have higher mortality rates, women often have higher **morbidity rates**, that is, the frequency with which a disease appears in a population. So, women are more likely to suffer from chronic diseases, illnesses, and disabilities, but their conditions are often less life-threatening.

II. Environmental and Socioeconomic-Related Health Disparities

As was mentioned before, areas with environmental hazards can negatively impact the health of a population. John Snow, a preeminent English physician at the vanguard of the practice and study of medical hygiene, helped establish the link between geography and health disparities. In 1854, he mapped out cases of cholera during an outbreak in London, examining concentrations of cases based on physical location. Through his analysis, he found an area with high cholera rates and a water pump in that neighborhood in large part responsible for the outbreak.

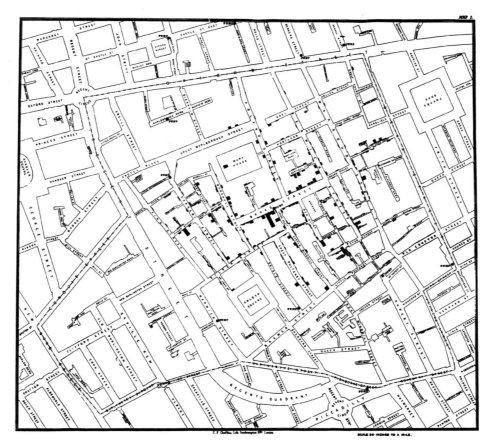

Figure 6. The Map John Snow Used to Study the 1854 Cholera Outbreak in London.

Socioeconomic status also factors into health disparities: those of the middle class and higher tend to have longer life expectancies than those of the lower, working, and impoverished classes. People of the lower classes have less access to nutritious food, healthcare, health insurance, and information about health. Moreover, people of lower classes are far more likely to view themselves in poor health in comparison to those of higher classes. This attitude affects behavior and can create a self-fulfilling prophecy.

III. Ethnicity and Race-Related Health Disparities

Due in large part to social and environmental factors, but perhaps also to biological reasons, there are notable disparities between the health of people belonging to different races and ethnicities. For example, African Americans have twice the infant mortality rate of white infants. Meanwhile, Asian-American infants have a lower mortality rate than white infants. In general, Asian Americans also have lower rates of mortality due to major diseases like cancer, diabetes, and heart disease.

8. Healthcare Disparities

Going hand in hand with health disparities between demographics and populations, healthcare is also not evenly distributed: higher quality healthcare generally goes to those of the higher social classes. Those of the higher classes are more likely able to take care of themselves, and when they are sick, they have typically little to no fear of going to the doctor. On the other hand, those of the lower classes have less ability to make healthy decisions and are often uninsured, meaning a doctor's visit or a trip to the hospital can end up costing a huge amount of money. For this

229

reason, poorer, uninsured people are likely to wait to seek medical attention, with conditions often worsening, making more medical intervention necessary (or else making it too late for medical intervention).

The Affordable Care Act, commonly known as "Obamacare," passed in 2010, seeks to alleviate the healthcare disparity problem in America by increasing the affordability of insurance coverage and lowering the overall cost of healthcare. The contentious law has alleviated the problem somewhat, allowing more people access to health insurance, but disparities are still rampant.

In terms of gender, women are generally favored by the healthcare system. As was mentioned before, men have higher mortality rates. As such, women are more likely to be insured. Moreover, women are more likely to use healthcare resources: they are more likely to go to the doctor when sick or to follow the doctor's orders or prescriptions. Moreover, the higher morbidity rates that women have mean they have more illnesses and diseases that require medical attention.

MCAT STRATEGY > > >

While many issues related to inequality and other sociological concepts can have political associations, the MCAT will expect you to stick strictly to well-established facts of sociology. MCAT prep is not the place to get political.

This page left intentionally blank.

Practice Passage

Approximately 1 in 5 U.S. children in grades K-12 display one or more mental health (MH) pathology and almost 1 in 20 have "extreme functional impairment." These MH issues are associated with an increased (100%) drop-out rate compared with youth without MH difficulties. Additionally, lower grades and lower standardized test scores are strongly correlated with behavioral difficulties and the resulting inattention.

More restricted settings and special-education accommodations may assist youth with untreated MH needs, but less than 30% of children in need receive these services. The cost of treating MH needs in schools is $15 billion dollars per annum, and total yearly social costs are estimated at $247 billion. Social costs include long-term costs to productivity, contagion effects, crime, etc. While social costs may not be entirely recoupable, it is possible to reclaim a great deal of it through effective interventions.

A meta-analysis of MH interventions at 987 secondary schools in the U.S. found a 64% improvement in student academic performance and MH functioning, and a 95% improvement in MH alone with intervention. Interventions also proved effective at reducing dropout rates, increasing academic performance and reducing behavior problems, which increases teacher effectiveness. Ideal services successfully address social, emotional, and behavioral health concerns. Table 1 summarizes results from a study comparing changes in indirect MH indicators at secondary schools with and without dedicated MH services.

Table 1. Effect of Mental Health Services on Secondary School Indicators

School	% Who Drop-out	% Passing Standardized Tests	% In Special Education
With Services	20	73	8
Without Services	42	61	12

There are long-term financial benefits to investing in MH services early in students' lives. Analysis of early intervention programs for low-income children indicate that there are potential savings in criminal justice, special education, and welfare-assistance costs. An audit of California school-based psycho-educational programs found benefits of $9,837 per student in long-term social cost aversion. School-based drug programs have been shown to provide $840 in long-term benefit compared with costs of $150 per student. Overall these programs can save well over their yearly costs, even if implemented with a layout of infrastructure.

1. Which of the following demographic changes will make it most difficult to implement and coordinate effective, centralized mental services in public schools?
    A. Urbanization
    B. Suburbanization
    C. Gentrification
    D. Industrialization

2. Which of the following could be a confounding factor in the research presented in the table?
    A. Special education is a type of mental health service
    B. Standardized testing test ceiling effects
    C. Schools with mental health services are likely different than schools without those services
    D. A higher dropout percent means fewer students are available for standardized testing

3. According to the passage, what is the social barrier to implementing mental health services at schools?
   A. Short-term costs
   B. Long-term costs
   C. Short-term benefits
   D. Long-term benefits

4. Why might it be beneficial to an individual without children in school to support mental health services in schools?
   A. Longer school hours for students
   B. Increased tax revenue from more productive graduates
   C. Improved student academics
   D. Increases in special education services

5. Students who witness their classmates benefitting from mental health services and become more willing to seek out these services themselves have directly benefitted from a reduction in:
   A. social facilitation.
   B. deindividuation.
   C. stigma.
   D. conformity.

6. According to the passage, which of the following is NOT a benefit to providing mental health services for students at schools?
   A. Improved academic performance
   B. Reduced mental health issues
   C. Improved family functioning
   D. Reduced social costs

7. Which of the following findings would lend the greatest support to the idea that mental health issues observed in students are a result of social constructionism?
   A. The total number of those diagnosed with MH issues in the U.S. is three times higher than in other western countries.
   B. The total number of those diagnosed with MH issues in the U.S. is three times lower than in non-western countries.
   C. The criteria for what constitutes MH pathology in the U.S. is three times higher than in other western countries.
   D. The criteria for what constitutes MH pathology in the U.S. is three times lower than in non-western countries.

Practice Passage Explanations

Approximately 1 in 5 U.S. children in grades K-12 display one or more mental health (MH) pathology and almost 1 in 20 have "extreme functional impairment." These MH issues are associated with an increased (100%) drop-out rate compared with youth without MH difficulties. Additionally, lower grades and lower standardized test scores are strongly correlated with behavioral difficulties and the resulting inattention.

Key terms: MH pathology, K-12 kids, inattention

Cause and effect: failure to address MH needs → 2x dropout, other problems

More restricted settings and special-education accommodations may assist youth with untreated MH needs, but less than 30% of children in need receive these services. The cost of treating MH needs in schools is $15 billion dollars per annum, and total yearly social costs are estimated at $247 billion. Social costs include long-term costs to productivity, contagion effects, crime, etc. While social costs may not be entirely recoupable, it is possible to reclaim a great deal of it through effective interventions.

Key terms: restricted settings, special education, cost, effective interventions

Opinion: few children get the MH services they need; wasted $ could be reclaimed through intervention

A meta-analysis of MH interventions at 987 secondary schools in the U.S. found a 64% improvement in student academic performance and MH functioning, and a 95% improvement in MH alone with intervention. Interventions also proved effective at reducing dropout rates, increasing academic performance and reducing behavior problems, which increases teacher effectiveness. Ideal services successfully address social, emotional, and behavioral health concerns. Table 1 summarizes results from a study comparing changes in indirect MH indicators at secondary schools with and without dedicated MH services.

Key terms: meta-analysis, ideal services, indirect indicators

Opinion: MH intervention → improvement; ideal services should address 3 concerns

Table 1. Effect of Mental Health Services on Secondary School Indicators

School	% Who Drop-out	% Passing Standardized Tests	% In Special Education
With Services	20	73	8
Without Services	42	61	12

Table 1 shows MH services may lead to lower dropout rate, better test scores, and fewer kids in special ed

There are long-term financial benefits to investing in MH services early in students' lives. Analysis of early intervention programs for low-income children indicate that there are potential savings in criminal justice, special education, and welfare-assistance costs. An audit of California school-based psycho-educational programs found benefits of $9,837 per student in long-term social cost aversion. School-based drug programs have been shown to provide $840 in long-term benefit compared with costs of $150 per student. Overall these programs can save well over their yearly costs, even if implemented with a layout of infrastructure.

Key terms: long-term financial benefits, California schools, drug programs

Cause and effect: early MH intervention → $ saved; program savings > costs

1. B is correct. Suburbanization is a population shift from central urban areas into suburbs, resulting in formation of suburban sprawl. This decentralization would make it more difficult to coordinate services as the population in need (students) will be more spread out.

2. C is correct. It is likely that schools with MH services have other resources available which can help students or likely have students with more resources themselves. Thus, better student outcomes may be attributable to these factors, rather than the MH services.

3. A is correct. According to the passage, there is a substantial immediate cost for providing MH services. However, there is a long-term savings from providing these services.

4. B is correct. A social benefit is that students receiving MH services tend to become more productive workers, which would lead to increased tax revenue.

5. C is correct. Witnessing other people doing something that may have previously seemed taboo can lead to the stigma being reduced. This can encourage people to do things like seek MH services.

6. C is correct. The passage does not cite findings of improved family functioning as a result of mental health services at school.

7. D is correct. Social constructionism proposes that everything people know as reality is partially, if not entirely, socially situated. For example, social construction of gender is the idea that gender difference (male vs. female) is socially constructed, and not primarily based in biology. Only choice D properly displays this idea in the context of mental health, as it implies cultural differences (western vs. non-western) impacts the criteria used to decide if behavior is indicative of an MH issue.

Independent Questions

1. Which of the following is NOT considered a demographic variable?
   A. Age
   B. Immigration status
   C. Fertility
   D. Sexual orientation

2. In the demographic transition model, the first stage is marked by high birth and death rates. As a society transitions from the first into the second stage, which of the following changes is expected?
   A. Death rates will increase.
   B. Death rates will decrease.
   C. Birth rates will increase.
   D. Birth rates will decrease.

3. According to the Malthusian theory, which of the following is considered a preventive check?
   A. War
   B. Birth control
   C. Famine
   D. Disease

4. Which of the following statements accurately describes a population with a bottom-heavy population pyramid?
   A. Fertility rate is smaller than mortality rate.
   B. Fertility rate is larger than mortality rate.
   C. The overall population is highly likely to decrease over time.
   D. No conclusions can be drawn without more information.

5. Urbanization is the migration of people into dense population centers, such as cities. Which of the following does NOT contribute to urbanization?
   A. Industrialization
   B. Urban growth
   C. Urban renewal
   D. Suburbanization

6. Globalization can directly lead to civil unrest through which of the following mechanisms?
   A. Cultural assimilation
   B. Promotion of inequality
   C. Consistencies in economic development between regions
   D. Terrorism

7. Which of the following is the correct definition of the total fertility rate?
   A. Births minus deaths in the entire population per unit of time
   B. Infants born in the entire population per unit of time
   C. Average number of births a woman will have during her lifetime
   D. Total number of existing infants in a population per unit of time

8. Chris is a public-school teacher, and today he is attending a march organized by a fellow teacher on social media. The purpose of the march is to resist recent legislative changes to the budget of the public school system. This social movement can best be described as:
   A. proactive.
   B. reactive.
   C. facilitated.
   D. relative.

Independent Question Explanations

1. C is correct. Fertility is not considered a demographic variable. Demographic variables include age, gender, race, immigration status, and sexual orientation, among others.

2. B is correct. During the second stage of the demographic transition, medical advancements are made and sanitation improves. As a result, death (or mortality) rates decrease. However, birth (or fertility) rates remain high.

3. B is correct. Thomas Malthus proposed the Malthusian theory, which relates to population growth. In particular, he proposed that a population will tend to outgrow its resources. Two different types of "checks" exist to limit this population growth: positive checks and preventive checks. Positive checks include disasters, like war, famine, and disease (eliminate choices A, C, and D). Preventive checks include actions intentionally taken to limit births, such as birth control or choosing to have children later in life.

4. B is correct. In a population pyramid, younger age groups are shown on the bottom of the pyramid, while older segments of the population are shown nearer the top. For this reason, a bottom-heavy population pyramid describes a society in which younger individuals predominate in the population. This implies that the fertility (birth) rate is greater than the mortality (death) rate. In such a situation, the overall population is likely to increase, not decrease, over time.

5. D is correct. Suburbanization is the migration of people into the suburbs, or less dense areas surrounding urban centers. This results in a depopulation of the cities.

6. B is correct. Inequality is the direct link between globalization and civil unrest. This inequality may result from some of the often-criticized facets of globalization, including colonialism and disparities in economic development. Inequality may then lead to civil unrest. Cultural assimilation, or the process by which a person or group grows to adopt the cultural traits of another group, is not typically a source of unrest in itself (eliminate choice A). Consistent economic development is the opposite of a situation that is likely to produce inequality or unrest (eliminate option C). Finally, terrorism is a potential symptom of civil unrest, not the link between globalization and unrest (eliminate choice D).

7. C is correct. The total fertility rate is the number of births that the average woman in the population will have over her lifetime (or more specifically, during the years she is able to bear children). The crude birth rate is the number of births per 1,000 individuals in the population over a given time period, typically a year.

8. B is correct. A reactive social movement is intended to resist change. Here, the change in question is the legislative update to the school system budget, and the teachers are acting to resist this change. Note that in this case, the movement is not considered facilitated because no organization is described as sponsoring the event.

This page left intentionally blank.

IMAGE ATTRIBUTIONS

Chapter 1

Fig 1: https://commons.wikimedia.org/wiki/File:Patellar-knee-reflex.png by Christina T3 under CC BY SA 3.0

Fig 3: https://commons.wikimedia.org/wiki/File:Ion_channel_activity_before_during_and_after_polarization.jpg by Rintoul under CC BY 4.0

Fig 4: https://commons.wikimedia.org/wiki/File:Action_potential.svg by Chris73 under CC BY SA 3.0

Fig 5: https://commons.wikimedia.org/wiki/File:Propagation_of_action_potential_along_myelinated_nerve_fiber_en.svg by Helixitta under CC BY SA 4.0

Fig 6: https://commons.wikimedia.org/wiki/File:1225_Chemical_Synapse.jpg by OpenStax under CC BY 4.0

Fig 7: https://commons.wikimedia.org/wiki/File:Components_of_the_Nervous_System.png by J. Fair under CC BY SA 3.0

Fig 8: https://commons.wikimedia.org/wiki/File:Brain_parts.jpg by A. Ajifo under CC BY 2.0

Fig 9: https://commons.wikimedia.org/wiki/File:Spike-waves.png by Der Lange under CC BY-SA 2.0

Fig 10: https://commons.wikimedia.org/wiki/File:Dissociative_identity_disorder_neuroscience_brain_imaging.png by Schlumpf under CC BY-SA 4.0

Chapter 2

Fig 2: https://commons.wikimedia.org/wiki/File:1416_Color_Sensitivity.jpg by OpenStax under CC BY 3.0

Fig 3: https://commons.wikimedia.org/wiki/File:Human_visual_pathway.svg by Miquel Petello Nieto under CC BY-SA 4.0

Fig 4: https://commons.wikimedia.org/wiki/File:Anatomy_of_the_Human_Ear_en.svg by Chittka L, under CC BY 2.5

Chapter 3

Fig 2: https://commons.wikimedia.org/wiki/File:Sleep_Hypnogram.svg by RazerM under CC BY-SA 3.0

Fig 3: https://commons.wikimedia.org/wiki/File:Broadbent_Filter_Model.jpg by Kyle.Farr under CC BY-SA 3.0

Fig 4: https://commons.wikimedia.org/wiki/File:Treisman_Attenuation_Model.jpg by Kyle.Farr under CC BY-SA 3.0

Chapter 4

Fig 2: https://commons.wikimedia.org/wiki/File:1605_Brocas_and_Wernickes_Areas-02.jpg by OpenStax under CC BY 3.0

Chapter 5

Fig 1: https://commons.wikimedia.org/wiki/File:Universal_emotions7.JPG by Icerko Lydia under CC BY 3.0

Fig 5: https://commons.wikimedia.org/wiki/File:HPA_Axis_Diagram_(Brian_M_Sweis_2012).svg by ShelleyAdams under CC BY-SA 3.0

Chapter 6

Fig 2: https://commons.wikimedia.org/wiki/File:Spreading_Activation_Model_Mental_Lexicon.png by Nathanael Crawford under CC BY-SA 3.0

Fig 5: https://id.wikipedia.org/wiki/Berkas:Pavlov%27s_dog_conditioning.svg by Maxxl under CC BY-SA 4.0

Fig 6: https://commons.wikimedia.org/wiki/File:Skinner_box_scheme_01.png by Andreas1 under CC BY-SA 3.0

Fig 8: https://commons.wikimedia.org/wiki/File:Bobo_doll-fr.svg by DMY under CC BY-SA 4.0

Chapter 7

Fig 3: https://commons.wikimedia.org/wiki/File:Maslow%27s_Hierarchy_of_Needs.svg by Factoryjoe under CC BY-SA 3.0

Chapter 8

Fig 1: https://commons.wikimedia.org/wiki/File:DSM-5_%26_DSM-IV-TR.jpg by F.RdeC under CC BY-SA 3.0

Fig 6: https://commons.wikimedia.org/wiki/File:Dissociative_identity_disorder.jpg by 04Mukti under CC BY-SA 3.0

Chapter 9

Fig 2: https://commons.wikimedia.org/wiki/File:Anon_London_Feb10_TCR_Protesters.jpg by Paul Williams under CC BY 3.0

Fig 5: https://commons.wikimedia.org/wiki/File:Apartheid_Museum_Entrance,_Johannesburg.JPG by Annette Kurylo under CC BY-SA 3.0

Fig 6: https://commons.wikimedia.org/wiki/File:Mixed_stereotype_content_model_(Fiske_et_al.).png by Sonicyouth86 under CC BY-SA 3.0

Chapter 10

Fig 2: https://commons.wikimedia.org/wiki/File:Social_Network_Analysis_Visualization.png by Martin Grandjean under CC BY-SA 3.0

Chapter 11

Fig 2: https://commons.wikimedia.org/wiki/File:Statue_of_liberty_01.jpg by Francisco Diez under CC BY 2.0

Fig 5: https://commons.wikimedia.org/wiki/File:Mother-Child_face_to_face.jpg by Robert Whitehead under CC BY 2.0

Chapter 12

Fig 3: https://commons.wikimedia.org/wiki/File:Distribution_of_Annual_Household_Income_in_the_United_States_2011.png by vikjam under CC BY-SA 3.0

Fig 5: https://commons.wikimedia.org/wiki/File:Life_expectancy.jpg by Ionut Cojocaru under CC BY 3.0

INDEX